THE FIFTH DIVISION IN
THE GREAT WAR

Xmas 1917.   *By Capt. Keesey, R.E.*

THE FIFTH DIVISION
IN THE
GREAT WAR

BY

BRIGADIER-GENERAL
A. H. HUSSEY
C.B., C.M.G.

AND

MAJOR
D. S. INMAN

WITH A FOREWORD BY

FIELD-MARSHAL
EARL HAIG OF BEMERSYDE
K.T., G.C.B., K.C.I.E., G.C.V.O., C.B.

London
NISBET & CO. LTD.
22 BERNERS STREET, W.1

First Published in 1921

TO THE MEMORY

OF

OUR FALLEN COMRADES

PREFACE

A T the Annual Dinner of the 5th Division held
in London on 26th June 1920 the idea was
mooted that the history of the Division should be
written. Brigadier-General Hussey and Major Inman
were asked if they would undertake the work. They
have done so, with much diffidence—with what success
must be left to the judgment of the reader.

The Authors wish to apologise for any short-
comings, mistakes, or omissions which may have
occurred. The War Diaries for the first few months of
the War are necessarily very meagre, and they have
had to rely upon private diaries and accounts kindly
lent by Officers, and books already published, for their
information. As the War went on, the Official Diaries
became much fuller, and the Authors have also drawn
largely from their own personal recollections.

They wish to express their thanks to Field-Marshal
Earl Haig for having so kindly written a Foreword,
to Major-General Romer for his help in the first two
chapters, to Major-General Lord E. Gleichen for permission to make use of his book, to the Royal Air
Force for permission to reproduce photographs taken
by them, to Captain Keesey for the frontispiece, to
Mrs. Edmond for the photograph of the Staff, to the
publishers, Messrs. Nisbet & Co., for the help they have
given and the interest they have taken in the book, and

lastly to the many Officers who subscribed towards the expenses of publication.

In conclusion, they wish to say what a pleasure it has been to them to have written the record of a Division, which not only has won such imperishable fame, but was also a very happy home to them during the greater part of the Great War.

A. H. H.
D. S. I.

LONDON, *March* 1921.

FOREWORD

FOR those who served in the 5th Division during the Great War this Foreword to their divisional history is not intended as an introduction, for they need none, but as a well-earned tribute paid to a very fine and gallant record.

Those who did not serve in the Division will find in this book a full and varied account, covering the whole period from August 1914 to the suspension of hostilities in November 1918, and embracing almost all the greater episodes of the War on the British front in the West.

The Division had its full share in the fighting during the opening months of the War, at Mons, Le Cateau, at the crossing of the Marne and the Aisne, and in the first battles in Flanders. The last battle of the War found it in the forefront of our advance, pressing on in pursuit of the retreating enemy East of the Sambre. In the interval between that early fighting and the final victory many a fine exploit had been set to the credit of the Division. In the Somme battle of 1916, the skilful and successful fighting about Falfemont Farm and Leuze Wood vies with the capture of Morval in its claim on our attention. In the Arras battle, 1917, the 13th Brigade of the 5th Division took part with the Canadians in the storming of the Vimy Ridge, and well upheld the honour of the Old Country by the share it took in a brilliant Canadian achievement.

Later in the same year the Division once more found itself in the old Ypres battlefield. It had heavy fighting there, and was pulled out of the line early in November, only to be hurried off to Italy. It returned to France in April 1918 just in time to be sent straight into the Lys battle where, East of the Forest of Nieppe, it helped to stop definitely and permanently the German advance in that direction. Finally, when our turn came to attack again, the 5th Division fought right through the August battle of Bapaume, and was engaged with equal success in all our subsequent advance—until the Armistice.

This brief summary of a splendid tale of achievement gives but an inadequate idea of the courage and devotion displayed through four and a half years of war. A more detailed account will be found in the pages of this book ; but the full story can only be understood by those who know from their own experience what it was our troops were called upon to do, and the spirit in which they accomplished their task. It is with that knowledge, and in the sense of gratitude which springs from it, that I have written this FOREWORD.

Haig

of Bemersyde.

15th December 1920.

CONTENTS

LIST OF ILLUSTRATIONS

xiii

MAPS

CHRONOLOGICAL TABLE OF EVENTS OF THE FIFTH DIVISION

1914

Aug.	16 . . .	Division landed in France.
„	23 . . .	Battle of Mons.
„	24 and 25 . .	Retreat from Mons.
„	26 . . .	Battle of Le Cateau.
„	27 to Sept. 3 .	Retreat from Le Cateau to Tournan Area.
Sept.	5 . . .	Advance commenced.
„	6 to 9 . .	Battle of the Marne.
„	13 to Oct. 2 .	Battle of the Aisne.
Oct.	12 to 30 . .	Fighting on La Bassée Front.
Nov.	1 to 29 . .	Messines. Ypres.
„	30 to March 1915	Wulverghem Front.

1915

April	17 . . .	Capture of Hill 60.
„	22 to May 24 .	Second Battle of Ypres, and Hill 60 Operations
May to July . .	.	Ypres Front.
Aug. to Feb. 1916 .	.	Bray Front.

1916

March to July	.	Arras Front.
July	19 . .	Into Line—Battle of the Somme.
„	27 . .	Capture of Longueval by 15th Brigade.
„	30 . .	Attack North of Longueval by 13th Brigade.
Aug.	2 to 23 .	Rest. Belloy-St. Leonard Area.
„	26 . .	Into Line, Maltz Horn Ridge.
Sept.	3 . .	Attack on Falfemont Farm.
„	5 . .	Capture of Falfemont Farm and Leuze Wood.
„	25 . .	Capture of Morval.
Oct. to March 1917	.	Béthune Front.

1917

April	9 . . .	Capture of Vimy Ridge.
„	23 . . .	Operations near La Coulotte.

1917 (*continued*)

May	3 . . .	Into Line, Oppy-Fresnoy Front.
„	8 . . .	Operations at Fresnoy.
June	28 . . .	Capture of German Line, Oppy Wood.
Sept.	7 to 29 . .	Rest. Le Cauroy and Éperlecques Areas.
Oct.	1 . . .	Into Line, Ypres Front.
„	4 . . .	Advance along Reutelbeek.
„	9 . . .	First Attack on Polderhoek.
„	26 . . .	Second Attack on Polderhoek.
Nov.	6 . . .	Third Attack on Polderhoek.
„	11 to 24 . .	Rest. Westoutre and Nielles Areas.
„	27 to Dec. 12 .	Entrained for Italy.

1918

Dec. 1917 to Jan. 1918 .	Area North of Padua.
Jan. to March 18 . .	In Line on River Piave.
March 19 to 26 . .	To Area East of Vicenza.
April 1 to 5 . .	Entrained for France.
„ 8 to 10 . .	Lucheux Area.
„ 12 . . .	Took up Line East of Forêt de Nieppe.
„ 12 to 14 . .	German Advance repulsed.
June 28 . . .	Capture of Line on the Plate Becque.
Aug. 8 . . .	To Compagne Area.
„ 13 . . .	To Frévent Area.
„ 19 . . .	To Area East of Doullens.
„ 21 . . .	Commencement of Great Advance. Capture of Achiet-Le Petit.
„ 23 to 24 . .	Capture of Irles, and Loupart Wood.
„ 26 . . .	Capture of Beugnâtre.
„ 30 . . .	Advance continued to West of Beugny.
Sept. 3 . . .	Capture of Beugny and advance to East of Vélu.
„ 18 . . .	Attack on African Trench.
„ 27 . . .	Capture of African Trench, and Beaucamp Ridge.
„ 30 . . .	Capture of Gonnelieu and Banteux.
Oct. 20 . . .	Crossing of River Selle forced.
„ 23 . . .	Capture of Beaurain.
Nov. 5 . . .	Forêt de Mormal cleared.
„ 7 . . .	Capture of Pont-sur-Sambre, and Crossing of River.
„ 8 . . .	Capture of St. Rémi-mal-bati.
„ 9 . . .	Line advanced to Damousies-Ferrière. Cavalry and Cyclists sent forward.
„ 11 . . .	ARMISTICE.

THE 5TH DIVISION IN THE GREAT WAR

CHAPTER I

MONS—LE CATEAU AND THE RETREAT

(For Operations dealt with in this Chapter, see Map 1)

SO many accounts have been written of the mobilisation scenes of the " Contemptible Little Army " which embarked for France in August 1914, and of their experiences on first arrival there, that it seems unnecessary to recount these events again. Suffice it then to say, that on the fateful 5th of August the mobilisation of the 5th Division at the Curragh and Dublin commenced, that it was carried through without a hitch of any sort, and that on the 10th the Division was fully equipped and ready to embark.

The troops left Dublin and Belfast amid patriotic cheering and waving of handkerchiefs, and after an uneventful passage arrived at Le Havre in the course of the next two days. Here they entrained and travelled through Rouen and Amiens to the Le Cateau-Landrecies area, arriving there on the 18th. The G.O.C., Sir Charles Fergusson, visited the Brigades in their billets and made them a stirring speech, giving many technical tips about the Germans and how to meet their various wiles. The Division together with

I

the 3rd formed the II. Corps, commanded by Lieut.-Gen. Sir Horace Smith-Dorrien; he had succeeded General Grierson, who had died suddenly from heart failure in the train on the way out.

On 20th August, orders were received for an advance in a Northerly direction on the next day. Every one was almost in complete ignorance as to the situation. It was known that the 3rd Division was to march on the right, and that the I. Corps were still farther to the East; but as to the enemy or the French, there was no information. As this was the first occasion on which the Division was to move as a complete unit, it was lucky that it was to all intents and purposes a " peace march," as it served to give the Staffs valuable practice, and helped the units to find their legs; it was a fair test, too, for the Reservists.

The weather on the 21st was fine; the country through which the Division passed looked very smiling with its clean and tidy cottages and farms, fields ripe for harvest, and orchards laden with fruit; and the country people were most attentive in offering drink and fruit to the thirsty men.

The Division billeted that night in and around Bavai, where they were vociferously welcomed. On the following day the march was resumed *viâ* Dour and Boussu, the latter part of the journey being through a crowded mining district, full of slag-heaps, mine-shafts, and small houses. The roads were mostly " pavé " of uneven sets, with great pits in them, just broad enough for one vehicle, and extremely painful to march on; on either side of the road, where this villainous " pavé " did not exist, it was either deep dust or caked mud, which became a morass after rain. The inhabitants here, most of them able-bodied young

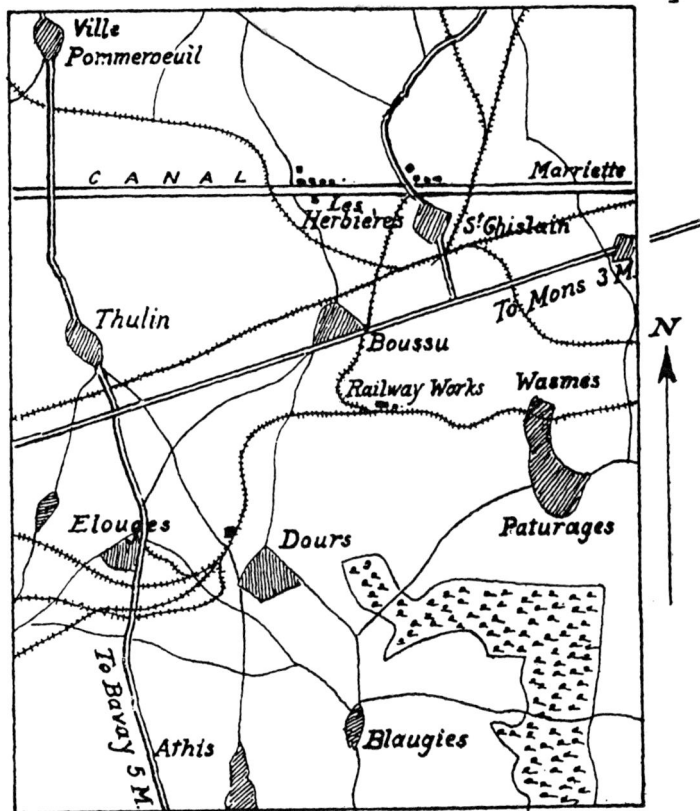

MONS.

Map 1

Ville
Pommerœuil

C A N A L

Marïette

Les
Herbières

St Ghislain

Thulin

To Mons 3 M.

N

Boussu

Railway Works

Wasmes

Elouges

Dours

Paturages

To Bavay 5 M.

Athis

Blaugies

Miles. 1 0 1 2 3 Miles

Scale 1/100,000

[To face p. 2.

men, were very friendly, but nevertheless had the air
of being benevolent spectators; one could not help
wondering why they were not fighting in the ranks.
Rumours of the approach of the Germans soon
began to come in, and were substantiated by the
receipt of orders from the II. Corps for the 3rd and 5th
Divisions to hold the straight reach of the Mons-Condé
Canal running due West from Mons. The left of the
5th Division was to be on the Pommeroeuil-Thulin
road, the right at Mariette in touch with the 3rd
Division. The front was divided up between the 13th
Brigade (Brig.-Gen. Cuthbert) on the right, and the
14th Brigade (Brig.-Gen. Rolt) on the left, while the
15th Brigade (Brig.-Gen. Lord E. Gleichen) remained
in reserve and prepared a defensive line about Wasmes
in case the Canal line was forced back. In the 13th
Brigade, the West Kents were on the right, with the
"Duke's" in support; then came the K.O.S.B. supported by the K.O.Y.L.I.; and in the 14th Brigade
the East Surreys and the D.C.L.I. held the front.
Each Battalion in the front line had a few men thrown
across the Canal as a screen.

The morning of the 23rd opened misty and wet,
but by 10 a.m. the weather had cleared, and there was
every promise of a hot day. The Divisional Mounted
Troops, consisting of A Squadron 19th Hussars, under
Major Parsons, and the Cyclist Company, under Major
Burnett, pushed forward to reconnoitre, and quickly
came into contact with the enemy, whereupon ensued
some spirited skirmishing. Exaggerated rumours of
calamities began to come in, but soon authentic reports
were received showing that the enemy was advancing
in strength. About 1 p.m. an attack developed on
the whole front, and both Brigades found themselves

hotly engaged. The German Infantry made repeated efforts to press the attack home, but the good work of our machine-guns and the steady rifle-fire of the men in the front line kept them in check, and they failed to reach the bridges.

About 3 p.m. the 19th Brigade was sent up to extend the line on the left of the 14th, and we appeared to be holding our own, although much harassed by the hostile Artillery. Two hours later, a barricade, which had been erected on the North side of the Canal, was destroyed by Artillery fire, and our troops on that side were compelled to withdraw. A gap also occurred between the two Divisions, and the German Infantry took instant advantage of it, crossing the Canal and penetrating through as far as Wasmes, where they ran up against the Bedfords and Dorsets of the 15th Brigade, who were holding the line of the railway. The right flank of the Division was thus in danger, and it looked as if a wedge were being thrust in between the 13th and 15th Brigades ; so menacing indeed was the situation that the II. Corps appealed to the I. Corps for help, with the result that General Haking's Brigade (the 5th) was sent by the latter to fill the gap.

After dark, German bugle calls were sounded all along the line, and died away in the distance Northwards ; they appeared to be sounded in order to give the impression that a withdrawal was taking place. Also, refugees came in, among them a priest, who declared that the enemy was retiring to the North, but no credence was placed in their reports.

At 9 p.m. the Brigades on the Canal fell back to the prepared position North of Wasmes, but, although the distance was not great, the country was so intersected with dykes, and the situation on the right flank was so confused, that it was practically daylight before all units were in position. The superiority of the German Artillery had been much felt during the day. Early in the morning four guns of the 120th Battery had been brought into action on the Canal bank near St. Ghislain, but they had had to withdraw owing to shell and rifle fire ; later another section of the same Battery was brought up ; they suffered many casualties, the C.O., Major Holland, being killed, and in the withdrawal in the evening one gun had to be abandoned. The 119th Battery was sent up to cover the retirement, and did some good execution against hostile columns moving through Pommeroeuil, and the 52nd and 124th Batteries were also moved forward later, but did not come into action. The remainder of the Artillery had been disposed to cover the Wasmes line.

During the night the G.S.O.1 was summoned to Corps Head-Quarters and received orders that a further retirement would be carried out, the general direction of which would be South-West. It looked as if this might be difficult to do, for not only were the Germans likely to make a strong frontal attack, but the evening reports also showed that there were large hostile columns on the left, which might interfere with a retirement to the South-West. Orders were accordingly issued, and all Transport directed to march at once.

The new line that had been taken up during the night ran from the small wood on the railway just North of Wasmes, past the railway works to Halte, and back towards Dour station. It was by no means continuous, but consisted of various " points d'appui " and patches of entrenchment ; the field of fire was bad except on the left, where the railway crossed the Boussu road. The ground was a mass of slag-heaps, mine-heads, and chimneys, with here and there a green field, the whole intersected with a network of railway lines. The trenches had been dug with the help of some pit-boys, who were at first somewhat unwilling, but buckled to with a little persuasion. The Dorsets and Bedfords of the 15th Brigade were still holding the railway at Wasmes with the right bent back towards Paturage, the other two Battalions (Cheshires and Norfolks) being kept in Divisional Reserve. On the left of the Bedfords came the 13th Brigade (K.O.S.B. and West Kents, with the " Duke's " and K.O.Y.L.I. in Brigade Reserve). Then came the 14th Brigade (Manchesters, D.C.L.I. and Suffolks, with the East Surreys in reserve). Covering the right were the 28th Brigade R.F.A., and on the left the 27th Brigade R.F.A., while the 15th Brigade R.F.A. and the 108th Heavy Battery were in position on the extreme left.

Very early in the morning the Germans began pushing forward. At first our Artillery and rifle-fire proved too much for them, and they suffered heavy casualties without achieving much result, but the right soon became outflanked, and, under the ever-increasing pressure, began to retire. On the left, too, the situation was threatening, the 14th Brigade being violently attacked about Dour station. A message was received at this time from General Allenby to the effect that his orders were to retire to a line some miles back, but the danger of the 5th Division left being enveloped was so evident, that Sir Charles Fergusson, who had been ordered to hold on in order to cover the withdrawal of the 3rd Division, pointed out in reply that it was of vital importance for the Cavalry to prevent the Germans outflanking us. The Cavalry responded splendidly to this appeal, with great gallantry standing their ground until the retirement was well under way. When this retirement took place, about 1 p.m., the Divisional Reserve, consisting of the Norfolks and Cheshires with the 119th Battery, under Lieut.-Col. Ballard of the Norfolks, was ordered to act as a flank-guard. Severe fighting now developed at Élouges and out to the West, and the 9th Lancers, of General de Lisle's Brigade, made a gallant charge against the enemy's guns, but they were held up by wire, and could not get through ; a heavy toll was taken from them, and only a small remnant, under Captain Grenfell, escaped the storm of shells and bullets. Later in the day Colonel Ballard's flank-guard became seriously involved near Élouges, and had some very stiff fighting, the Cheshires losing some five hundred men. The Battery, too, was in trouble ; one Section was detached about four hundred yards to the right, under Lieut. Preston ; they fired on the German Infantry until orders to retire were received, and then came into action again against the German Cavalry, when a machine-gun was brought against them at a range of four hundred yards. Lieut. Preston, though four times wounded, made repeated efforts to get his guns away, but had to give it up and was eventually taken away in an ambulance. With the other guns the casualties were so great that Lieut.-Col. Ballard ordered their withdrawal ; most of the detachments had been wiped out, and it was only a matter of minutes before the rest went. Captain Grenfell, 9th Lancers, with his small remnant of men, saw their difficulties and offered to help ; and with their assistance the guns were dragged out singly, limbered up, and got safely away. Both Captain Grenfell, who had already been wounded, and Major Alexander, the Battery Commander, received the V.C. for their gallantry.

Meanwhile the main column of the Division got clear of the mining area, with its maze of villages and pits, and retired to the vicinity of St. Waaste-La-Vallée, where it billeted. The 3rd Division, in its withdrawal, had crossed behind the 5th, and was billeted, or bivouacked, West of it. The German Cavalry made no attempt to pursue in the afternoon, but heavy firing was heard to the North-West, and a defensive position was taken up for a short time North of Athis. The plight of the unfortunate inhabitants was most pitiful. Mystified children and women, with glazed, resigned eyes, were standing about, and to their anxious inquiries as to why the British were retreating the only answer that could be given was that it was a strategical movement to the rear, " pour mieux sauter."

On the next day the 5th Division was allotted the Bavai-Le Cateau road. In order to use this road they would have to make practically a flank march into Bavai with a superior enemy threatening on the North ; such a march could not but cause the G.O.C. much anxiety. The 14th Brigade, with adequate Artillery, was therefore ordered to form the rear-guard and to occupy a position covering this road, while every effort was made to get the Transport clear of Bavai as soon as possible. The Germans soon began to make this pressure felt ; some Jaegers attacked, and a couple of field-guns opened fire at a close range—luckily the range was not exact, and there were only a few men wounded. The anticipated danger appeared to be imminent, but the 14th Brigade had no difficulty in keeping the enemy off, and the whole column cleared Bavai in safety.

The march was then continued in sweltering heat along the dead straight road on the Western edge of the Forêt de Mormal, whose tall trees, mostly oak, beech, and hornbeam, acted as a suffocating blanket and kept off any breeze there might be. The roads in many places were blocked with ox-wagons, and streams of refugees trundling along their worldly possessions in wheelbarrows or perambulators ; one had to be hard on them and turn them off to the side roads till the columns had passed. Engelfontaine and Montay were passed, and Le Cateau was reached in the course of the afternoon. To the disappointment of all, the orders were to continue the retirement next day, and it was not till early in the morning that these were cancelled. Sir Horace Smith-Dorrien had decided that the II. Corps was to stand and fight.

Le Cateau lies in the valley of the Selle River, which is little more than a stream; the rolling, billowy nature of the country, cut up here and there into deep valleys, made the position a difficult one to defend. A spur lay to the East of the village running in a Northerly direction, parallel to the stream, and a similar spur with a branch towards Troisvilles lay on the Western side. The country was principally cornfields, but the corn was nearly all cut and stood in stooks; the only restriction to free movement of all arms was an occasional wire fence. Some trenches had been dug by the civilians to the West of the village, but they were nothing like deep enough and were badly sited ; starting on the right, a little beyond the Reumont-Le Cateau road, the line ran to Troisvilles ; from that place to Caudry it was held by the 3rd Division, and from Caudry to Haucourt by the 4th Division, just arrived from home ; these trenches had been taken up as an outpost line during the evening. As soon as it was known that the Corps was to make a stand, the 14th Brigade was allotted the right sector, the 13th the centre, and the 15th the left; it was a long line for one Division to hold, and the Corps Commander consequently placed the 19th Brigade at Sir Charles Fergusson's disposal. Covering this line was the Divisional Artillery—a Brigade, with a proportion of howitzers, to each sector. Divisional Head-Quarters were at Reumont, where the R.E. constructed a platform on one of the houses, whence a view could be obtained of the battlefield.

The disposition of the Brigades was as follows :

14th Brigade—Suffolks, South of the Reumont road, half the East Surreys and Manchesters in support.

13th Brigade—K.O.Y.L.I. and K.O.S.B., the former with their right resting on a point just East of the Reumont road, with the West Kents and " Duke's " in support.

15th Brigade—Bedfords and Dorsets (the latter in Troisvilles in touch with the 3rd Division), with the Cheshires and Norfolks in the second line.

The troops occupied the sodden, cheerless trenches in thick mist; little could be done to improve them, for there were no entrenching tools available—only a few picks from the neighbouring farms. The battle opened with an unfortunate incident. The D.C.L.I., two Companies of the East Surreys, and two Companies of the Suffolks, under Lieut.-Col. Longley, which had formed part of the rear-guard the day before, had bivouacked on the outskirts of Le Cateau, S.E. of the

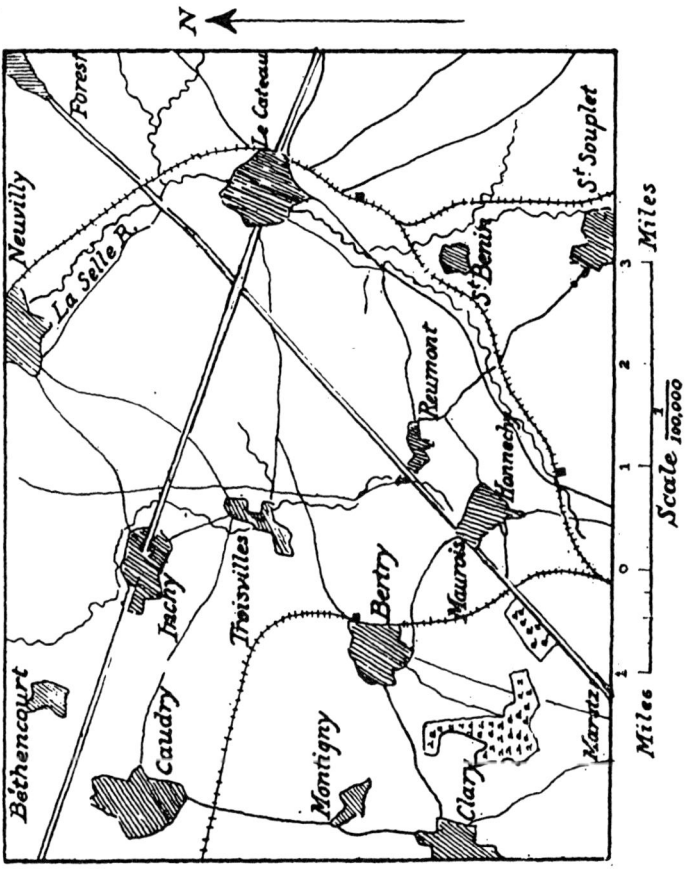

LE CATEAU.

Map 2

N

Forest

Neuvilly

La Selle R.

Le Cateau

St. Benin

St. Souplet

Reumont

Honnechy

Béthencourt

Caudry

Fachy

Troisvilles

Bertry

Maurois

Montigny

Clary

Maretz

Miles

3   2   1   0   1

Scale 1/100,000

Miles

Miles

[To face p. 10.

town, with a view to joining up with the I. Corps.
They were preparing to rejoin the rest of the Brigade
and resume the retirement, not having heard of the
change in the orders, when, at 6.30 a.m., a sudden
volley rang out from the houses just beyond the railway.
Men fell in all directions. Taken by surprise and
massed in column along the exposed side of the road,
there was only one thing to be done--they were turned
about and doubled to the high ground South of the
town. It then became evident that not only was the
enemy occupying the Southern part of the town, but
that he also held the railway for a considerable distance to the South. So Lieut.-Col. Longley determined
to move still farther South, but each attempt to do so
was headed off, until the timely arrival of some of the
16th Lancers of General Gough's Brigade enabled them
to rejoin the Division ; but there had been a heavy
tale of casualties, the Suffolks alone losing over 200
men. The East Surreys were then ordered up to cover
the right flank East of Maurois.

About 6 a.m. the weather cleared, and the German
Artillery opened fire, at first with comparatively few
guns, but their numbers gradually grew until
by noon their superiority was almost overwhelming. The enemy attacked all along our line, but
his principal efforts, on the 5th Division front, were
against the right and right centre. This was our
vulnerable flank, for beyond Le Cateau there was
nothing except Briggs' Cavalry Brigade, and they
could give little assistance. The I. Corps had been
heavily engaged near Landrecies, and there was no
hope of their being able to come up in time ; the
danger of envelopment was so evident that two Battalions of the 19th Brigade were ordered up to support

the right flank. Up to about 11 a.m., however, we
seemed to be holding our own in spite of the tornado
of Artillery fire. It was about this time that a message
was received from the II. Corps saying that the situation
was most critical at Caudry (some three miles to the
West), and asking if Sir Charles Fergusson could send
any assistance. Although the situation on his own
front was by no means encouraging, the G.O.C., in view
of such an urgent appeal, decided to send the remaining two Battalions of the 19th Brigade and a Battery
towards Caudry. As the engagement developed on
the right front, the trenches, which afforded little
protection to the firing-line, became quite untenable,
and the casualties mounted up in an alarming way.
Wounded men were coming back in a continuous
stream. Strong hostile columns were seen advancing
against the whole front, and the direction of the enemy's
Artillery fire showed that they were outflanking us
more and more ; it seemed doubtful whether our line
could hold out any longer. To quote the Commander-
in-Chief's dispatch : " It became apparent, if complete
annihilation was to be avoided, that a retirement must
be attempted, and the order was given to commence it
about 3 p.m."

The K.O.Y.L.I., on the right of the 14th Brigade,
had in the morning received a written order : " There
will be *no* retirement for the fighting troops—fill up
your trenches, as far as possible, with water, food, and
ammunition." And later this order was repeated
verbally by a Staff Officer. Surrounded on three sides,
swept by a concentrated rifle and machine-gun fire
from front and flanks, battered by shells, and with
their ammunition exhausted, the Battalion stayed
to its death, faithful to the order. Lieut. Denison,

though mortally wounded in the head, and blind, continued to encourage his men until he became insensible. As the final German rush came, Major Yate gave an order to meet it with a charge, refusing the call to surrender. Sixteen Officers and three hundred and twenty rank-and-file of this gallant regiment were captured, and there were many more killed and wounded.

On the left, the 15th Brigade was faring better at first ; Inchy was in flames, shelled by both sides, British and German, and the Dorsets were so happy (?) at Troisvilles that they asked permission to counter-attack on that flank, but as the day wore on the shell-fire increased, they saw the right first and then the centre falling back, and finally the 15th Brigade too had to give way. The Norfolks, on the right of the Brigade, stuck to it bravely and covered the retirement of the 13th Brigade, till they were taken to form the rear-guard of the Division. The rest of the Brigade followed the K.O.S.B., and fell back in good order to the St. Quentin road, South of Maurois.

To turn to the fortunes of the Artillery :—

As stated before, a Brigade of Artillery (18-prs.), with a proportion of the Howitzer Brigade, was attached to each of the three sectors of the line, the 108th Heavy Battery and 61st Howitzer Battery being at first kept in Divisional Reserve. On the right the 15th Brigade R.F.A., with the 37th Howitzer Battery, covered Le Cateau and the ground East of it, being posted on the right of the Reumont-Montay road, from 200 to 400 yards in rear of the Infantry. The first German shells came from about 5000 yards distant on the slopes North-West of Le Cateau. Some of these Batteries were quickly silenced, but more and more

German Batteries were brought up, and a heavy fire also opened from the North of Inchy. Our Batteries had to fire in all directions, the most extreme case being that of the 11th Battery, which had in the first place to swing the left half Battery back in order to fire to the right rear, and later to run up a gun to meet an Infantry attack on the right front of the original line. Commencing at between 2000 and 3000 yards, the range quickly dropped, as the enemy advanced, to 1000 yards, and eventually to 600 yards. Casualties mounted up rapidly ; in the 11th Battery every Officer, the two Staff-Sergeants, and half the Sergeants were either killed or wounded, and what with casualties to men, horses, and material, and in some cases to shortage of ammunition, the number of guns in action was gradually reduced, until eventually only five out of the eighteen guns were firing in the Brigade, one in the 11th Battery, and two in each of the 52nd and 80th. Advantage was taken during a cessation of fire to attempt to withdraw the guns to a position farther back, and the limbers and wagon-teams came up, but two teams were at once blown to pieces. In the 52nd Battery it was found impossible to get any of the guns away, so the breech-blocks were removed, and the survivors among the men withdrawn. Eventually the reduced Brigade was re-assembled behind the village of Reumont, and the five guns were brought into action again to cover the retirement of the Infantry. Of the eighteen Officers of the Brigade only four, one Captain and three Subalterns, were left unwounded. The 37th Battery maintained its fire to the end, and was particularly valuable when the Germans had reached the dead ground close in front of our firing-line. In the first attempt at withdrawal four guns were brought away, but when they tried to save the remaining two, all the horses of one team were shot down and the gun had to be abandoned; the other one, however, was safely brought away. Captain Reynolds and two Drivers, Drain and Luke, received the V.C. for this gallant exploit.

In the centre sector the 28th Brigade R.F.A. took up a very similar position to that of the 15th Brigade, but on the opposite side of the Reumont-Montay road. The German Artillery, after dealing with the 15th Brigade, turned their attention on to the 28th guns, and to such a concentration of fire, our guns, in their exposed position, fighting almost back-to-back, could make no adequate reply. The O.C. the Brigade, Colonel Stephens, with the whole of his Staff, and two Majors, Nutt and Jones, had been captured in the observation station on the right, and the C.R.A. decided that the only thing to be done was to take advantage of any lull in the firing to get at any rate some of the guns away. Only three could be limbered up, and the horses of one of these were almost immediately shot down, so that only two guns in the whole Brigade were saved.

In the left sector the ground offered greater facilities for concealment than in the other two, and the Battery positions of the 27th Brigade R.F.A. were never accurately located; casualties were therefore comparatively light, and the Brigade was successfully withdrawn from action on the retirement being ordered.

The 61st Howitzer Battery and the 108th Heavy Battery, which had been kept in reserve at the commencement of the action, had taken up good positions and were never discovered by the enemy; they had been first employed against the enemy's guns in the neighbourhood of Forest, and afterwards, when the Infantry gave way in the centre, the 61st Battery established a belt of fire in front of the abandoned trenches, denying the ground to the enemy, none of whom gained the crest while the Battery remained in action. The 108th Heavy Battery moved a Section back to a position North of Maurois when the retirement began, one gun of which got stuck in a ditch ; the other Section remained in action against the enemy's guns and advancing Infantry until the end, and this unit was the last to leave this part of the field. The G.O.C., after congratulating them, personally gave the order to leave, which they did reluctantly ; they only had nine rounds left, and said they were having " the time of their lives."

By 4 p.m. the Division was retiring along the St. Quentin road covered by a rear-guard of the Norfolks and some Companies of the 19th Brigade, which were hastily got together and placed under the command of Lieut.-Col. Ballard. Transport, guns, and Infantry were hopelessly mixed up, and the confusion was increased by some of the Transport and troops of the 3rd Division coming on the main road at Maretz. This road presented a truly alarming spectacle ; it was packed with vehicles, double-banked, and moving at a snail's pace with frequent blocks—guns, ambulances, and small bodies of tired Infantry without Officers were crawling along past derelict motor-lorries and wagons. The hungry and exhausted men plodded along in a hopeless way, many men lying down by the roadside utterly worn-out and broken, and every carriage was crowded with wounded, the Artillery outriders and even the horses of the teams being used to carry them. To make matters worse

The Staff of the 5th Division, August 1914.

[To face p. 16.

a steady rain set in and continued throughout the
pitch-dark night. It is difficult to say what would
have happened had the Germans followed up and
shelled the road; luckily the battle had exhausted
them too, and they made no attempt to pursue. The
Staffs worked hard to improve matters; organised
bodies of the Train were moved off to side roads, and
the wandering groups of Infantry were formed into
temporary Platoons, and placed under the nearest
available Officer. At the cross-roads South of Estrées
a short halt was made, and the column was further
re-organised. All mounted troops and Train were
ordered to continue their march into St. Quentin;
Infantry of the 3rd Division were directed to wheel to
the right, and that of the 5th Division to the left;
they were then collected into Brigades, and finally into
Battalions. Throughout the retirement successive
positions were taken up by Batteries, Sections, or
guns, wherever the ground offered; that the help
thus afforded by the Gunners was appreciated by their
comrades of the Infantry was touchingly shown next
morning; exhausted as they were by the long night-
march, many a man stepped out from the ranks, as
they passed, to silently pat the guns drawn up on the
roadside. Daylight of the 27th of August found most
of the Transport through St. Quentin, and the Infantry
within a few miles of the town. Another rest was
allowed and food distributed to the hungry men; but
rumours arrived that the Germans were approaching
St. Quentin, and the Division had to deploy quickly
and get into readiness South of the town, once more
becoming a fighting force. Fortunately the rumour
was false, the weary and footsore troops were again.
put on the move, and it was only in the afternoon that

2

they finally reached their billets in and around Ollezy, having marched some thirty miles in a little over twenty-four hours after a desperate battle. During the night a further retirement *viâ* Guiscard and Noyon was ordered, the hour of starting being 5 a.m. The long line of Transport moved off at that hour, but shortly came to a standstill, and it was discovered that some of the wagons of the Divisional Ammunition Column had broken down in a narrow part of the road ; there was a delay of almost an hour, and much anxiety was felt, as the rear-guard was holding the line of the Somme Canal at no very great distance from the blocked Transport. The Germans, however, never came into touch with them, and the rear-guard finally withdrew, after having destroyed the bridges and boats on the Canal. Before coming to Guiscard the 5th Division came on to the main Ham-Noyon road, which was also being used by the 3rd Division, and there was naturally some delay. The Commander-in-Chief, Sir John French, met them here and watched the Division on the march, and called up the Battalion and Battery Commanders in order to express to them his satisfaction, telling them that a message had been received from the French to the effect that the action of II. Corps had saved the left wing of the Allied Armies ; and in truth not only had they held, but they had also broken the German attack, thereby saving Paris. This speech had a most encouraging effect on the exhausted troops.

On reaching Noyon the Division was diverted to Pontoise, where it was to billet. The crossing of the Oise was by a narrow and shaky bridge, which was only just passable for the Transport, and which caused so much delay that the rear-guard did not get into billets for some seven hours after the leading troops. Hopes of a prolonged rest at Pontoise had been dangled before our eyes, but, as the billets were commanded by high ground, it was thought better to move on to Carlepont ; and here too their hopes were dashed to the ground, as orders came to move on at midnight. The march across the plateau between the Oise and the Aisne was a most trying one, as the weather was extraordinarily sultry. The Aisne was crossed at Attichy, and billets were taken up at Croutoy. German Cavalry patrols followed the rear-guard, but made no attempt to delay the march. The next day, 31st August, there was another hot and trying march, with constant halts, to Crépy-en-Valois ; here we had rumours that the German Cavalry had swept round the left flank of the Army and had got in rear of the British ; in fact, a German motor-car did approach our outposts in the dark, and the occupants were killed.

Early in the morning of 1st September the Germans attacked the rear-guard just as the Division was moving out of Crépy, but the 13th Brigade repulsed the attack, and then, after falling back through Crépy, took up a defensive position South of the town. The "Duke's" here put up a very pretty little ambush, capturing a car containing a German General and his Staff. The 15th Brigade, too, with guns and a Squadron of North Irish Horse, was sent off to the left to support the 4th Division, which, it was rumoured, was being attacked. Its co-operation was not required, but, as there were again persistent rumours that the German Cavalry were in our rear—in fact, a patrol of six Uhlans had got across the river at Meaux—the 15th Brigade was detailed to march on the left, while the orderlies accompanying the G.O.C. and the Divisional

Staff scouted ahead in the woods. However, no Uhlans were met with, and the Division marched without further incident to Nanteuil. On the 2nd the march was continued to Cuisy, and on the 3rd to Boulers, the Marne being crossed at Isles-Les-Villenoy, where the bridges were destroyed after the troops had crossed. Lieut.-Col. Tulloch, the C.R.E., had now become very expert in blowing up bridges, and so many had he demolished that, when the Division had to submit a name for the Légion d'Honneur, Tulloch was unanimously voted as most worthy to receive the decoration. Eleven bridges in all had been destroyed, and the two Field Companies, the 17th and the 59th, had carried out their task with conspicuous bravery. On the 13th August a Subaltern of the 59th Company had gone back 7 or 8 miles behind the rear-guard in order to complete the destruction of the suspension bridge at Pontoise, which was reported not properly done ; and at Mons a Subaltern of the 17th Company had set off a miss-fired charge with a revolver shot, though he must have been dangerously close to bring off the coup. On this day a German wireless was intercepted ordering their Cavalry to strike at the left flank of the British Army ; firing was heard in that direction, but there were no further signs of an attack.

On the 4th the Division had a trying night-march to Tournans, only 15 miles from Paris, starting at 9 p.m. There were numerous delays caused by one thing or another ; the advance-guard took a wrong turn in the Forêt de Crécy, a Battalion fell asleep at the hourly halt and lost touch, and the 3rd Division crossed our road. There was a good deal of straggling, which naturally annoyed the G.O.C. He met one man, a Reservist, crawling along and using his rifle as a support ; to his stern inquiry why he had fallen out the man replied that he was exhausted ; and well he might have been—for slung over each shoulder was an enormous Belgian hare, three huge round loaves took the place of his knapsack, and tied to his belt was a colossal frying-pan.

CHAPTER II

THE AISNE AND LA BASSÉE FRONT

Maps 3 and 4

AT Tournans, appropriately so named, the Army was turned about. The retreat was at last over, and late in the afternoon of the 5th of September the joyful order was received, " Army is advancing—Be prepared to move at a moment's notice." The effect was electrical ; the men's spirits rose to the highest pitch, the difference in their bearing on the march was most marked, and there were no stragglers on that day. Perhaps what pleased every one most was the knowledge that the Germans were now going to suffer for the savage way in which they had burnt and pillaged the farms on their way South. This day brought home to one some of the horrors of war ; wagons, guns, dead horses, and every sort of material lay strewn about the sides of the road ; but the most maddening spectacle was the wanton wreckage of the farms and houses ; ricks were burnt, dismembered cattle, pigs, and sheep were flung about indiscriminately, and the stench was appalling ; furniture out of the cottages (much of it old and priceless) was broken and thrown aside ; and perhaps the most blatant sight of all was the pile of empty wine bottles which marked the bivouacs of the retreating savages.

The first part of the march was to Villeneuve, then

through the forest of Crécy to Mortcerf, and here Head-
Quarters stopped, the advance-guard (15th Brigade)
pushing on 3 miles farther to La Celle. Small
parties of stray Uhlans were met with in the forest,
but they did not offer any opposition, and evinced no
sorrow at being captured. On the 7th the advance was
continued to Coulommiers and Boissy-le-Chatel, and on
the 8th to Doué, where a short halt was made. On
passing through Doué the advance-guard (13th Brigade
with the 27th Brigade R.F.A.) found themselves
opposed by rifle-fire, and had to deploy. It soon
became clear that the German rear-guard meant to
make a stand, and defend the line of the Petit Morin,
evidently in order to cover the crossing of their main
body over the Marne. The 14th Brigade were brought
up, and the two Brigades, well supported by two
Brigades of Artillery, plunged into the wooded valley,
and occupied the hamlets of St. Cyr and St. Ouen with
little opposition ; then, after a pause, they pushed up
the steep Northern slopes, gained the top of the ridge,
and from there neared the La-Ferté-Boussières main
road. By this time the 5th Division had gained so
much ground, that they were some 2 miles in advance
of the 3rd Division on the right and the 4th on the left,
both of which seemed to be heavily engaged ; and the
G.O.C. decided to send the Cyclist Company along the
main road to Boussières, in order to strike at the rear
of the Germans opposing the 3rd Division. No sooner
were the cross-roads at Montapeine in our possession
than the Cyclists were let loose, and in a short time
they had captured a hundred Uhlans ; unfortunately
some British guns opened an accurate fire on them,.
killing a few of our Cyclists, and forcing the remainder
to retire, with the result that many of the Cavalrymen

escaped. As it was getting nearly dark now the advance was stopped, and the tired troops bivouacked where they stood.

The task of the 5th Division the next day (9th September) was to cross the river Marne, and continue to press the enemy. The bridge leading to Méry was found to be intact, and the Division crossed at Saacy without difficulty ; but when the advance-guard (14th Brigade) reached the plateau near Le Limon, it was met with heavy Artillery and rifle-fire, both from Hill 189 (South-East of Montreuil), and from its left front. The position of the 5th Division was at the North end of a big loop of the Marne, some 3 or 4 miles in advance of the III. Corps on the left, who were held up at La Ferté at the Southern end of the loop, and the Germans on the ridge running from La Ferté to Montreuil were able to enfilade the left flank of the Division with impunity. In the thick woods it was impossible to say exactly where the enemy was, and a concealed German Battery near Hill 189 seized every opportunity of shelling any of our troops that emerged on to the open ground. It was not till the evening that a flash betrayed the whereabouts of this persistent Battery, and enabled our Artillery to deal with it effectively. The D.C.L.I. charged through the woods, but were brought up by a hail of bullets from a wood 80 yards on their right flank ; to meet this opposition they had to change direction to the right, so exposing their left flank to the main trenches 300 yards away ; thus they remained on the edge of the wood unable to move. The 15th Brigade was then sent up and deployed on the right, connecting up with the troops the 3rd Division ; even so it was found impossible to push on, although the Bedfords and Dorsets, supported by the Norfolks, managed to reach Bézu, where they dug themselves in in the dusk.   In the late afternoon, too, the 13th Brigade was sent forward into the loop to see if it could get across at the railway bridge and attack the ridge, but nightfall put an end to the battle, and by next morning the enemy had cleared out, after having fought a very successful rear-guard action.   In the dark the D.C.L.I. were withdrawn to a road at the back of the position, where an amusing incident occurred ; dog tired, they had thrown themselves down on the road and were soon wrapt in sleep, when a swelling shout, mingled with many invectives, aroused the Officers ; at once the Battalion was ordered " Fall in — Fix bayonets — No firing," and they momentarily expected a night-attack ; but the shouts came from the men themselves, whose feet, sticking out into the road (as T.A.'s feet always do when wagons or guns are passing), were in jeopardy of being driven over by the G.S. wagon bringing up their rations !   The episode ended in much laughter, and joy at the prospect of biscuits and bully-beef.

These difficulties had prevented much progress being made, and the holding up of the 5th Division, too, had delayed the advance of the 3rd Division.

On the 10th September a start was made at 4 a.m. towards the valley of the Aisne, the 15th Brigade leading as advance-guard, covered by the 3rd Cavalry Brigade.   Hill 189 was passed, where stood the derelict German Battery, or what remained of it, with some twenty corpses lying around.   The enemy was in full retreat, and the Cavalry had an exhilarating time, bringing in many prisoners ; and occasionally the Divisional Artillery had the chance of shelling a hostile column.   During this and the following day traces of the precipitate retreat of the Germans were very manifest, the roadside was littered with cast-off equipment, rifles, clothing, etc. The Division bivouacked for the night near Chézy, and continued the march the following day *viâ* St. Quentin to Billy-sur-Ourcq without any incident worth recording.

The Sixth French Army was now close on the left, moving towards Soissons and Noyon, and a short march on the 12th, in pouring rain, through Hartennes and Nampteuil, brought the head of the Division to the edge of the plateau overlooking the Aisne Valley. The 13th Brigade, close on the heels of the Cavalry, were the advance-guard, and, as they approached the Aisne, they could see ahead of them the strong position on the Northern bank, 2 miles or so on the other side. The Aisne is a sluggish river, 60 or 70 yards across ; on the North side the hills stand out like a wall, with the thickly wooded spurs dipping down sharply into the valley, while on the South of the river lay the heights of Champagne, practically a tableland, whence a series of ridges sloped down towards the river ; the valley in between these heights was a veritable death-trap ; no living creature could exist there except in the hours of darkness. The German guns posted on the heights commanded all the crossings, and the enemy was fully prepared to hold up by every means the advance of the British. It was clear that a formidable task lay in front of the Division, and the position was not one to be lightly rushed ; nobody could say whether the German Army were awaiting us, or whether, as at the Marne, they were only rear-guards. Definite orders, however, were received from Corps Head-Quarters that the advance was to be pushed on strenuously.

THE AISNE.

Map 3

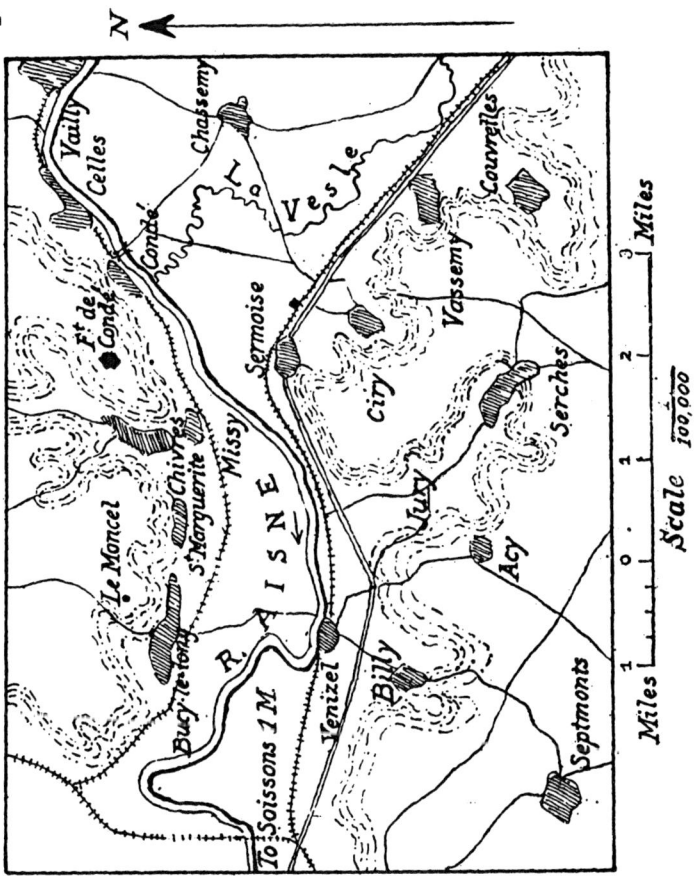

N

Vailly
Celles
Chassemy
La Vesle
Condé
F.t de Condé
Sermoise
Courcelles
Vassemy
Chivres
St. Marguerite
Missy
Ciry
Acy
Le Moncel
Bucy le long
R. AISNE
Serches
Venizel
Billy
Jury
Septmonts
To Soissons 1 M

Scale $\frac{1}{100,000}$

Miles

Miles

[To face p. 26.

By dusk the Cavalry reported that the bridges had been destroyed, and that they could do no more. There was, however, one left, the Condé Bridge, which was allotted by the II. Corps for the crossing of the 5th Division, but this was held by the Germans. Early on the 13th, the 13th Brigade, led by the West Kents, set out to reconnoitre the river line, and Lieut. Pennycuick, 59th Company R.E., reported two out of the three piers of the Bridge at Missy broken. The time was short, the R.E. had nothing with them but what they carried in their tool-carts, so, with ready resource, after the West Kents had cleared the enemy from the piers, they set to work to build rafts, and by the evening had five ready, two made of planks and three of straw and wagon-covers, in which two Battalions were ferried across. While the 13th were down by the river their Transport was stampeded by shell-fire as it tried to cross the plateau, and many men and horses were killed. The Artillery also found itself being heavily shelled without any chance of replying, as the range to the Chivres heights was too great. The 3rd Division on the right had crossed the river at Vailly, and the 4th Division on the left at Venizel—it was imperative that the gap between these two Divisions should be filled at once. The 17th Field Company R.E. had built a pontoon-bridge at Venizel, and during the night the 14th Brigade got across. The Manchesters and East Surreys advanced to St. Marguerite to support the 12th Brigade of the 4th Division, who had seized the high ground about Le Moncel, and soon became hotly engaged in Missy. Captain Johnston and Lieut. Flint, 59th Company R.E., greatly distinguished themselves here, working for all they were worth ferrying the wounded across and bringing

up ammunition into the village. Captain Johnston,
who afterwards became Brigade-Major of the 15th
Brigade and was killed at "Hill 60" in May 1915,
was awarded the V.C., and Lieut. Flint the D.S.O.
In the afternoon the German Artillery had grown more
active, and big howitzers (8-inch and 5·9) came into
play ; it was improbable that a rear-guard should
have such heavy Artillery, and the certainty that the
Germans were in strength had to be faced. The 14th
Brigade made some progress on the left, and were
now on the line St. Marguerite-Missy, but the G.O.C.
decided that no further advance could be hoped for
until the plateau on which stood the Fort de Condé
was in our hands. Accordingly, orders were issued
for the 13th Brigade to be withdrawn South of the
river, and for the 15th Brigade, who had crossed at
Venizel, to move through Missy, and, with the 14th, to
attack the Chivres Ridge on the 14th. It was difficult
to discover the Battalions asleep in the fields in the
early morning, and to collect the Brigade together ;
St. Marguerite was being heavily shelled, and it was not
till 4 p.m. that the two Brigades advanced to the attack.
The Artillery crossed the river at Venizel, the only
available bridge, in full view of the enemy—fortunately
it was a misty morning, and most of the Batteries of
the 8th and 15th Brigades R.F.A. got across unnoticed ;
the 27th Brigade R.F.A. were in action on the plateau
above Missy ; and the 28th Brigade, consisting now of
only two guns of the 122nd Battery, had the misfortune
to drop one of them in the river while crossing the
bridge, which was, however, afterwards recovered by
the R.E. Owing to the shape of the ground there was
great difficulty in finding positions, the only suitable
ones for 18-pounders being right out in the open, firing

up the Chivres valley ; these were occupied, but soon had to be given up when the German fire became too hot. The howitzer positions were an easier job, and the 61st (Howitzer) Battery found an excellent one near St. Marguerite and did some useful work there. It was near here, in some dead ground, that the entire Transport of two Artillery Brigades, together with that of one Infantry Brigade, were assembled together in a mass, when the enemy's guns unfortunately found them out, and created great havoc among them.

As has been said before, it was about 4 p.m. that the Infantry advanced. In the 14th Brigade the Manchesters and D.C.L.I. were in front, with the East Surreys echeloned in the right rear. In the 15th Brigade the Norfolks were leading, then the Cheshires and Bedfords, while the Dorsets remained at St. Marguerite and improved the defences there. Progress was very slow, direction was lost in the thick woods, and the men surging inwards on to a horseshoe-shaped road got inextricably mixed up ; a high wire-netting fence, together with some wire entanglements, added to the difficulties. Men began firing at each other in mistake for the enemy, and, though the casualties were few, many men turned about and retired down the hill into Missy ; the stream of men increased, the little village was heavily shelled, and the 15th Brigade lost many men. The attack had been a failure, and the Brigades found themselves back on the St. Marguerite-Missy line.

The R.E. had by now built a trestle-bridge near Missy bridge, and in the night Sir Charles Fergusson met the Brigadiers of the 13th and 15th Brigades there, and gave them orders for another attack on the Condé plateau next day. The Artillery started by

shelling the Chivres spur, but their fire produced little
effect, as the Germans were all hidden and scattered
about the wood. The 15th Brigade, with the Norfolks
in front and the Bedfords in support, pushed on a
short way, but the attack gradually came to a standstill, whereupon orders were issued to take up a defensive line and consolidate the positions held. The
14th Brigade, reinforced by the West Kents and the
K.O.S.B., of the 13th Brigade, garrisoned the line
St. Marguerite-Missy, and the 15th Brigade was brought
back during the night to Jury, crossing by a pontoon-
bridge which had been made between Missy and
Venizel; the remaining two Battalions of the 13th
Brigade watched the Condé bridge from the low
ground between Sermoise and Chassemy. The troops
on the North side of the river were placed under the
command of Brig.-Gen. Rolt, commanding the 14th
Brigade, Head-Quarters being at an insalubrious farm
known as " Rolt's Farm."

The attack had passed into defence, and for the
next fortnight it was stalemate. The Division was
astride the Aisne, half the Infantry and two Batteries
of Artillery being on the right or Northern side, the
enemy trenches 200 to 300 yards from ours, dominating
them from the higher ground. The ground was a
bog, and in the damp, foggy woods water was struck
only a foot below ground ; consequently most of the
line there had to be constructed of breastworks, where
the men lived in shanties made of faggots and water-
proof sheets. It rained incessantly, and our trenches
in the low ground were continuously being sniped by
the Germans from the heights above ; the woods were
daily subjected to searching salvos of shrapnel, up
and down, backwards and forwards ; on these occasions

the men bolted, like a lot of rabbits, into their little cubby-holes till the storm was over, when a prospecting head was to be seen popping out, followed by another, and another, till it was safe to emerge altogether; it was a marvel how few casualties there were. St. Marguerite and Missy were fiercely bombarded with H.E. every day; the Eastern end of the former, where the road turned sharply to the right, was a most "unhealthy" spot, for it was in full view of the Germans, and anything that came in sight of them was instantly shelled; the place was called "Hell's Own Corner." The bulk of our Batteries were on the Southern side of the river (some in silent positions in case of counter-attack), covering the front at a range of about 4000 yards; those on the North side had at last found some good positions, and were never discovered by the Germans. It must be remembered that at this period we had no Heavy Artillery, beyond the normal Divisional Artillery, which included the 108th 60-pr. Battery, and a great event was the arrival of some 5-inch howitzers from South Africa; they were given positions near Jury, whence they plumped lyddite shells around Fort de Condé.

Divisional Head-Quarters were in the school buildings of Serches, a quiet little hamlet tucked away in a ravine. The Reserve Brigade (15th), at Jury, were given the task of constructing a defensive system on the left bank, under the guidance of Colonel Tulloch, the C.R.E. The 14th Brigade remained on the front until the 24th, when they were relieved by the 15th, Brig.-Gen. Lord Edward Gleichen taking over from General Rolt.

Only one little episode needs recounting. Early in the morning of the 27th of September an Officer's patrol of the 13th Brigade sent in a report that the Germans were seen crossing the Condé bridge in force. Everybody had long felt anxious about the gap between the 3rd and 5th Divisions, and consequently this report caused great commotion. Orders were given to load up and be ready to march at a moment's notice, the 3rd Division and the II. Corps were warned, and the 14th Brigade was moved from Jury to the cross-roads East of Serches; the 15th Brigade sent one Battalion back to the pontoon-bridge, and even the Cavalry were turned out of their comfortable quarters in Braisnes. But a misty dawn brought forth no Germans; it was nothing but a scare, brought about by a patrol, who had lost their way, being mistaken in the dark for Germans; eventually everybody, in a somewhat ruffled frame of mind, returned to their normal stations.

It will not be out of place to quote here Lord French's words; he says in his Dispatch: "With great skill and tenacity Sir Charles Fergusson maintained this position throughout the whole battle, although his trenches were necessarily on lower ground than those of the enemy on the Southern edge of the plateau, which was only 400 yards away."

At the end of the month orders came that the whole of the II. Corps was to be moved to another sphere of operations, and there was much surmising as to where this would be. The trenches were taken over by the 6th Division, and, as this was the first occasion on which a Division in close contact with the enemy had been relieved, everybody regarded it as a most critical operation. The problem was to withdraw in the dark without letting the enemy know; guides had to be provided who had reconnoitred every inch

LIEUT.-GEN. SIR CHARLES FERGUSSON, BART.,
K.C.B., K.C.M.G., D.S.O., M.V.O.

[To face p. 32.

of the ground, and the strictest silence had to be observed. But all went well, the enemy never discovered the relief, and in the morning of the 2nd of October the 15th Brigade were across the river, and Sir Charles Fergusson had handed over the command of the Front.

Now ensued a very pleasant week's marching through one of the most beautiful parts of France with grand Autumn scenery. The weather was fine, with gorgeous days and cold nights, and, above all, shells, Missy, and the trenches were left behind. Desperate secrecy was observed, marching was only by night, and troops were enjoined not to show themselves during the daytime for fear of the enemy's aeroplanes. Evidently some great object was in view, though what it was could only be conjectured. Above was a bright clear moon—fortunately night-bombing was unknown then. What caused much joy was that a German wireless message had been intercepted to say that "all six British Divisions were still on the Aisne." On 7th October the Division entrained at Pont St. Maxence and neighbouring stations; rumour had it that Calais, or even Ostend, or Bruges, would be the detraining station, but it turned out to be Abbeville—rather a disappointment, as it was hoped it would be farther afield. French motor-buses were to have been ready to take the troops from their billets on to the Dieval area, but they arrived late, and then were too few, so there was great delay, and many of the men had to spend the day and the greater part of the night lying in the fields by the roadside. However, by the afternoon of the 10th the Division was concentrated round Brias. Rumours came that the French were being hard pressed round Arras, that the German Cavalry were trying to

3

get round our Northern flank, and that Lille was surrounded by the enemy, but was still holding out with
a few French Territorial Battalions in it. Hence the
hurry ; but no one seemed to know anything definite
except that the Division would soon be fighting
again.

La Bassée Front

(Map 4)

An early start was made on the 11th of October
towards Béthune through the mining district of Bruay.
The Corps urged the Division to hurry, but the G.O.C.
pointed out that this was somewhat difficult as our
road was being crossed by a British Cavalry Division
moving from East to West, and by a French Cavalry
Division moving from West to East, while a long French
convoy was trying to get through both columns. On
nearing Béthune, the Division was ordered to occupy
the high ground South of Hinges, and the Divisional
Mounted Troops were dispatched in all haste to the
objective. They approached it with every military
precaution, watched by an admiring Staff, but, on
arrival at the top of the hill, they found to their disappointment and annoyance only a French ammunition
column peacefully slumbering there ! That night the
Division billeted in Béthune, and, during the evening,
orders and definite information as to the situation were
received. The French Army was being outflanked ;
they had been driven out of Vermelles, and, it was
believed, out of Givenchy ; the II. Corps, 5th Division
on the right, 3rd on the left, was to advance North of
the Béthune-La Bassée Canal, and to swing round gradually on to La Bassée, pivoting the right on the Canal.

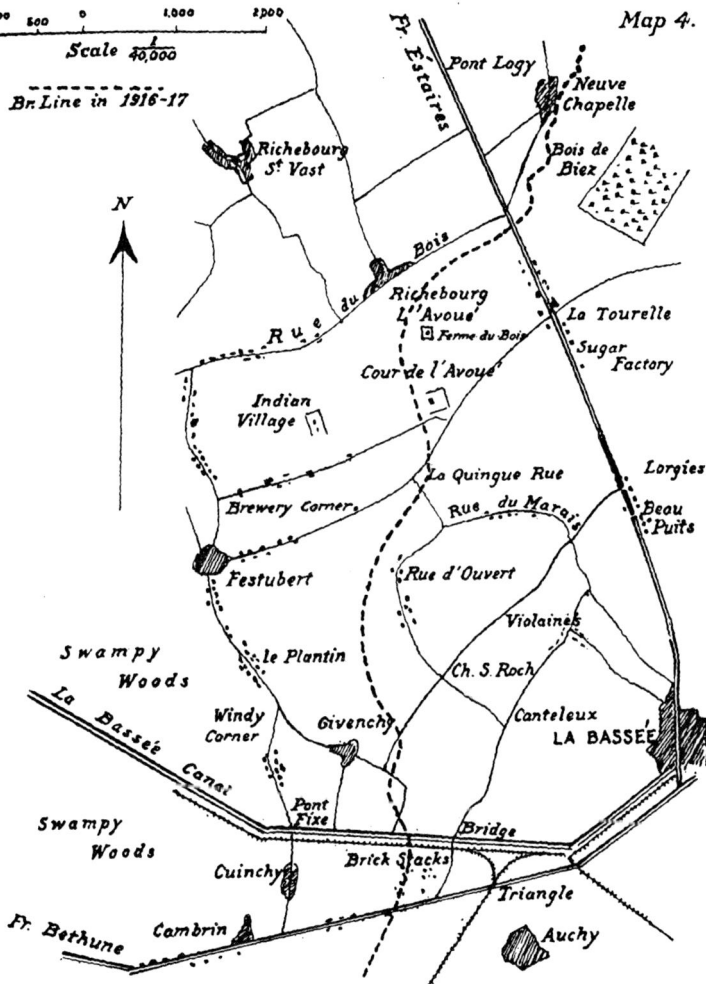

LA BASSÉE FRONT.

Map 4.

Scale $\frac{1}{40,000}$

Br. Line in 1916-17

N

Ft. Estaires
Pont Logy
Neuve Chapelle
Bois de Biez
Richebourg St Vast
Bois
Rue du
Richebourg L'Avoué
Ferme du Bois
La Tourelle
Sugar Factory
Cour de l'Avoué
Indian Village
La Quingue Rue
Lorgies
Rue du Marais
Beau Puits
Brewery Corner
Festubert
Rue d'Ouvert
Swampy Woods
le Plantin
Violaines
Ch. S. Roch
La Bassée Canal
Windy Corner
Givenchy
Canteleux
LA BASSÉE
Swampy Woods
Pont Fixe
Bridge
Cuinchy
Brick Stacks
Ft. Bethune
Cambrin
Triangle
Auchy

The Division was from the outset allotted a very extensive frontage, the original line being from the Canal South of Givenchy to beyond Richebourg L'Avoué (about 4 miles), but this frontage was very much increased when it was ordered to take over ground South of the Canal as well. The 13th Brigade (Brig.-Gen. Hickie, who had replaced General Cuthbert) was sent to Annequin with orders to act in co-operation with the French troops attacking Vermelles; to the North of the Canal came the 15th Brigade, and then the 14th, who had the 3rd Division immediately on their left. With such a big front it was only possible to keep two Companies of the Devons (who had recently replaced the Suffolks in the 14th Brigade) in reserve. The Divisional Artillery, which had been re-equipped and brought up to strength before leaving the Aisne area, was disposed to cover this front. Head-Quarters of the Division were at Gorre Brewery.

The country North of the Canal is perfectly flat, with the exception of a slight rise at Givenchy; near the Canal, on both sides, are some " marais," or swampy woods, but farther North it is mostly arable land, intersected with muddy dykes, and rows of trees which much impede the view; to the South are the villages of Cuinchy and Cambrin, and the mining village of Annequin with its big slag-heap; farther on, towards Vermelles, the ground is of chalk formation, and becomes more undulating.

It was a cold morning on the 12th; the freezing fog was so thick that one could hardly see 50 yards in front of one. On the right, General Hickie dispatched the West Kents, "Duke's," and K.O.S.B. to co-operate with the French; the 15th Brigade took up the line from the Canal at Pont Fixe with the Dorsets;

then came the Bedfords at Givenchy, and the Cheshires holding Festubert; the 14th continued the line with the D.C.L.I., Manchesters, and East Surreys at Richebourg L'Avoué, where, after some fighting, touch was gained with the 7th Brigade of the 3rd Division. During the afternoon the Germans attacked along the Canal bank, but they were repulsed by the Dorsets, Lieut. Roper being killed whilst gallantly leading a bayonet charge.

The night passed off fairly peaceably, except for a half-company of the Cheshires, who were captured in Rue D'Ouvert. It appears that a patrol reported Rue D'Ouvert free of Germans, and that this half-company was sent to make sure of the fact, when they found themselves surrounded by superior forces and violently attacked. The brave little band, though they had lost heavily, succeeded in getting into a farmhouse, which they held all day till the Germans set fire to it; having no water they tried to put the fire out with some wine there was in the farm, but in the end they were compelled to surrender, their numbers reduced by this time to thirty.

The 13th October was not a happy day for anyone. In the first place, the 13th Brigade could make little progress South of the Canal; they were up against an extraordinarily strong position in the famous " Railway Triangle," which remained in German hands till almost the end of the war; the empty trucks, from which the enemy fired, had been fortified with stockades of sleepers, and the position was well-nigh impregnable. The French could make little progress against Vermelles, though they made attempts both on this day and the next to capture it. On the left, the 14th Brigade made some progress, but the advance was very slow, for every house and hamlet had to be fought for. But it was in the centre, on the 15th Brigade front, that the trouble arose. Givenchy was heavily bombarded by the Germans for hours, and rendered quite untenable ; the Bedfords held out gallantly, but, after losing some sixty men, many of the wounded being buried by the falling houses, gradually fell back to the trenches in rear of the village. The Dorsets, who had advanced a bit and dug themselves in, were violently attacked at the Pont Fixe on the Canal, fire being opened on them from their left flank, which was now uncovered, and also from the railway embankment on the South. An act of treachery on the part of the Germans was responsible for many men being killed ; a party of some twenty of the enemy advanced holding up their hands, and, as the Dorsets advanced to take their surrender, these twenty suddenly fell flat down, and a fusillade was opened on our men from a flank. The Battalion retired slowly in admirable order to Pont Fixe, which they still held, though much shaken and pitifully thinned ; they had lost some four hundred casualties ; and two guns of the 11th Battery, which had come up in close support, had also to be abandoned. Colonel Bols, the C.O. of the Dorsets, was severely wounded in this attack, and was actually taken prisoner and stripped of his clothing, but in the confusion he managed to crawl away, and regained his freedom, to become afterwards Chief of the Staff to General Allenby in Palestine.

Reports now came in that the enemy was advancing in large numbers along the Canal bank, and the situation appeared to be most critical. The two Companies of the Devons, which were in reserve, were hurried up to the assistance of the 15th Brigade, but by nightfall things had quieted down, and there were no attacks.

The next day (the 14th) the remainder of the Devons
went up to the 15th Brigade, and a concerted attack by
the 13th and 15th Brigades was arranged for the afternoon ; but little could be accomplished. The second
French attack on Vermelles had failed, the 13th Brigade
could make no progress towards the Triangle, and this
prevented the 15th Brigade from advancing ; but the
14th Brigade, with the 3rd Division on their left, made
some advance towards the Éstaires-La Bassée road.
In the evening the French extended their left to the
Canal, thus relieving the 13th Brigade, who were sent
back in reserve.

The 15th October was comparatively uneventful ;
the men were much exhausted by the continuous hard
fighting ; but on the left the 14th Brigade again made a
little progress, and the 3rd Division gradually wheeled
round to the South-East.

The 16th and 17th showed a welcome advance. The
whole of Givenchy fell once more into our hands, and
the Bedfords, who occupied it, found some of their
buried and wounded men there ; Rue D'Ouvert was
taken by the Cheshires, Canteleux by the Norfolks, and
in the 14th Brigade the D.C.L.I. and East Surreys
seized Lorgies ; later, Violaines was occupied by the
Cheshires, and the 14th Brigade took Beaux Puits.
Astride the Canal, the Devons, who were ordered to
make good the bridge on the Canteleux road, came in
for some very heavy shelling ; one Company was on the
South side, and two on the North side, and as they
advanced to their objective a tornado of shells was
poured into them, coming straight down the Canal into
the ditch they were holding, and setting fire to some
stacks behind which they were taking refuge. Under
cover of the smoke they fell back, taking their wounded

with them, and many acts of bravery were performed there, notably by Lieut. Worrall (later in the war C.O. of the Bedfords).

La Bassée was now almost within our grasp, and the Corps urged the importance of capturing it, but, although a general attack was delivered on the 18th, no further ground could be gained. The D.C.L.I. in their advance met with a hail of bullets from machine-guns and rifles in a sugar-factory on the Éstaires-La Bassée road, and though the place, which was a regular fortress, was bombarded by all our available guns, it resisted our efforts to capture it.

Hitherto the II. Corps had been advancing, even if slowly, but the enemy was now reinforced by apparently the VII. and XIV. Corps, set free by the fall of Antwerp, and on the 20th of October the whole line was violently attacked. The pressure became greater on the 21st; the enemy penetrated between the 14th Brigade and the 7th Brigade on their left, and the D.C.L.I. found their flank in the air; they rushed up a Platoon, which took up a position facing half-left, but they were enfiladed by machine-guns and were forced to retire; the Manchesters also at Trois Maisons made a fine bayonet charge when the enemy were within 200 yards, but they, too, were caught in enfilade and lost heavily. Early in the morning of the 22nd, when the foggy dawn was just breaking, the Cheshires were surprised while digging, and were driven back to Rue D'Ouvert, taking some of the Dorsets with them, and losing some two hundred casualties; and the 13th Brigade Battalions, too, which had been sent up to reinforce the 14th, were fiercely attacked, the three Companies in reserve in the 15th Brigade having to be sent to their assistance. Later a counter-attack under Lieut.-Col. Martyn (temporarily commanding the 13th Brigade vice General Hickie, sick), composed of the Manchesters, D.C.L.I., and Worcesters, was organised, but they could not gain much ground; it had, however, the effect of stopping the German pressure for the time being.

The Corps Commander now decided to fall back to a defensive position, which had been partially prepared; and, accordingly, on the night 22nd–23rd October, the 5th Division withdrew to the line running just East of Givenchy and Festubert, then through La Quinque Rue, and West of the Bois de Biez to Neuve Chapelle. Owing to the heavy fighting and the severe losses of some units, the proper organisation of the Infantry Brigades had to be departed from; it was necessary, for example, to withdraw the Cheshires and Dorsets from the front line, but they could not be sent to the rear for a real rest because the Division was holding such a wide front and being constantly attacked; instead, they were billeted in barns round Hamel and Rue de Béthune, where they were being constantly turned out ready to return to the front line in the many critical moments of the next few days. It is interesting to note that these Battalions persistently complained of being fired at by night from the houses in the village, thus starting the delusion which afterwards affected all newly arrived Divisions. The 15th Brigade was reinforced by the "Duke's," while the Bedfords in their turn had got mixed up with the 13th Brigade.

The French now re-inforced their troops North of the Canal both with Infantry and Artillery, and for a few days they came under the orders of Lord E. Gleichen, but eventually they sent over a General, who assumed full responsibility for the defence of the trenches held by them—roughly from Givenchy (inclusive) to the Canal.

The next seven days were a lively period for the 5th Division. In the space of sixty days it had fought at Mons, stood the brunt of the battle of Le Cateau, taken part in the terrible retreat, fought again on the Marne and the Aisne, and already on this front had almost reached its limit ; it was now holding a long line with worn-out and exhausted troops, with no reserves, and was attacked all day and every day. The Division and Brigade Staffs were continually being faced with a crisis ; either a Battalion appealed for help, which could not be sent, or a report arrived that the enemy had broken through ; but the men fought stubbornly, lost trenches were recovered, heavy shelling, wet, and exhaustion were borne unflinchingly, and a standard of human endurance established that no one hitherto thought possible ; the Staffs, too, learnt that though the Germans might capture a trench it did not mean that they could break through. The two most critical periods were on 26th October and 29th October. On the former day the Germans pierced the centre of the 7th Brigade of the 3rd Division, and captured Neuve Chapelle, and at the same time attacked the trenches of the West Kents to the South of the village. Exposed to terrific shelling, with their left flank uncovered, the West Kents immortalised themselves by repulsing the German attack and holding their own ; they lost most of their Officers and were sadly reduced in numbers, but they stuck to their trenches, and were finally brought out of action by two Subalterns, one with two years' and the other with six months' service. The situation at Neuve Chapelle was so critical that Brig.-Gen. Maude (commanding the 14th Brigade),

with the Bedfords, Cheshires, and Dorsets, was ordered
to counter-attack in co-operation with the 3rd Division,
but the situation had meanwhile improved, and the
attack was never launched.

The arrival of the Indian Divisions on the 29th removed a certain amount of anxiety from the Divisional
Staff, although it did not at first help the troops in
the trenches. Orders were received for the 5th Division
to be relieved by the Lahore Division, and some of the
latter's Battalions at once took over the trenches.
Early on 29th October the Germans made a fierce
attack on the trenches North of Festubert, held by
the 1st Manchesters (of the Lahore Division) and the
Devons, who had been in the firing-line for practically
sixteen days. The attack was repulsed, but was
renewed again about 10 a.m. with equal vigour. The
Germans continued to shell the trenches, although their
Infantry did not advance ; they could be seen digging
in and driving saps forward to our lines. In accordance
with the plan of relief the 2/8th Gurkhas took over
during the night the trenches held by the 1st Manchesters. The Germans resumed their desperate
assaults on the 30th, and pressed the Devons and
Gurkhas very hard ; at one moment they reached the
wire in front of the Devon trenches, but, although
almost at the limit of human endurance, the Devons
held firm. The attacks continued during the whole
morning, after which the enemy gave up his Infantry
assault and settled down to bombard our trenches.
With the dying down of the Infantry fire it was thought
that the crisis was over ; it was therefore a shock when,
late in the afternoon, news came from the Devons that
the Gurkhas on their left had been driven by shell-fire
out of their trenches, which had promptly been occupied

by the Germans.   The relief had to be suspended, and
the Devons were re-inforced by their reserve Company,
who restored the situation on the left, while one of
the relieving Battalions, the 58th Rifles, recovered the
trenches on the right.   The Devons had had a heavy
toll of losses in the past week : Captains Besley and
Elliot, and Lieutenants Ditmas, Dunsterville, and
Hancock had all been killed, and many men too—
heroes all, of whom Devon may well be proud.

After this the relief was proceeded with, and Major-
Gen. T. L. Morland, who had succeeded Sir Charles
Fergusson (promoted to Lieut.-Gen.) in command of
the Division, handed over to the Lahore Division,
leaving in six of his Battalions to strengthen the line,
together with most of the Divisional Artillery.

In these accounts of lurid battles, and intricate
operations and marches, one is apt to overlook the very
necessary and excellent work done by the Divisional
Supply Column of the R.A.S.C.   Never once during
the past two months' fighting, during the retreat and
during the advance, had the rations failed ; it speaks
highly of the organisation, and the devoted work of
the Officers, and of the lorry and G.S. Wagon Drivers,
many of whom had to run the gauntlet of the enemy's
shells and bullets in bringing their loads up to the
troops.   Nor would any history be complete without
paying the very highest possible tribute to the R.A.M.C.,
who, in their advanced dressing-stations in ruined
cottages, nearly always under shell-fire, carried on their
noble work night and day, often having to go without
sleep for days at a time ; their record of self-sacrificing
devotion is indeed a magnificent one.

CHAPTER III

NOVEMBER 1914 TO MARCH 1915

(MAPS 5 AND 6)

AT the end of October the Germans opened their great offensive at Ypres, in their vain endeavours to reach the Channel Ports, their attacks extending down to Messines. Sanguinary battles were going on at Ypres, where the immortal 7th Division held the front so heroically against the furious onslaughts of the German hordes, until the I. Corps came to their assistance.

The 5th Division, with no time to rest or recover from their hard fighting, were pulled out from the Neuve Chapelle-La Bassée front and sent up North. In common with other Divisions, they became much split up ; in fact, there was a regular jumble everywhere ; Brigades, Battalions, and Batteries were sent hither and thither to patch up the holes in the strained British front, and many units had no notion to what formation they belonged ; Battalions were attached for a day or two to a Division or Brigade, and then spirited away elsewhere as the circumstances demanded. For some time the Division was one only in name, and it was not till near the end of November that the component units forgathered together again.

It will be convenient, therefore, to follow briefly the doings of each Brigade separately ; but, before

MESSINES FRONT. Map 5.

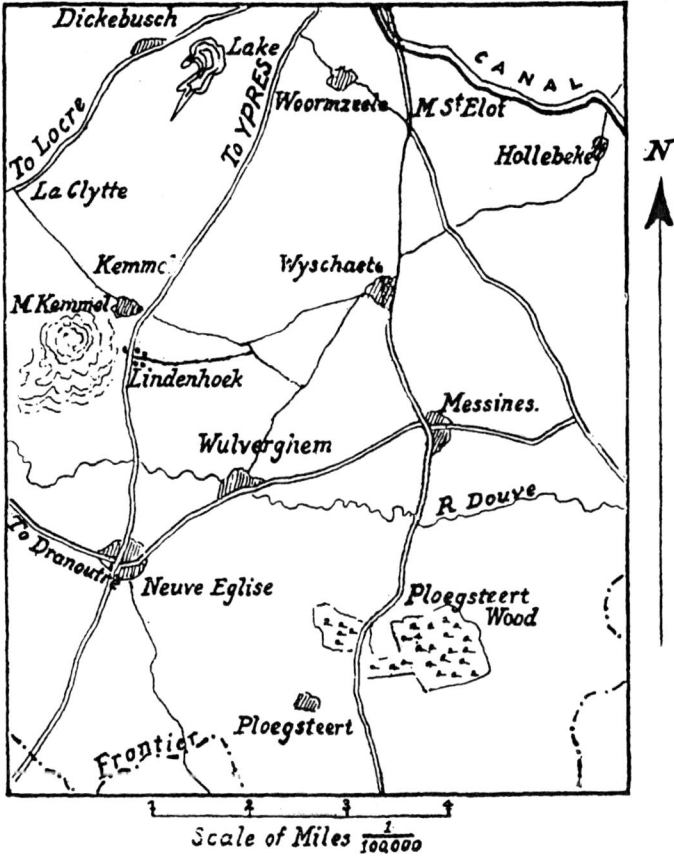

Dickebusch

Lake

To Locre

CANAL

To YPRES

Woormzeele

M St Eloi

Hollebeke

N

La Clytte

Kemmel

Wyschaete

M. Kemmel

Lindenhoek

Messines.

Wulverghem

R. Douve

To Dranoutre

Neuve Eglise

Ploegsteert Wood

Frontier

Ploegsteert

Scale of Miles $\frac{1}{100000}$

[To face p. 44

doing so, it is necessary to glance at the operations of the Cavalry.

On the 30th of October the Cavalry Corps, under General Allenby, were holding a long thin line against overwhelming masses of the enemy, from Hollebeke, South of the Ypres Salient, to Messines inclusive, together with Conneau's French Cavalry; to their right was the 4th Division of the III. Corps, holding the Eastern edge of Ploegstreet Wood and St. Yvon, facing somewhat North-East. That evening the 2nd and 3rd Cavalry Divisions, under Generals Byng and Gough respectively, were compelled to fall back to the Canal, and Hollebeke was captured by the Germans; the 1st Cavalry Division, under General de Lisle, was also hard pressed at Messines, where the Germans, who had gained a footing in the town, were soon driven back again. Early in the morning of the 31st a strong attack forced the Cavalry out of Messines, and at the same time the 4th Division were seriously engaged farther South. No supports were available until 11.45 a.m., when the K.O.S.B., the K.O.Y.L.I., and the London Scottish came up, and were sent forward at once to re-capture the ridge. The K.O.S.B. on the right, and the K.O.Y.L.I., London Scottish, and 3rd Hussars on the left, advanced to the attack, and by 1 p.m. had made considerable progress in the Western edge of the town; but during the night there was another violent attack on the exhausted 2nd Cavalry Division, who were forced back towards Kemmel, thus laying bare the left flank of the London Scottish. The latter at once threw back a defensive flank, but the enemy was by this time round both sides, and a retirement of the whole force became inevitable. In the nick of time the XVI. French

Corps arrived on the scene, and, together with Conneau's Cavalry, they held the prepared trenches in front of Wulverghem, with the British Cavalry and Battalions of the 5th Division in support. In these two days' fighting there had been many casualties ; the K.O.Y.L.I. lost 5 Officers and 150 other ranks, Captain Carter and 2nd Lieut. Corballis being the only Officers left with the Battalion.

To turn now to the Brigades of the 5th Division :

13TH BRIGADE

The K.O.S.B., after taking part in the attack on Messines, were sent up to Ypres on 5th of November in company with the 9th Brigade to join the 3rd Brigade of the 1st Division, and to take over the trenches South of Hooge on the Menin road. Here they remained for thirteen days in the front line, suffering much from sniping, shell-fire, and " Minnies " ; though there were no regular attacks, the strain on the Officers and men, tired as they were, was very great, and it was with much joy that they were relieved on the 20th and rejoined their Brigade at Locre at the end of November.

The K.O.Y.L.I. and West Kents were likewise first engaged on the Messines front in support of the Cavalry until the middle of the month, when they were also sent up to Ypres, and took part in an attack on Hooge Château, occupying the trenches in the thick woods East of Zillebeke. Both Battalions rejoined the Brigade at the end of the month.

The " Duke's " were attached to the 15th Brigade, and went up with them to Ypres, where they were at first in support of the Cheshires and Bedfords at

Hooge, and, on the 10th, took over the trenches near
Weldhoek Château ; here they had some heavy fighting
on the 11th and 13th, and lost altogether 14 Officers
and 380 other ranks. They were relieved on the 15th
by the 11th Hussars, and returned to Locre on the
21st November.

14TH BRIGADE

The whole Brigade was at first kept back as a
reserve to the Indian Corps, marching and counter-
marching to support or re-inforce any threatened
point, until the 7th November, when it was sent up
North to take over the trenches at Laventie, relieving
the 8th Brigade and part of the Indian front. The
fire trenches were in fair order, but there were no
communication, support, or reserve trenches, and there
was no wire in front ; their line ran along the Rue
Tilleloy, from near Fauquissart on the left, to the
cross-roads of Chapigny on the right, the German
trenches being from about 200 yards distant on the
left, to only 25 yards on the right. There is little to
record of their week's stay here ; opposite to them
were the 32nd Jaeger Regiment, who possessed some
active and accurate snipers, and on two or three
occasions they were subjected to mild bombardments,
but on the whole they had a quiet time, and they
were enabled to improve their trenches and put some
concertina wire out. These Jaegers were inclined to
be facetious, and used to put up a spade on their
parapet on which they marked the hits or misses
of our snipers, and on the right, where the trenches
were so close, some back-chat and mutual taunts were
exchanged between the opposing sides. On the 15th
the Brigade left, and marched to Méteren, with orders

to take over the trenches East of Wulverghem from
the 39th French Division, which ran from the Wulverghem-Messines road to the Messines-Wystchaete road ;
there was a perfect network of trenches here, all very
narrow and shallow, and tenanted by many gruesome
relics of the hard fighting which had taken place.
On the 28th November they were relieved by the
15th Brigade, just arrived from Ypres, and sent to
the reserve area at St. Jan Capelle.

15TH BRIGADE

The 15th Brigade were at Dranoutre on 1st Novem-
ber, and, like the other Brigades, were for the first
four days employed in support of the Cavalry and the
French. On the 5th they combined with the 7th
Brigade (General McCracken) and marched to Ypres,
taking with them the " Duke's " and the two R.E.
Companies of the Division (17th and 59th). At dusk
they relieved the 21st and 22nd Brigades of the 7th
Division East of Hooge, with the Bedfords and
Cheshires in the front line ; Head-Quarters were at
Beukenhorst Château, afterwards so well known as
Stirling Castle. Nothing much happened till the afternoon of the 7th, when a sudden rifle-fire broke out on the
left ; the troops on the left and some of the Bedfords
were seen to be retiring, and the enemy broke through ;
it seems that an order to retire was given, but by whom
no one could find out—possibly by a German in British
uniform. Captain Monteith and the Adjutant of the
Bedfords quickly rallied the men, and succeeded in
driving some of the enemy back, and another party,
led by Q.M. Sergeant Byford, charged with a cheer and
bayoneted fifteen or twenty Germans in their trenches ;

the 9th Brigade supports also counter-attacked on the left, and the position was restored, twenty-five prisoners being captured. The Bedfords were again heavily attacked on the 14th, the day on which the Flower of the German Army, the Guards, was launched against the front, and, as every one knows, completely repulsed. The fighting on that day on the 15th Brigade front was perhaps not so severe as at other parts ; but in one place the enemy managed to push a machine-gun through the woods, which enfiladed the Cheshires, forcing them and the Bedfords to retire. There was much confused fighting in the woods, and it was only by the grit of the men that the line was held ; among the many instances of individual gallantry one may be mentioned : Sergeant Mart, with only one other man of the Bedfords, succeeded in recovering some of the lost Bedford machine-guns by stalking and rushing the Germans in their trenches. On the 7th again there was heavy firing, but no attack supervened ; in fact, the Germans on the immediate front seemed to have retired a bit. At length on the 20th the two Battalions were relieved by French troops, and on the 21st marched back to Locre ; they had been fourteen days in the front line, and, in addition to the stiff fighting, had suffered much from the bitter cold and wet. At Locre a well-earned rest was enjoyed ; on the 25th the Brigade moved back to St. Jan Capelle, and on the 28th took over the trenches at Wulverghem from the 14th Brigade.

ARTILLERY

The 8th (Howitzer) Brigade remained with the Meerut Division for another month ; at this time the need was much felt for more howitzers, both heavy and

4

light, and the Divisional 4·5 Howitzers of nearly every Division were scattered about in different places. The Divisional 18-pr. Brigades (15th, 27th, and 28th) and the 108th Heavy Battery left the Indian Corps on 1st November, and marched to Bailleul; on the following day they took up positions covering the Cavalry and French on the Messines front, as follows:

> 27th Brigade (on the right), near Neuve Église.
> 15th Brigade (centre), West of Kemmel-Neuve-Église road.
> 28th Brigade and 108th Heavy Battery (left), near Lindenhoek.

A 6-inch gun and a 6-inch Howitzer Battery were attached, and were in action also near Lindenhoek; later, another 6-inch gun and a Battery of 4·7 guns (115th) joined, and " D," " J," and " E " Batteries, Royal Horse Artillery, also worked with the Division Artillery during the latter part of the month.

The guns supported the French attacks on Messines on the 6th and 7th November, both of which attacks failed, and again the 39th French Division on the 14th. The 8th (Howitzer) Brigade on the whole had a quiet time with the Indians, and, with the exception of the 37th Battery, which remained with them until the end of January, rejoined the rest of the Artillery at the end of November, taking up their positions with the others.

By the 29th November the Division was collected together again, with the exception of the 37th Battery, and the Cheshires, who were so weak in numbers that they were kept back in Corps Reserve. As the line now taken up was to be the home of the Division during the Winter, it merits some further description. It ran from La Petite Douve in a North-Westerly direction up the slope to the Wulverghem-Messines road, and thence along the crest of the ridge East of Wulverghem to Hill 75—a frontage of approximately 3500 yards. The German line was roughly parallel to ours, at a distance varying from 30 yards on the left to about 800 yards on the Messines road. The trenches were poor ; owing to the water-logged nature of the ground, digging beyond a depth of a foot or two was impossible, and protection could only be obtained from breast-works ; these were neither high nor of sufficient thickness, and in places gaps of as much as 200 yards separated the occupied portions. Wire entanglements were practically non-existent, and on dark nights the lack of them, and the gaps, led to some awkward incidents ; on one occasion a ration party nearly delivered their loads to the enemy in place of our own troops, but, realising their position just in time, reached our lines from the front. The Messines Ridge completely overlooked the forward area, and rendered movement by day impracticable ; the few communication trenches which did exist were a nightmare of mud and water.

Some 2 miles behind our lines rose the wooded slopes of Kemmel Hill, which afforded grand observation over the enemy's lines, and was a frequent resort of Artillery Officers, Generals, and Distinguished Visitors to the Front. Although bombarded from time to time, the mill on the top of the hill continued working for some considerable time, the farmer being apparently unconcerned by the battle being fought around him.

After the heavy fighting in November in this area both Armies had settled down to their first Winter of trench warfare, and, except for one occasion, no attacks were made by either side. On this occasion (14th December) the French XVI. Corps with the British II. Corps undertook an offensive between Hollebeke and Messines. The rôle of the 5th Division Infantry was to demonstrate, and to lead the Germans to believe an assault was intended, while the Divisional Artillery, much re-inforced, supported the attack of the 3rd Division, in addition to carrying out heavy bombardments on their own front. The attack was a failure ; no progress was made, and, after another attempt on the following day, the operation was stopped.

Although the fighting activity, with this one exception, was small, the period spent in this sector was an extremely arduous and trying one for the troops. There were none of the amenities, such as duck-boards, iron-arch shelters, braziers, etc., which afterwards made life in the trenches bearable ; the Winter was one of continuous rain, and as a consequence the men lived in trenches half full of water and mud, often knee-deep, and the complaint of " trench feet " became common. Various expedients were tried to minimise this danger, the most successful one consisting of square wooden tubs for the men to stand on, made by the R.E. ; it was necessary to provide a cross-bar of wood for a seat, or the men preferred to turn the tubs upside down and sit on them with their feet in the slush ! But there was very little real sickness, and this was no doubt due to the excellent food and warm clothing provided. The ground near the trenches, which was mostly ploughed land, quickly became a morass, which, owing to the scarcity of hurdles and fascines, made the movement of reliefs and ration and fatigue parties a tiring process with many slips and falls, and the many drainage operations undertaken failed to make matters any better.

All through the long Winter nights the R.E. and Infantry worked hard to improve the defences, but it was a very labour of Sisyphus ; no sooner had one part been built up, than, weakened by rain, another portion slid down into the water at the bottom of the trench, and the work was endless. By dint of much hard work, though, the position was gradually improved, until, by the Spring, the conditions in the trenches were tolerable, and a large amount of wire too had been put up in front. Whilst the units holding the line lived in such condition, those in support fared little better ; at first these were located in positions close behind the line, sheltered from view as much as possible. Accommodated as they were in shallow holes, scooped out of the ground, conditions were little better than those in the front line ; later, farms, or the remains of farms, were lived in ; these were usually roofless shells, but, having hard floors, they were infinitely preferable to the dug-outs, and, where cellars existed, there was comparative comfort. Brigade reserves were lodged in the villages of Neuve Église and Dranoutre ; the former was occasionally shelled, and many houses were damaged, but the latter place was untouched, and remained so until the Division left the area. The Divisional Reserve was billeted on Bailleul, in normal times an uninteresting town, but to troops returning from the line a veritable paradise. Billets were good, and at the shops, of which there were a good few, much could be got to supplement the ration fare ; at the Asylum on the Locre road very welcome and necessary hot baths could be obtained, while there were facilities for football and other recreations in and around the town. The many cafés and estaminets provided a further condition of civilisation, and at the " Faucon " in the " Place " a very passable dinner could be obtained.

The Artillery remained in much the same positions as they took up on first arrival, the Batteries in each Brigade relieving each other every second or third night. Activity on both sides was slight; nearly all firing was done by day, night-firing being very occasional; facilities for close observation were limited, as it was impossible for F.O.O. to approach the line by day; in some cases farm buildings close up were used as O.P.'s, but the life of a F.O.O., who had taken up a position on the roof-beam of a barn before dawn and was compelled to remain there until darkness made his return to the Battery possible, was not a happy one. When telephone communication remained intact, Infantry Officers would occasionally observe for the Artillery, but, owing to the want of technical knowledge and the lack of Artillery maps, the results were rarely satisfactory. The first 18-pr. H.E. shells were issued about this time, and were highly approved of. The wagon-lines were an orgy of mud, horses generally standing in the open up to their hocks in slush. About the end of February the British Artillery was divided up into " Divisional," " Army," and " G.H.Q.," the former consisting only of 18-pr. and 4·5 Howitzer Batteries, and the 108th Heavy Battery consequently left the Division.

The Divisional R.E. had their quarters in Neuve Église and Dranoutre, and were fully employed in making fascines and hurdles by day with the help of Infantry fatigue parties, and in improving the trenches by night. Dressing-Stations were established at Neuve

Église and Dranoutre, the three Field Ambulances relieving one another in turn. Divisional Head-Quarters were at first in the Convent at Locre, but moved later to the Château at St. Jan Capelle, where they remained for the rest of the time. During the Winter the system of reliefs varied ; at first the front was held by two Brigades, with the 3rd Brigade in reserve, and " triangular " reliefs were carried out ; afterwards the 14th Brigade had a short sector in front of Neuve Église, whilst the 13th and 15th relieved each other on the Wulverghem front.

As previously stated, activity was slight ; the enemy's Artillery fire was only occasional, being mostly directed on the trenches, Wulverghem, Neuve Église, and Kemmel Hill. Among the German troops opposite were many snipers, who, having the advantage of a slightly commanding position, made things very uncomfortable for the front-line troops ; most of our casualties were caused by their fire, though the shelling of Neuve Église contributed to the toll, the 14th Field Ambulance being particularly unfortunate in having a shell fall into their Dressing-Station.

Daily, or rather nightly, patrolling in No Man's Land took place, and the Germans conceived the ingenious idea of tying chickens to their wire, which warned them by their clucking of the approach of our men ; the same thing happened two years later when geese were discovered acting as sentinels in No Man's Land.

On Christmas Day occurred the much-discussed truce, which (leaving aside all questions of right or wrong) gave our troops the unique opportunity of inspecting No Man's Land and the enemy position at their ease. On that day every Officer and man in

the Division received a Christmas card from Their
Majesties, and, in addition, a present of a pipe, tobacco,
and cigarettes from Princess Mary. The King and
the Prince of Wales visited the Divisional area on
14th December, the D.C.L.I. on that occasion cheering
the Prince as " Duke of Cornwall "; and the King of
Belgium also honoured the Division with a visit, and
inspected the 15th Brigade, who were in reserve in
Bailleul.

Two Territorial Battalions, the 9th London Regiment (Q.V.R.) and the 6th Cheshire Regiment, joined
the Division, and were sent into the trenches with the
regular Battalions for training ; the 6th Cheshires were
withdrawn on 1st March, and replaced by the 6th
King's Liverpool Regiment. Re-inforcing drafts arrived
and brought the Battalions up to an average strength
of 850, except in the Cheshires, who still remained at
300. In March, Brig.-Gen. Lord E. Gleichen, having
been promoted Major-General and ordered to take
over the command of one of the new Divisions forming
in England, handed over command of the 15th Brigade
to Brig.-Gen. Northey ; about the same time Brig.-Gen.
J. G. Geddes succeeded Brig.-Gen. J. Headlam as
C.R.A., and Brig.-Gen. Wanless O'Gowan assumed
command of the 13th Brigade.

On the 17th February orders were received for the
13th Brigade to join the 28th Division (General Bulfin)
in the Southern part of the Ypres Salient ; and ten
days later the 15th Brigade were also ordered to join
the same Division, the exhausted 83rd and 84th
Brigades coming down South to take their place ;
at the same time the 37th and 65th (Howitzer)
Batteries were sent to the 27th Division.

13TH AND 15TH BRIGADES WITH THE 28TH DIVISION

The line taken over ran from the Mound at St. Eloi to the Bluff on the East side of the Ypres-Comines Canal, but early in March it was shortened by the 27th Division taking over the Mound; it consisted mostly of breastworks, and was commanded by the enemy position at White Château opposite the left centre. On the left of the position, at the Bluff, a curious situation existed in the "International" trench; part of this trench was held by the British and part by the Germans, the occupying troops being divided by blocks; some wag suggested that the repairs should be undertaken by each side on alternate days! The trenches were a slight improvement on those at Wulverghem as regards drainage conditions, but the fighting was a great deal more lively. The ground immediately in rear of the trenches was swept by rifle-fire by day and night, and a number of casualties used to occur while reliefs were going on. The enemy's Artillery, too, was very active, using mostly 5·9 or 8-inch Howitzers, of which he appeared to have a great number; our own covering Artillery was the 28th Divisional Artillery, but they had a miserable allowance of ammunition, which was mainly shrapnel and very little use against the enemy's deep trenches. There was also a Belgian Battery of 75 mm. guns, which apparently had a more liberal supply, most of which was H.E.; this Battery was frequently called upon by the Infantry, and its rapid fire and satisfactory bursts had a most heartening effect on them.

All was quiet till the 14th March, when the enemy opened a bombardment on the British position from the Canal to St. Eloi; simultaneously a mine was exploded under the Mound, and a formidable Infantry attack was launched. At the first onset they succeeded in forcing back the troops of the 27th Division on the right of the 15th Brigade, and captured the village of St. Eloi, thus threatening the flank of the 15th Brigade ; supports were rushed up, and the 13th Brigade (in reserve at Kruistraat) moved up their Battalions to be ready for further developments. During the night the 27th Division by a very gallant counter-attack re-captured St. Eloi, and re-established the original line with the exception of the Mound, which remained in the enemy's hands. The Germans appeared to be well acquainted with our dispositions, as, simultaneously with their attacks, a bombardment was opened on Kruistraat ; the Norfolks, who were on their way up from there for a trench relief, had a lucky escape, as the shell-fire did much harm to the village, and would just have caught them had they been there.

The enemy made no further attempts to take St. Eloi, and, after a short period of liveliness, conditions returned to " normal."

Map 6

YPRES.

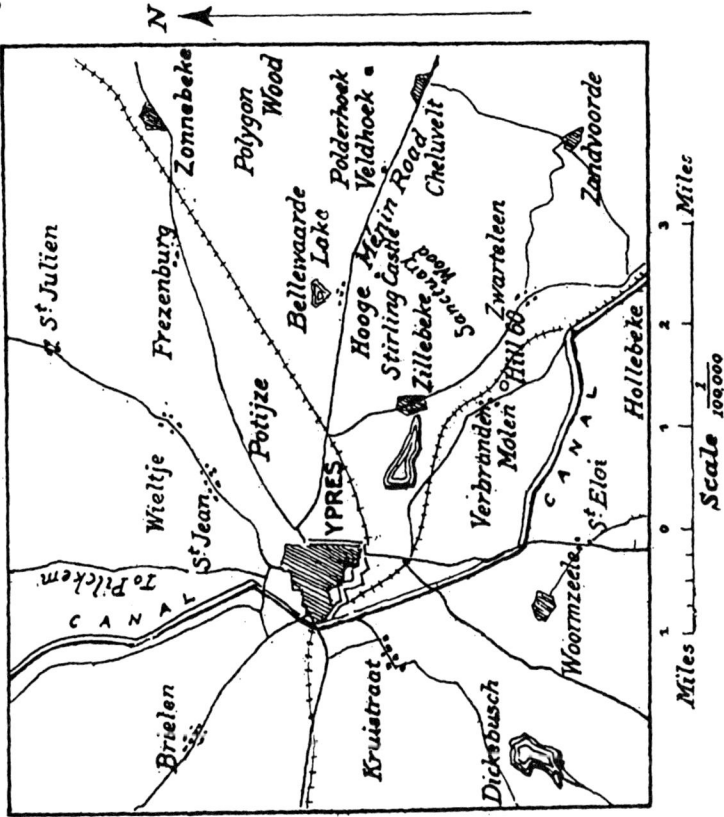

N

To Pilckem

CANAL

Brielen

Wieltje

St Jean

St Julien

Potijze

Frezenburg

Zonnebeke

Polygon Wood

Bellewaarde Lake

Hooge

YPRES

Kruistraat

Dickebusch

Stirling Castle

Zillebeke

Sanctuary Wood

Menin Road

Polderhoek

Veldhoek

Cheluvelt

Zwarteleen

Verbranden Molen

Hill 60

Woormzeele

St Eloi

CANAL

Hollebeke

Zandvoorde

Miles 1   0   1   2   3   Miles

Scale $\frac{1}{100,000}$

CHAPTER IV

"HILL 60," YPRES

(Maps 6 and 7)

THE relief of the Division from the Wulverghem Front was completed at the beginning of April, and on the 6th, General Morland assumed command of the new sector in the Ypres Salient.

The new line ran from the East of the Mound at St. Eloi by the Bluff, " Hill 60," and Zwartelen, to the Western edge of Armagh Wood. The 15th Brigade remained in position in the right sector, and the 13th Brigade in the left sector, the 14th Brigade being at first in reserve.

Weather conditions were now more favourable, and consequently the state of the trenches, and of the troops therein, was much better. The trenches, or rather breastworks, were rapidly improved, and soon formed a solid line of defence, though not yet continuous or adequately provided with support positions.

On the taking over of the sector, preparations for the attack on " Hill 60 " were proceeded with. As in all mining operations, large Infantry working parties were required nightly by the Engineers to carry up the necessary stores and dispose of the spoil from the mine-shafts. The Engineers and Territorials worked gallantly and with cheerful determination, so that, |by the middle of April, their preparations were completed, and the scene set for one of the most sanguinary and hard-fought encounters of the War.

From the village of Zillebeke the ground to the South slopes gently up for some 2000 yards to the Zwartelen-Zandvoorde ridge. Running approximately from North-West to South-East through the position are the roads from Ypres through Verbrandenmoelen to Hollebeke, and from Zillebeke through Zwartelen to Zandvoorde. Between these roads, and roughly parallel to them, runs the double line of railway from Ypres to Comines, which, some 600 yards from Zillebeke, enters a cutting ; this cutting extends beyond the crest of the ridge and is some 15 or 20 feet in depth. The earth excavated has been deposited on either side, and has, in course of time, formed small hillocks. On the West side are two of these hillocks, one a long, irregular mound on the top of the ridge, which, owing to its shape, became known as " the Caterpillar," and the other, a smaller mound some 300 yards down the slope towards Zillebeke, more conical in shape, known as " the Dump." On the East side of the cutting is a third mound, more or less regular in shape, and situated on the highest point of the ridge. It is this mound of excavated earth that has become famous as " Hill 60." To call it a hill gives a somewhat false impression, as, in fact, it is merely a small protuberance on the crest of a gently sloping ridge ; its position on the highest portion of the ridge, however, rendered it an excellent post for observation of the ground around Zillebeke and Ypres.

Prior to the attack, Brigade reliefs had been carried out, and, on April 16th, the 14th Brigade was holding the right sector of the Divisional Front, and the 15th Brigade the left sector, around " Hill 60." The 13th Brigade had been withdrawn on the 10th, and were at

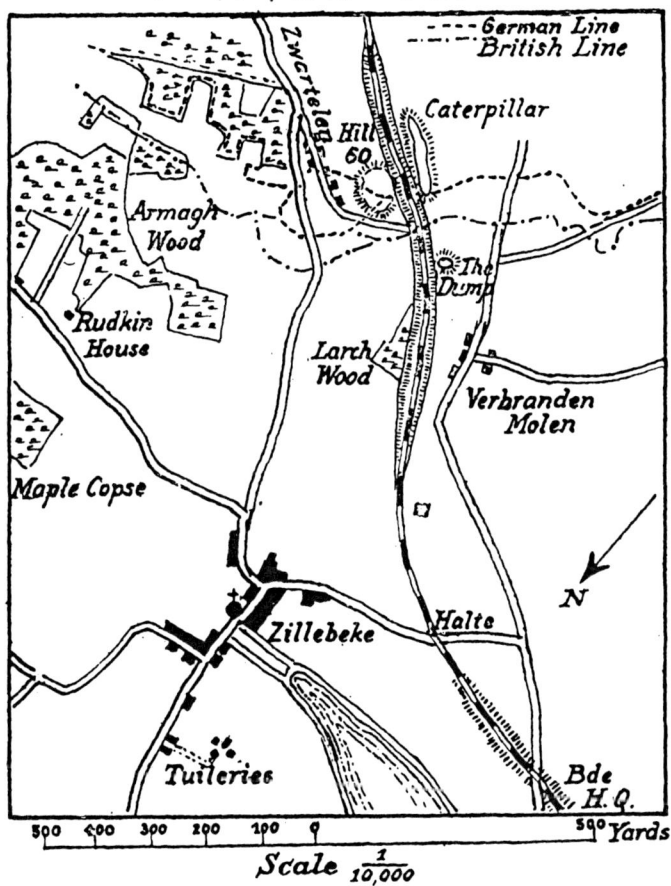

--- German Line
--- British Line

Caterpillar

Zwarteleen

Hill 60

Armagh Wood

Rudkin House

The Dump

Larch Wood

Verbranden Molen

Maple Copse

N

Halte

Zillebeke

Tuileries

Bde H.Q.

500 400 300 200 100 0 500 Yards

Scale $\frac{1}{10,000}$

[To face p. 60.

Ouderdom training for the attack. The 15th Brigade dispositions were : Norfolks on the West of the railway cutting, Dorsets on the East, at the foot of "Hill 60," and Bedfords and Cheshires continuing the line through Zwartelen to Armagh Wood. Brigade Head-Quarters was at Transport Farm near Zillebeke Lake.

On the night of the 16th–17th the 13th Brigade moved up, the West Kents and K.O.S.B. taking over the trenches in the vicinity of "Hill 60," the "Duke's" being held in support at Zillebeke Lake, and the K.O.Y.L.I. in reserve. The 13th Brigade Head-Quarters were located in the railway embankment in dug-outs near Transport Farm. The 15th Brigade adjusted their position around the Hill to allow of the concentration of the attacking troops, but otherwise remained in position ; and their line was strengthened by the distribution of the machine-guns of the 13th Brigade and a Battery of motor machine-guns. The 27th Brigade R.F.A. were in positions near Kruistraat, 28th Brigade R.F.A. near Zillebeke Lake, and the 15th Brigade R.F.A. East of Ypres ; in addition, various other units of Field and Heavy Artillery were placed under the orders of the C.R.A. for the attack. Divisional Head-Quarters were on the Vlamertinghe road, about three kilometres West of Ypres.

On the 17th the day passed quietly until the evening, the Germans being apparently unaware of the concentration of troops which had taken place. The weather was fine and sunny, and the ground dry. For some half-hour before the attack absolute calm prevailed, hardly a shot being fired by either side. At 7.5 p.m. the first mine under the Hill was exploded, and our bombardment commenced ; simultaneously rapid fire was opened by our Infantry and machine-guns along the whole of the 15th Brigade front. The synchronisation was perfect, and the sudden change from absolute calm to pandemonium was most striking. The second and third mines were fired at fifteen-second intervals, and at 7.6 p.m. the West Kents, supported by the K.O.S.B., advanced and captured the Hill, penetrating into the enemy's position some distance beyond the crest. The casualties in this first rush were very light, and some of these few were caused by falling débris from the mine explosions. The surprise was complete. Practically the whole of the German garrison on the Hill was destroyed by the mines, and, in addition, numbers of men in the neighbouring positions, rashly exposing themselves in their curiosity to see what had occurred, were caught by the rifle and machine-gun fire. For some little time after the assault the enemy Artillery, realising that an attack had taken place, but not knowing the exact position, fired wildly in all directions. The railway cutting was heavily shelled, as were also the trenches on either side of the Hill, and it was during this bombardment that gas and lachrymatory shells were first used against the Division. Naturally the troops were unprovided with any defence against such barbarous methods of war, and some confusion was caused by the lachrymatory shells, mainly in the Battery positions.

The West Kents and K.O.S.B. were now hard at work consolidating the captured position, and by 12.30 a.m. on the 18th they reported themselves entrenched on the Hill, with two communication trenches linking up with our old front line. About 4 a.m. a heavy counter-attack was launched by the enemy, and a fierce struggle ensued : some of the K.O.S.B.,

who were entrenching, did not wait to pick up their
rifles and bayonets, but rushed at the Germans armed
with picks and shovels, which they used with great
effect. The enemy were not prepared lightly to
surrender their position, and pressed their attacks with
great determination. As the day wore on the fight
continued, but by this time our position was known,
and was subjected to bombardment by Heavy Artillery
and "minenwerfers." Owing to the curve of the
salient the enemy were able to bring almost enfilade
fire to bear from the direction of Zanvoorde, in addition
to the fire from the guns on our front, and the trenches
rapidly disappeared under a deluge of high explosive.
Overwhelmed by this fire, and taken in enfilade by
rifles and machine-guns on " the Caterpillar," our troops
were gradually forced back, until, by the evening,
they were holding a line below the crest. The " Duke's "
were brought up from Zillebeke Lake, their position
there being taken by the K.O.Y.L.I., and a counter-
attack was made at 6 p.m., our position on the Hill
being re-established after a stubborn encounter. The
enemy Artillery fire throughout the day had been
heavy both on our forward positions and back areas.
The 13th Brigade Head-Quarters were unlucky in having
a shell fall outside their dug-out where some of the
Staff were standing, and the Staff Captain was killed.

Before dawn on the 19th the 13th Infantry Brigade
were withdrawn, except the Q.V.R., who were left
under the command of the 15th Brigade, and the G.O.C.
of the latter assumed responsibility for the front. The
East Surreys of the 14th Brigade had also been attached
to the 15th Brigade, and they, with the Bedfords, took
up the forward positions. No respite was given to
these troops, who were continually subjected to bom-

bardments and bombing attacks ; and the casualties mounted up steadily.

During the night the activity increased, and throughout the 20th furious attacks were made, mainly by bombing, on our position. In repulsing these attacks the East Surreys immortalised themselves, and for their magnificent conduct on this day Captain G. R. Roupell and Corporal Dwyer of this Battalion were awarded the V.C. Their losses were heavy, amounting to some 250 men, including the C.O. (Major W. H. Paterson) and the Adjutant, both of them owing to Battalion Head-Quarters being blown in. Later, when in rest at Ouderdom, the Battalion was visited by the Corps Commander, who complimented them on one of the finest actions of the War, and told them that, when in reply to a query, he informed Sir John French who was holding the line, the latter remarked, " Thank God ! the East Surreys are there."

Nightfall brought no relief. The enemy, in spite of severe losses, continued to attack the Hill with fury.

Our troops there were rapidly diminishing owing to casualties, until at length only one Officer and a handful of men remained in the position. This Officer (Lieut. Woolley, Q.V.R.) displayed the utmost gallantry, and continued to hurl bombs and encourage his men, with such effect that the position was held against all attacks, until supports could be rushed up to re-inforce the line. This action earned for Lieut. Woolley the distinction of being the first Territorial Officer to be decorated with the V.C., and for his Battalion undying fame.

Still the battle continued, and the tenacity with which the position was maintained was almost superhuman. Trenches or breastworks were practically non-

existent, as, no sooner were they made, than they were
obliterated by shell and " minenwerfer " fire. Amid
the débris of the mine explosions and innumerable
craters of shells and bombs, over ground covered
with our own and the enemy dead and wounded,
the fierce hand-to-hand struggle had swayed to and fro
for more than three days ; but still the Hill was held.
The losses on both sides had been heavy, and on the
21st the Devons were attached to the 15th Brigade and
relieved the shattered Battalions on the Hill.

On 22nd April the focus of attention on the
Salient of Ypres moved farther North, as on that day
commenced the second great struggle for Ypres and the
Channel Ports.

About 5 p.m. the Germans, unable to attain their
ends by fair means, resorted to the use of poisonous
fumes, and released a cloud of chlorine gas against the
Allied Front from Bixschoote to Langemarck. They
hoped by this means completely to overrun the Allied
position, and advance victoriously on Calais. But
once again they made the fatal mistake of under-
rating their opponents. The history of this and subsequent attacks, and the glorious record of the troops who,
half suffocated, stemmed the rush of the Kaiser's
hordes, are written elsewhere. But there was one
result of the employment of gas which must be referred to here. Up to this time real hatred of the
enemy had formed no part of the British soldier's
fighting equipment. Campaigning in another nation's
country, the destruction of hearths and homes had not
touched him as it had the soldier of our Allies, and he
had treated the German as a more or less honourable
opponent (as witness the Christmas Day episode).
Now, however, a change appeared. After witnessing

5

the results of this latest abomination, there was born in the heart of every man such a hatred of a dastardly enemy as nothing else could have engendered. This was a consequence which had not been fully reckoned on by the Germans, but which was perhaps as far-reaching as any, and cost them dear. The effect was immediate ; few prisoners were taken in the subsequent operations in this area, and the determination to overcome such a barbarous foe at all costs was inestimably strengthened.

The 13th Brigade, who had been resting at Ouderdom, were setting out in the evening to relieve the 15th Brigade, but, when on the road, received orders to march and report to the 1st Canadian Division to the North of Ypres. On their arrival in this area they found that the French Front had been broken, and that the Germans were advancing towards the canal South-East of Boesinghe. The Canadians were also being heavily attacked, and had to throw back their left wing to cover the flank. With a view to easing the pressure on this flank, the 13th Brigade, in conjunction with other troops, were ordered to carry out a counter-attack Northwards along the line of the Ypres-Pilckem road : at the same time the French were to make an attack, in order, as far as possible, to regain their position. The attack was ordered for 3.45 p.m. (23rd), but it was impossible to get the troops into position until 4.15 p.m., at which time the assault was launched. The 13th Brigade attacked on the West side of the Pilckem road on a two Battalion front ; the K.O.S.B. were on the right and the West Kents on the left, with the K.O.Y.L.I. and Q.V.R. in support. Owing to the difficulties of communication the arrangements for Artillery support were not completed in time, with the result that, when the attack commenced, there was no supporting fire. The guns, however, soon commenced firing, and greatly facilitated the advance, doing an enormous amount of damage to the enemy, who were more or less in the open. The ground over which the K.O.S.B. had to move was open, and, having suffered heavy casualties from the numerous machine-guns brought forward by the Germans, they were brought to a stand before they had advanced very far. On the left the ground was more enclosed, and the West Kents made good progress, but, as their attack was proceeding, the French, attacking from the East, moved completely across their front, and masked their fire. At dusk the position gained was consolidated. There was a good deal of confusion in the front line, as the French Zouaves had got mixed up with our own troops, whilst, on the right, near the Pilckem road, the line ran back and was very sketchily garrisoned. During the night the 4th Rifle Brigade was attached to the Brigade, and relieved the K.O.S.B. and the West Kents in the line, the Battalions of the 13th Brigade remaining in support.

On the 24th the French carried out an attack on our left, and some ground was gained. Orders were received for two Battalions to be moved to occupy the trenches on the Wieltje-Poelcapelle road, and the K.O.Y.L.I. and Q.V.R. were sent to take over the position. At the same time the K.O.S.B. and West Kents were moved up from farther back into the close support position. By evening the Allied Line ran from Zonnebeke through St. Julien to the canal South-East of Boesinghe ; and the Germans were still attacking vigorously. On the 25th another violent attack was made on the Canadians and their line was forced back. On the 13th Brigade front the trenches held by the

Rifle Brigade were very heavily shelled, but no assault developed.

On the 26th the Lahore Division arrived, and launched an attack at 2 p.m., which was driven back by gas, and the line remained unaltered.

On the 27th the 13th Brigade were relieved by the Lahore Division. They did not, however, return to the Division at once, being kept in the area North of Ypres, and were constantly moved from place to place as the situation demanded, finally rejoining at Ouderdom on 4th May.

The line now ran some thousand yards South of St. Julien. The German attack still continued, whilst practically all the available reserve British troops had been used up. A glance at the map will show that the position of the 5th Division and the other troops in the South-East portion of the Salient was fraught with considerable danger. A further advance by the enemy in the North, or a successful attack about St. Eloi, would render the withdrawal of troops East of the Ypres-Lille road a matter of extreme difficulty, if not impossibility. On instructions from the Higher Command, therefore, provisional orders had been issued for the evacuation of the forward positions, and for the retirement to a line running East of Ypres; but, thanks to an improvement in the situation farther North, these orders were later cancelled.

Although on the 5th Division front the retirement did not take place, a withdrawal of the line from our left was decided on, the trench in Armagh Wood on our extreme left being the pivot of the movement. A new line was prepared running from Armagh Wood, East of Sanctuary Wood and Bellewarde Lake, to near Frezenburg.

While the events narrated above were taking place, the fighting round " Hill 60 " had abated in fury, though counter-attacks took place from time to time. The 15th Brigade still maintained their position on the Hill, but at a considerable cost. In order to give some relief, the Camerons from the 27th Division were attached to the Brigade for a few days, and did most excellent work.

On 1st May gas clouds were launched by the Germans against the Dorsets, who were holding the position ; this Battalion suffered heavily from the gas, losing some 300 men, but gallantly maintained their line.

During the night of 4th–5th May the Dorsets were relieved by the "Duke's," who had been lent to the 15th Brigade, and withdrew to Larch Wood. The Norfolks were now holding the line to the right of the cutting, and the Bedfords the line from Zwartelen to Armagh Wood.

At 8.35 a.m. on 5th May the Germans again released a cloud of gas against our positions on the Hill. The " Duke's " lost very heavily from the gas, and the half-suffocated remnants of the Battalion were overwhelmed by the Infantry attack which followed. At the first alarm the Dorsets had been rushed up to reinforce, and succeeded in maintaining our original line for some 80 yards to the East of the railway cutting : but the Germans obtained possession of our front-line positions, from " Hill 60 " to Zwartelen, and were now able to take the Bedfords and Dorsets in enfilade. Some two hours later they released another cloud of gas against the Bedford positions in Zwartelen, and succeeded in driving them out of the village.

In the meantime, orders had reached the Cheshires,

who were in reserve in and around Ypres, to move up and counter-attack the Hill ; this Battalion had been out all night digging trenches near Hooge, and had only arrived back at dawn. They were directed to move to Battalion Head-Quarters in Larch Wood, but on the way General Northey detached one Company to take up a position covering Zillebeke and the Lake, as there were no troops between the Germans and that village ; the remaining three Companies proceeded by the line of railway to Larch Wood. The gas clouds had almost disappeared and caused no trouble to these troops ; in fact, the mist that remained somewhat screened their movement.

On their arrival the situation was as follows : Immediately to the East of the cutting the Dorsets, consisting of but 3 Officers and about 100 men, held the original position; from their left, to a point some 150 yards East of the Zillebeke-Zwartelen road, our line had been completely broken, but the Bedfords maintained the position thence to Armagh Wood. The Germans were pouring a heavy fire into the Bedford trenches from flank and rear, and endeavouring to extend their captured position Eastward : parties were also advancing down the slope towards Zillebeke, and some of the enemy were in possession of a farm between Larch Wood and the front line.

The Cheshires re-inforced the Dorsets in the line and formed a defensive flank facing East, from the front line to the Eastern edge of Larch Wood. Two Companies then deployed between the railway and the Zwartelen road, and commenced an advance with the object of re-capturing the position. They suffered considerably from rifle and machine-gun fire, the C.O. (Colonel Scott) being killed, but by 1.30 p.m. they had

LIEUT.-GEN. SIR T. L. MORLAND, K.C.B., D.S.O.

[*To face p* 70

driven the Germans back, and were occupying the
old support trenches. They were unable to advance
farther, but the gap was now filled, and the situation
was more secure ; the 6th Liverpools had also come
up, and were placed in Larch Wood as supports.

On the left the Bedfords had put up a most gallant
resistance, and maintained their trenches East of
Zwartelen. The trenches held by the enemy in Zwartelen formed a salient into our line, and it was only by
erecting a parados, under heavy fire at close range,
that the Bedfords were enabled to make their position
tenable. They had sustained considerable loss, and
the Company of the Cheshires, which had been covering
Zillebeke, was moved up to re-inforce them.

About 9 p.m. three Battalions of the 13th Brigade
came up from Ouderdom with orders to counter-attack
and re-take the Hill. These troops had only been
withdrawn from the fighting North of Ypres on the
4th, the units had not been made up to strength, and
the men were far from fresh. The counter-attack
was arranged to take place at 10 p.m., after a twenty-
minute Artillery bombardment. The night was dark,
and this, and the irregularities of the position, rendered
the forming up extremely difficult. At 10 p.m. the
attack was launched, the K.O.S.B. on the right directed
on the Hill, and the K.O.Y.L.I. on the left directed
on the position thence to Zwartelen. The bombardment had been ineffective, and the K.O.S.B. were soon
held up by rifle and machine-gun fire. On the left the
K.O.Y.L.I. formed up, and attacked from a position
in rear of the Cheshires, with the result that some
confusion occurred ; after a short delay they continued
their advance. What actually occurred is not quite
clear ; some were driven back, but the greater part of

two Companies completely disappeared ; they probably advanced too far and were surrounded. By midnight all troops had fallen back to the positions held prior to the attack.

The following day was spent in consolidating the position and re-organising units which had become mixed in the fighting. Enemy Artillery fire continued to be heavy, and there was much bombing and sniping in and around the old front line. Preparations were made for a further counter-attack, to take place at dawn the following morning ; the objective was our original line from the railway to Zwartelen, and this was to be obtained by bombing along the trenches from either flank.

At 4 a.m. the Cheshires commenced the attack from the railway end, and, after hand-to-hand fighting, succeeded in reaching the point of the salient in Zwartelen. The trenches here were practically back to back, and a heavy fire was opened on them from the East side of the salient at point-blank range. Attacked from three sides, they were forced back out of the village, but succeeded in establishing a block in the trench West of it, which they maintained. Thus some hundred yards more of our line was restored. The Royal Irish Rifles of the 3rd Division were relieving the Bedfords to the East of Zwartelen, but, as the relief was not completed until 4.30 a.m., the attack from that flank never got going.

In consequence of the exhaustion of the Battalions of the 13th and 15th Brigades, the 3rd Middlesex, Royal Irish Rifles, and South Lancashires were lent to the 15th Infantry Brigade to effect much-needed reliefs. The Royal Irish Rifles relieved the Bedfords, as referred to, and, after another day of Artillery and bombing activity, the other two Battalions were moved up to the " Hill 60 " area, and the shattered remnants of the 13th and 15th Brigades were withdrawn.

The battle of " Hill 60 " had now come to an end. After three weeks of very severe fighting we had gained no ground; in fact, we had lost that portion of our position astride the Zwartelen road, which, although it was of little tactical importance to us, when occupied by the Germans became a continual source of trouble and annoyance. Being slightly in rear of our positions farther East, it became a nest for German snipers, who made movement by daylight in these trenches a dangerous proceeding unless strict precautions were taken. The losses on both sides had been heavy ; the casualties of the 13th Brigade in the original attack, 17th to 19th April, amounted to 62 Officers and 1300 men, and those of the 15th Brigade in the period 1st May to the 7th were 33 Officers and 1553 men. The losses of the Germans were certainly as heavy as, if not heavier than, our own.

The results of the battle of " Hill 60," however, must not be judged by territorial gains or losses. When taken, the Hill position formed a sharp and pronounced salient into the enemy's lines. Certainly it was on high ground, but the eminence was not sufficient to afford command over the neighbouring German lines. Thus, open to attack on three sides, and with the German Artillery very greatly superior both in number and calibre, the position was extremely costly to hold. It was only due to the incomparable gallantry and dogged determination of the British Infantry soldier that the Hill was held as it was. The effects of the operation are to be looked for elsewhere than on the battered mound by the railway. Coming, as it did, five days before the opening of the great German drive for Ypres and the Channel Ports, there is little doubt that it was in that sphere that the results were felt. Complete surprise as it was, it certainly succeeded in pinning a considerable number of enemy troops to their ground, and also there is no doubt that it necessitated certain modifications in the original German plans, in that troops destined for the operations farther North had to be diverted to re-inforce and replace those shattered in the constant attacks and counter-attacks on the Hill. Only when the full facts are known will it be possible to give an answer to the question asked by many at the time—" Was it worth it ? "

The withdrawal of the troops from the Gheluvelt Polygon Wood area had in the meantime taken place. The retirement was most skilfully and successfully carried out, and it was some time before the Germans realised what had occurred.

On 8th May, having re-adjusted their positions to conform with the new line, the enemy made a furious onslaught against the British position in the vicinity of Wieltje and Frezenburg. Fighting continued in this area until the 17th, but no material success was gained by the Germans, in spite of the employment of gas and masses of Heavy Artillery.

Foiled in their attempts to capture Ypres the Germans, with characteristic childish spite, were engaged in the systematic destruction of that unhappy town. The use of incendiary shells caused fires to break out in several places, and for three or four days the town was in flames. By night it formed an unforgettable scene, the shattered tower of the Cloth Hall standing out gaunt against the crimson background of the conflagration.

Since the conclusion of the first battle of Ypres in 1914 the town had been left in comparative peace, and had been little shelled. On our arrival there in March 1915 many of the houses were in good repair, and the town presented the usual aspect of civilian life in the battle zone. Many shops were still open, the tobacconist, and the grocer who did business in the " Grande Place," being particularly enterprising in catering for the Army's needs. Other places which remain in the memory are the excellent American Bar in the " rue de la Gare," the tea-shop in the " rue de Lille," the barber's shop in the same street, where the proprietor continued shaving though shrapnel was bursting on his roof, and that favourite rendezvous, the " Hôtel du Nord," near the station. The popularity of the latter place was enhanced by the presence of two fair damsels (whom Rumour later declared to be spies), who served the meals and exhibited the greatest friendship to the troops in occupation.

There were many comfortable billets in the town, and the Cavalry and Infantry Barracks provided excellent accommodation for the Engineers and Quartermasters, and their personnel and stores.

In the middle of April the second bombardment commenced suddenly with an outburst of fire from a large number of guns of all calibres, up to and including 15-inch Howitzers. Much damage and loss immediately resulted, the bursts of the 15-inch shells being particularly awe-inspiring. It was no uncommon sight to see two or three houses collapse like a house of cards when struck by one of these projectiles, whilst a cloud of red-brick dust rose high in the air over the doomed city. The Quartermaster's stores were hurriedly evacuated to the units' Transport lines in the area around Ouderdom, and as many of the troops as possible were moved into the old casemates in the Ramparts, which afforded a very fair measure of protection. The plight of the civilians was pitiable. Numbers fled from the town carrying what belongings they could, and the roads to Vlamertinghe and Dickebusch presented a heart-rending spectacle. Others took refuge in the cellars ; some of these made their escape later, but a number perished owing to the houses and cellars being blown in. The lot of the aged and infirm, and the sick, was terrible, as, unable to do anything for themselves, they had to wait in the pitiless rain of shells until arrangements could be made to move them. The conduct of the Sisters who tended to these, moving from house to house along the shell-swept streets, was magnificent, and was a superb example of unselfish devotion.

The bombardment continued daily, the number and natures of the guns used by the Germans being extensive and peculiar. In accordance with his habit of finding nicknames for the unpleasant implements of warfare, the British Soldier set to work to name his new acquaintances. Sound was the basis of these names, and soon one heard of " The last tram Home " (15-inch Howitzer), " Bouncing Bertha," " Whistling Willy," " Perishing Percy " (the H.V. gun)—the last named became very familiar, owing to our meeting with its relations on many fronts later in the War.

Within a month or six weeks Ypres was reduced to a mass of smouldering ruins. Houses had disappeared, and only in the case of a few of the stronger buildings, such as the Cathedral, the Cloth Hall, the Barracks, and the Prison, could the original be recognised. For the accommodation of troops, only the casemates, and cellars here and there, remained ; but for reserve troops Ypres had ceased to be a desirable locality, and alternative positions had to be found outside the town. The civilians had all gone, and the streets were deserted except for the passage of troops and Transport, who did not spend more time than necessary in traversing the stricken town.

On 24th May commenced the fighting which may be said to terminate the second battle of Ypres. Early in the morning a gas attack was made on the British positions from Hooge to Wieltje, accompanied by the usual intense Artillery fire. A number of trenches near Hooge were lost, and a gap existed at this point for some time, which caused disquietude to the 15th Infantry Brigade on the left of the Divisional Line. During the next day the line was re-established.

Throughout the operations in April and May the Divisional Artillery were constantly and heavily shelled both by gas shells and H.E. Owing to the commanding positions held by the enemy the conceal-ment of Batteries was extremely difficult, and few escaped detection. No large dumps were kept at the guns, and ammunition supply was carried out from the rear echelons by day or night as the situation de-manded. In spite of the difficulties by which they were hampered, they never failed when called upon, and throughout showed the greatest gallantry in serving the guns, whatever the conditions. When the need arose they switched their guns to fire on the enemy masses attacking farther North, and did much execu-tion. The 37th Battery, which was attached to the 28th Division and engaged on the front about Wieltje, did particularly effective work, firing on an average

600 rounds daily—at that time an unprecedented expenditure.

A feature of this period was the bombardment of all the roads and other prominent places within the Salient, which continued day and night. Through this rain of shells the Battalion and Battery Transports had nightly to proceed with their loads of stores and ammunition. Many acts of bravery were performed in this connection, and it is the proud boast of these men that never did the supplies fail to arrive, though rarely a night passed without casualty to men, horses, or vehicles. In order to avoid Ypres, and that dread of Transport Officers, the " Menin road," tracks were made across country, and bridges were built over the canal South of Ypres, which, when completed, rendered the task of supply less hazardous.

Towards the end of May the units of the Division had been re-organised into their proper formations, and the 13th Brigade held the sector South of Woormezeele through St. Eloi ; the 14th Brigade the sector in the centre, astride the Comines Canal ; and the 15th Brigade the " Hill 60 "—Armagh Wood sector. The fighting on our own front had died down, and the period until the end of July was one of comparative quiet, if such a term can be applied to the Salient at this time ; but to our left fighting occurred at Hooge from time to time.

Mining activity continued in St. Eloi and " Hill 60 " areas, and, later, one of the first Tunnelling Companies, consisting of miners from home, untrained in anything else, came up and commenced operations in Armagh Wood. The only operation of importance took place at St. Eloi in June, when the enemy exploded a mine under the trench held by the K.O.Y.L.I. astride the

LILLE GATE, YPRES.

[To face p. 78.

Lille road. The Company holding the trench was almost annihilated by the mine and the shower of paving stones caused by it, but the enemy was prevented from following up his success by the heavy covering fire opened by the troops on either flank.

After the end of May the German Artillery fire decreased considerably, but, as far as the Infantry was concerned, this was counterbalanced by the increase in " minenwerfer " ; many of the latter were in action along the front, the heaviest types being much in evidence. The effect of these projectiles on the breastworks was appalling, a direct hit making a gap of 15 feet or more in the defences ; luckily the shooting was erratic, although on one occasion, near " Hill 60," many of the Norfolks and Dorsets were literally blown out of their trenches, and the latter demolished. Our own armament of trench-mortars was confined to one or two amateur weapons of the drain-pipe order, firing canisters or old jam-tins filled with explosive and shrapnel bullets, stones, or boot-nails. Owing to the retaliation provoked by their use, those operating them were very unpopular with the occupants of the various trenches, and considerable cunning was needed before the Officer-in-Charge could get them into action.

The Batteries were only occasionally shelled ; their allowance of ammunition was wretchedly insufficient, and on occasions they were unable to fire at all in retaliation, when called upon by the Infantry—a very disheartening state of affairs for both arms.

It was during this period that the " liaison " between the Artillery and the Infantry, which developed into that complete understanding, friendship, and mutual confidence between the two, and which was so marked a feature of the Division in later operations, was first established. An Artillery Officer in direct communication with the guns was attached to each Battalion Head-Quarters, thus enabling Battalion Commanders and Artillery Brigade and Battery Commanders to keep close touch with each other, without having to communicate through Brigade or Divisional Head-Quarters—an obvious advantage, especially during operations. The 15th Brigade suffered a spell of particularly bad luck, losing both their G.O.C. and Brigade Major within a short period; Brig.-Gen. Northey was wounded by a rifle shot when walking between his Head-Quarters and the trenches, and his wound, though fortunately not a very severe one, necessitated his evacuation; his valuable services were thus lost to the Division, but he was destined to win greater fame as the conqueror of German East Africa. Captain W. H. Johnston, V.C., who had won his V.C. at Missy, was killed by a sniper when in the trenches near Zwartelen; the gallantry and resource constantly displayed by him had earned him great popularity in the Brigade, and his loss was keenly felt by all ranks.

Towards the end of July the Division was relieved by the 46th Division, and withdrawn to the area between Poperinghe and Hazebrouck; great secrecy was observed and all marching done by night. Here we remained for about a week, and the opportunity for exercise after the prolonged tours of trench duty was most welcome; parades and recreations filled the day, and the 15th Brigade held a most successful Gymkhana. This was the first rest the Division had had since embarking from Ireland in August 1914, and was all too short.

Major-Gen. T. L. N. Morland was promoted to the

Command of the X. Corps, then in course of formation, his place in command of the Division being taken
by Major-Gen. C. T. McM. Kavanagh.

After many rumours, orders were received for the
Division to proceed to the Somme area to relieve the
French, and the entrainment was carried out on the
last days of July and the first days of August. We
turned our backs on Ypres without regret.

6

CHAPTER V

THE BRAY FRONT AND ARRAS

(Maps 8 and 9)

AFTER detrainment at the beginning of August,
the Division was concentrated in the area between Bray and Querrieux, and preparations were
immediately commenced for the relief of the French
troops holding the front from the Somme to near La
Boisselle. In the first few days of August the reliefs
were completed, the 14th Brigade taking over the
sector on the right from the Somme, near Frise, to
a point North-West of Maricourt, the 13th Brigade
thence to the top of the ridge overlooking Mametz,
and the 15th Brigade the left sector through the Bois
Français to the "Tambour," between Fricourt and La
Boisselle. On our right the French held the line South
of the Somme, and on our left were the 51st (Highland)
Division, who, with ourselves, formed part of the newly
formed X. Corps.

The terrain was the typical undulating country
of Picardy, open, with woods dotted about here and
there. Our extreme right rested on the marshes of
the Somme at the Moulin de Fargny, where the river
makes a horseshoe bend towards the North ; on the
left bank of the Somme lies the village of Frise, which
was held by the French, and on the right bank lie
the villages of Vaux and Curlu, facing each other on

BRAY FRONT 1915.

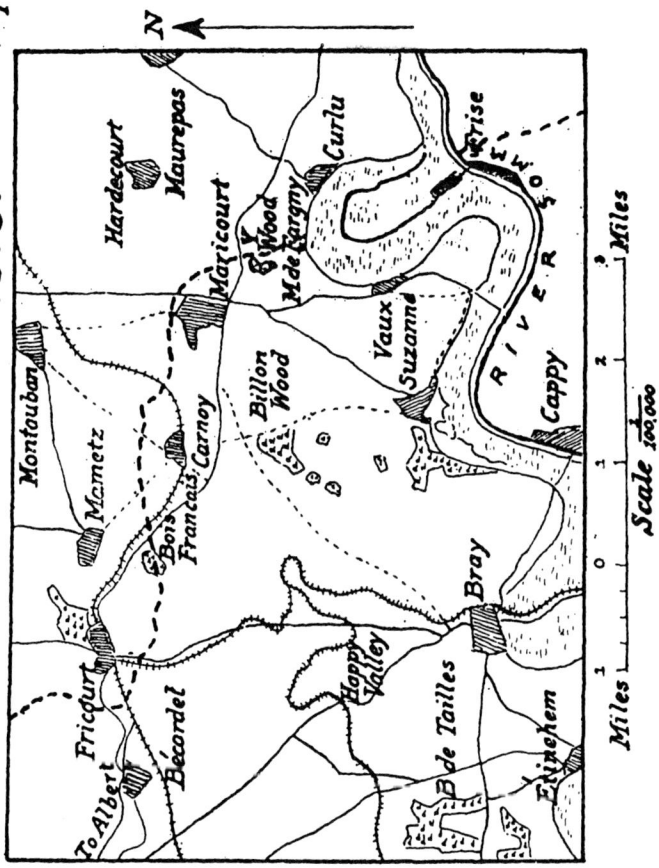

Map 8

N

Hardecourt
Maurepas
Curlu
Maricourt
B⁵ Wood
M de Fargny
Montauban
Mametz
Bois Francais
Carnoy
Billon Wood
Vaux
Suzanne
La Vise
W O O D
Bray
Happy Valley
B de Tailles
Beaucourt
To Albert
Fricourt
Etinehem
Cappy
R I V E R

Miles
Scale $\frac{1}{100,000}$
Miles

[To face p. 82.

either side of the horseshoe, while at the top is the Moulin de Fargny. From the high ground just above Vaux we could distinctly see the German Company Head-Quarters in Curlu, with the sentry walking up and down outside, and a cow tethered in the field behind ; no doubt from Curlu they could see all that went on in Vaux. The space between the two villages is a large expanse of marsh, in which no permanent defences could be formed ; in order to defend this gap, punts were used by night to patrol the marshes, armed with rifles and a machine-gun. From the Moulin de Fargny Northwards runs a ravine, known, owing to the shape of a wood situated therein, as " Y " Wood ravine. Along the West side of this ravine ran our line, whilst the opposing forces occupied the East side ; at the river end was situated the Chapeau de Gendarme, a curious-looking bluff of chalk, shaped like a cocked hat, of which the Germans held the top, with a listening post half-way down, within a few yards of a post of ours. From the top of " Y " Wood ravine the line ran about 200 yards East of Maricourt Wood, and then, making a sharp bend to the West, continued some 300 yards North of the wood and village. To the West of Maricourt a valley runs to Carnoy, and thence North-West to Fricourt ; to the North of this valley the ground rises gradually to the ridge on which is situated Montauban and the road thence to Mametz, a village on the Western end of the spur. Owing to the prominence of a group of apple-trees midway along this ridge it was known as the Pommier Ridge ; in connection with these apple-trees a rather amusing incident occurred. For many weeks they were used by our Artillery for registration purposes, until it became a daily habit ; one night the Germans felled and removed the trees, and the ensuing consternation of F.O.O.'s the following morning was most entertaining to those not directly concerned. The width of No Man's Land varied generally from 50 to 150 yards, but at the Chapeau de Gendarme and the Bois Français the lines were very close together ; at the latter place the distance was less than 5 yards, and it was almost like the mythical position where the British and Germans took it in turns to use the same loophole.

Observation was excellent from our positions, the whole of the enemy's front-line system and much of his rear areas being plainly visible ; in this respect we had the superiority, as, owing to the high ground in rear of our forward positions, practically the whole of our back areas was free from enemy observation, except from balloons and aeroplanes.

Up to this time the Division had always been in areas where the digging of trenches was impossible, and consequently the defences taken over from the French came as a revelation. The front-line system consisted of firing, support, and reserve trenches, with many communication trenches in between, and also long *boyaux* by which the lines could be approached from the rear. The trenches themselves were 8 to 10 feet deep, dug in the clay and chalk, which was the nature of the soil in these parts ; the freedom of movement and greater protection which they afforded was a much-appreciated novelty after the low breastworks of Flanders. The line was completely continuous along the whole front, and the trenches were well supplied with dug-outs and shelters ; many of these latter gave protection against the lighter natures of shells, whilst some were even furnished with bunks made of timber and rabbit wire, and lined with wood—comforts hitherto undreamt of.

On our arrival, the trenches were clean and dry, and our first impressions were that they were ideal; later, our views regarding the desirability of clay and chalk as a ground to dig and maintain trenches in underwent a very great change. It is, in fact, doubtful which of the two necessitated most work during the winter months, either the breastworks in the Northern area, or the trenches in the area of the chalky ground extending from Vimy Ridge to the Somme. Some of the communication trenches extended for a long way in rear of the line, and it was possible to approach all parts by daylight, under cover all the way. At one point, near the Bray-Fricourt road, a trench had been dug sufficiently deep and wide for a horse to be ridden along it, a refinement never met with on any other front.

As regards fighting activity the situation was very quiet indeed, shells were few and far between, and practically no sniping was being done; mining was in progress near the Carnoy-Montauban road, at the Bois Français, and at the "Tambour" near Fricourt; but, except in these places, the troops at first had a most peaceful time—so peaceful, indeed, that in the millpool at the Moulin de Fargny, which was in our front line, fishing was indulged in.

The Infantry reliefs took place before the Divisional Artillery arrived in the line, and for one or two days the French Artillery covered the front. By them an elaborate scheme of Artillery retaliation had been worked out, which in a great measure accounted for the general calm prevailing; the Germans were permitted to fire two shells on to each sector per day; as soon as they were impertinent enough to exceed this allowance word was sent by the Infantry to the Artillery, who immediately opened a burst of rapid fire with their 75's on the German trenches opposite ; if the Germans still persisted, the Frenchmen kept up their barrage until the hostile shelling had ceased. In the same way the shelling of any village in our line immediately drew a counter-blast on to a village in the German line ; thus, Mametz was shelled in retaliation for the shelling of Carnoy, Montauban for Maricourt, and Curlu for Vaux ; this scheme was retained with modifications throughout our stay in the area.

The Divisional Artillery, on arrival, took up positions in the valley North of Suzanne, behind the crest of the ridge near Billon Farm, and in the Happy Valley area North of Bray ; all these positions were screened from direct observation from ground in the enemy's possession, and, generally, the Batteries had a comfortable time, and were rarely shelled.

During August the situation remained quiet. The 18th Division of the New Army (K 1) had been allotted to the X. Corps, and took over the sector between the 5th and 51st Divisions, who both shortened their front ; and the 15th Brigade was relieved by them from the sector in front of Fricourt, where there had been some mining and a certain trench-mortar activity. After this re-adjustment Brigade reliefs were carried out, the front being held by two Brigades, the Reserve Brigade being in rest at Morlancourt, Sailly, and Chipilly. Division Head-Quarters were established in Étinehen, where it remained throughout our stay here.

In connection with the Loos offensive, in September, an attack was projected on the Divisional Front against the Pommier Ridge ; this was to have been carried out by the 13th Brigade, supported by the 15th Brigade, the objective being the summit of the Ridge. On 17th September the 13th Brigade were withdrawn for rest and training over dummy trenches, their place in the sector North of Carnoy being taken by the 15th Brigade. All the preparations were completed, assembly trenches were dug, and large quantities of stores were brought up, including short ladders to enable the attackers to climb out of the trenches; wire cutting was carried on by the Artillery, and on the afternoon of 25th September a bombardment of the enemy's position took place. After the bombardment, a form of entertainment popular with the Higher Command at this time, and known as a "Demonstration," took place; the Infantry having fixed their bayonets waved them above the parapet of the trench, at the same time emitting lusty cheers. This was supposed to delude the Germans into thinking an attack was imminent, but the usual result of this behaviour was that the enemy was distinctly annoyed, or if not annoyed, at any rate he had every reason to know that our trenches were fully occupied, and he at once subjected the Infantry to a severe Artillery "strafe." On this particular occasion, however, he did not play up, and the only retaliation provoked was four tired "whizz bangs," which exploded harmlessly behind our front line. Owing to the failure of the attack at Loos to do all that was expected, the Pommier Ridge attack was abandoned, and on 3rd October the 13th Brigade again took over the Carnoy sector.

The front was now held by three Brigades, the 14th being on the right, the 13th in the centre, and the 15th on the left, and this disposition was maintained until January. The situation was still quiet, although more " lively " than when the position was taken over ; the increase in activity was due to our own initiative, as, so soon as we had settled down in the positions, various means were employed to help on the war of attrition. Sniping was organised on scientific lines, and we soon gained the mastery in this branch of warfare, in which up to now the enemy had had the advantage ; this superiority was maintained until the end of the War. In addition to ordinary service and telescopic-sighted rifles, General Kavanagh had obtained three elephant rifles, which were distributed along the front ; to the uninitiated these weapons were as dangerous to the firer as to the target, and several men who thoughtlessly sniped with them found themselves at the bottom of the trench with a feeling as though a mule had kicked them ; they were, nevertheless, excellent weapons for the destruction of loophole plates, and, when used on one occasion against a ration party carrying hot soup up a German communication trench, the results were startlingly satisfactory.

In the search for weapons suitable for modern war recourse was had to an implement used by the Legions of Julius Cæsar—the catapult ; those used were of the conventional " Y " type, with several thongs of elastic bound together, and a leather cup forming the sling ; some 12 feet long, they were erected in the trenches and used for hurling bombs into the enemy's lines. An improvement on this was the " West Bombthrower " ; this engine of war had a spring-actuated arm, at the end of which was a wooden cup holding the bomb ; the arm was compressed on to the spring and released by a trigger, the bomb being hurled upwards and forwards ; it was adjustable for range, and a quite accurate and rapid fire could be obtained with it.

At this period also appeared the first satisfactory British trench-mortar; this was the 1½-inch mortar, which fired a projectile of some 30 lb. in weight, in the shape of a football attached to an iron rod; it had a range of 600 to 700 yards, was accurate, and the bursts of the bombs did much damage. When roused by the offensive use of such weapons, or by our Artillery, the Germans retaliated in kind, and their Artillery fire gradually increased; at first they had only used field guns and 4·2-inch Howitzers, but, later, 5·9-inch Howitzers appeared on the scene; mining and trench-mortar activity continued in the Carnoy and Bois Français areas, but there was no operation of any note.

Our own Artillery situation was much improved towards the end of the year; ammunition became more abundant, and a good proportion of the 18-pr. shells were H.E. ; Heavy Artillery had also increased, and there were some Batteries of 6-inch Howitzer and 4·7-inch guns covering the front; two 6-inch guns, which used to shell the slopes of Mont St. Quentin, where the Germans were often seen drilling, were permanently under the command of the C.R.A., and Field Artillery Batteries of the New Army were attached for training from time to time; during December, " A " Battery R.H.A. (the Chestnut Troop), and, later, " Q " Battery R.H.A., were attached to the Division.

In November the conditions of comfort prevailing in the trenches terminated with the arrival of wet weather. The rain quickly made the ground sodden, and the sides of the trenches rapidly slid downwards until the bottoms became seas of water and mud; the clay formed into mud of a peculiarly sticky nature, in which movement was a matter of the utmost difficulty, and most exhausting. With the continuance of the rain the state of the trenches became deplorable, and it was soon apparent that it would be impossible to maintain all of them in a state of repair ; the less important subsidiary and communication trenches were therefore abandoned, and all efforts directed on the upkeep of the others. General Kavanagh offered a prize, in a competition open to all, for the best suggestion for either a system or an implement to get rid of the mud and water from the trenches ; many suggestions were sent in, some practicable, and some of the " Heath Robinson " type, but no really effective remedy was forthcoming. Work was carried on incessantly, and the task was a heart-breaking one ; the mud stuck to the shovels or scoops, and could not be thrown out of the trenches, whilst the water appeared to remain at the same level whatever attempts were made to drain it away. At times the mud was so bad that men got stuck in it, and were totally unable to get themselves out without assistance, and frequently their boots were pulled off their feet in the effort of walking. On many occasions trench reliefs were carried out over the top of the trenches to avoid the interminable delays and the exhaustion caused by the journeys along the communication trenches.

At the beginning of December the 95th Infantry Brigade of the New Army, which was destined to take the place of the 14th Brigade in the Division, arrived from home ; this new Brigade, consisting of the 14th, 15th, and 16th Battalions Royal Warwickshire Regiment (being the 1st, 2nd, and 3rd Birmingham Battalions of that Regiment), and the 12th Battalion of the Gloucester Regiment, was split up among the three Brigades of the Division. The troops were sent up for training in the trenches, first by Platoons and

MAJ.-GEN. SIR C. T. M'M. KAVANAGH,
K.C.B., K.C.M.G., C.V.O., D.S.O.

[*To face p* 90.

Companies attached to the regular Battalions holding the line, and, later, as complete Battalions holding sectors of the front under the guidance of Officers of the old Battalions. For new troops, fresh out from home, their ordeal was a severe one owing to the physical conditions prevailing, but they acquitted themselves well. The fighting conditions were fairly quiet, although the 16th Warwicks were particularly unfortunate in this respect ; on their first tour in the trenches as a Battalion, which coincided with Christmas Day, they were subjected to a heavy shelling by 5·9 Howitzers, which caused a number of casualties, whilst on another occasion, very shortly afterwards, a mine was exploded under their trenches, from which they suffered somewhat severely ; the gallantry they displayed on both occasions augured well for the future.

Trench-raiding activity had been increasing on the front ; the initiative in most of these enterprises was ours, although the Germans occasionally retaliated with a raid on our line. On the night of 6th–7th December a raid was launched by each Battalion on the Divisional Front ; they met with varying fortune, the most successful one being that made by the Cheshires at the Bois Français, in which two prisoners were captured and many of the enemy killed ; the " West Bomb-throwers " and trench-mortars gave great assistance in this raid, their fire being directly controlled by the Battalion Commander (Lieut.-Col. Oldman).

At the New Year the Division bade farewell to the 14th Brigade Head-Quarters, the K.O.Y.L.I., the "Duke's," the Manchesters, and the Dorsets. The 95th Brigade Head-Quarters (Brig.-Gen. Ballard) took over the three remaining Battalions of the 14th Brigade and the 12th Gloucesters, the 14th and 15th Warwicks replaced the K.O.Y.L.I. and "Duke's" in the 13th Brigade, and the 16th Warwicks joined the 15th Brigade in place of the Dorsets. The parting was a sad one, but the splitting up of the New Army troops among those more experienced in war was a sound policy, although at first perhaps unpopular on account of the severing of old war comradeship.

Early in January occurred one of the most extraordinary exploits of the war, which reads more like fiction than fact. For some time there had been a suspicion that the Germans had commenced mining operations in "Y" Wood, and patrols and raids had been carried out with a view to ascertaining if it was so, but no definite information could be obtained. Knowing this, Lieut. Eaton, of a Tunnelling Company R.E. working on the Divisional Front, determined on a bold plan. Without saying anything of his purpose, he proceeded one night on a patrol in the marshes near the Moulin de Fargny, where he had always maintained a path could be found into the German lines. He succeeded in reaching the North bank of the river near Curlu, and, avoiding that place, struck North with a view to reaching " Y " Wood ; he was now alone, undisguised in any way, inside the German lines in a much-frequented area, but the danger of his situation in no way turned him from his purpose. Having proceeded for some distance he found himself approaching a German supply dump, at which wagons had been loaded up and were standing ready to leave ; posted over the dump was a German sentry, and near him a small flag indicating the identity of the dump. Approaching this sentry from behind, Lieut. Eaton felled him with a blow on the head from his revolver ;

he then secured the flag and put it in his pocket to pro-
duce as a *bona fide* on his return. Fearing the sense-
less guard would be observed and a commotion arise, he
climbed into the back of the last of the wagons, which
were just moving off, and lay hid until clear of the
dump ; then, covered by the noise of the wagons, he
jumped out and gained the open country. Seeing a wood
to the North, and thinking that perhaps it was " Y "
Wood, he made his way thither, but when he was close to
it a Battery fired from it, and he realised that he was
farther in rear of the German line than his objective ;
he noted the position of the Battery, however, and on
his information the Battery was shelled and silenced
the next day by our guns. Turning Westwards he
cautiously approached " Y " Wood from the rear ; he
was now in the enemy front-trench system, and, crawling carefully along the tops of the trenches, hiding as
far as possible behind the earth thrown up from them,
and keeping a wary eye on the Germans below him, he
made a thorough reconnaissance of their position in " Y "
Wood, and he was able to establish the fact that no
mining operations were in progress. Having gained the
required information, he turned homewards ; passing
safely to the rear of the enemy front-line system, he
proceeded to crawl along the back of the German
reserve line, in order to keep his direction ; whilst doing
this he perceived a German dug-out in which were
several Officers, and, not content with the success of
his exploit so far, he determined to make things unpleasant for them. He had all this time been carrying
in his pocket a bomb in case of eventualities ; setting
the fuse of this, he threw it into the dug-out, and,
removing himself as far as possible from the scene,
took cover. The explosion of the bomb caused much

activity in the area, but he remained undiscovered. When all was quiet again, he continued on his way, but, on approaching the Chapeau de Gendarme, he was startled to hear bombing and rifle-fire break out immediately to his right; not knowing what was occurring, he decided that it behoved him to return to our lines as soon as possible. Moving forward quickly, he was precipitated down the steep slope to the river-bank, and, being luckily unhurt, made his way, partly by swimming, partly by walking through the marshes, to the shelter of our lines. On return he was, of course, at first received with incredulity, but the facts of his long absence and the evidence of the dump flag soon convinced his hearers that he had, in fact, spent the greater part of the night within the enemy's lines, and gained the most valuable information. Readers can judge for themselves the quality of his performance and the degree of courage required to carry through such an astounding exploit. The bombing and rifle-fire which hastened the completion of the reconnaissance had been caused by a raid in the vicinity of the Moulin de Fargny. Lieut. Eaton was awarded the D.S.O. as an "immediate award."

Early in January the 30th Division had come to the X. Corps, and orders were issued for them to relieve the 5th Division in the line. By the 20th the relief of the 13th and 95th Brigades and the Divisional Artillery had been completed, and on that date General Fry, of the 30th Division, took command of the front; the 15th Brigade remained in the line in the left sector and came under the orders of the 30th Division. The 5th Division, less 15th Brigade, then withdrew to rest in the area round Corbie.

During the relief there had been a marked increase

in the German Artillery activity, both the trenches and Battery positions having been shelled more than usual ; some of the Battery positions were subjected to very heavy bombardments, especially at the hour of relief, a fact which gave rise to a suspicion of espionage, but luckily no damage was done. This activity culminated on 28th January in a heavy hostile attack on the French trenches South of the river Somme ; the village of Frise was cut off and the garrison was captured, and the Germans advanced to a depth of more than one and a half mile along the South bank of the river ; during the attack the 30th Division front was subjected to an Artillery bombardment, but there was no Infantry action. The village of Suzanne was heavily shelled, both with gas and H.E., and the river crossings from Frise to Bray were kept under continuous fire. To guard against the development of an attack from the right flank, the two Battalions in reserve to the 15th Brigade in Bray took up positions on the North bank of the Somme, near Cappy and Suzanne ; the 27th Brigade R.F.A. and 65th (Howitzer) Battery were ordered to re-inforce the 30th Division, and the 65th Battery gave great assistance to the French, receiving a special message of thanks from them. The following day the attack was brought to a stand by the French, and some of the lost ground was regained.

On 2nd February the 15th Brigade marched out from Bray and rejoined the Division at Corbie. Four days later the Division marched to the area immediately North of Amiens, and, after resting there some four or five days, to the Picquigny-Cavillon-Molliens-Vidame area.

In September, Brig.-Gen. L. O. W. Jones took over command of the 13th Brigade, and early in October

Brig.-Gen. A. H. Hussey replaced Brig.-Gen. J. G. Geddes as C.R.A. of the Division.

Our sojourn in the Somme area saw the birth of three of the Divisional institutions. In August was formed the Divisional Band, from bandsmen available in the various units ; up to this time bands of any kind had been forbidden, the only music available for marching being that of voluntary performers on the mouth-organ. Later in the autumn the Divisional Concert Troupe, " The Whizz Bangs," was formed under the organisation of Lieut. Wooley, attached to the Division as extra A.D.C., and early in 1916, when Lieut. Wooley left the Division, the management of the Troupe was taken over by Lieut. Forsyth, Q.V. Rifles, under whose able guidance it remained until 1918, and attained a high standard of performance. About the same time the Divisional School was started ; at first this was only a bombing school at Chipilly, but after the move to Arras it became a school for the general training of Officers and N.C.O.'s in other branches of warfare as well.

We had been hoping to enjoy an extended period of rest and training in the Cavillon area, but, once again, our hopes were doomed to disappointment. On 21st February the Germans commenced their mighty and costly attacks against the fortress of Verdun, and, as a result, on the 24th, orders were received for a sudden move to relieve the French troops holding the front about Arras.

The following day the Division commenced to march into the teeth of a North-East blizzard. The roads were covered with ice and snow, on which men or horses could get little foothold ; progress was very slow ; every hill meant a halt for the Transport, as

ARRAS FRONT
Map 9.

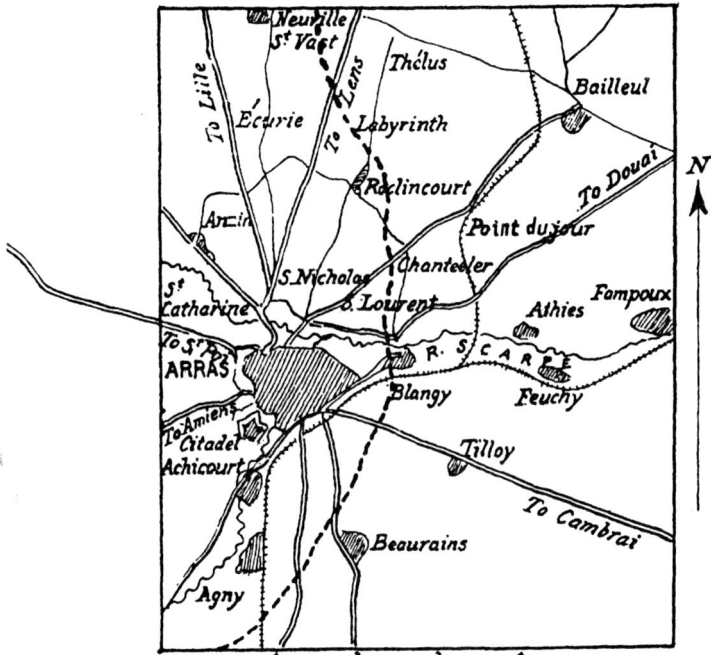

Scale of Miles $\frac{1}{100,000}$

- - - - - - - - - -
Br. Line in 1916.

horses had to be unhooked from other wagons to pull each vehicle up; in some cases it was a question of hours before they could get to the top; horses were continually stumbling, and whole wagons slid off the road. To add to the difficulties, other British Divisions, marching towards Arras, and French troops with long columns of lorries, marching South, were using the same roads; the Infantry completed their march very late and exhausted, but many of the mounted units and transport wagons were unable to reach their destinations until the following day. This march was always subsequently referred to as " The Retreat from Moscow."

ARRAS

After a short rest, the march was continued by Doullens to the area between Avesnes and Arras, and arrangements were made for the relief of the French on the front from the River Scarpe to the South end of the "Labyrinth" North-East of Roclincourt. The relief was completed by 4th March, on which date General Kavanagh assumed command of the new front. The Division formed part of the VI. Corps (Lieut.-Gen. Sir J. L. Keir); on our right the 14th (Light) Division of the same Corps held the line to the South of the River Scarpe, whilst on our left we had once again the 51st (Highland) Division of the XVII. Corps.

The front was held by two Brigades, the 13th Brigade taking over the right sector from the River Scarpe to the North side of the Arras-Bailleul road, and the 95th Brigade the left sector from that point to the Labyrinth; the 15th Brigade was in reserve at Wanquetin and Hauteville, and Divisional Head-Quarters was at Duisans, with Head-Quarters R.A.

7

and R.E. at Wagnonlieu, where also dwelt the French Sound-ranging Section, known as " Les Sorciers."

On our right the line was among the houses of St.-Laurent-Blangy, on the river-bank, and consisted of barricades, trenches, and fortified houses, access to some portions being through cellars and tunnels under the houses ; here our own positions and those of the Germans were very close together, and difficult to locate among the ruins. To the North of the village the trenches ran approximately parallel, due North to Chantecler, a ruined inn on the Arras-Bailleul road, up the gradual slope of the South-Western spur of the Vimy Ridge ; to the North of Chantecler they continued, still due North, over the crest of the spur, and down the slope of the valley in which Roclincourt is situated ; after passing some 700 yards East of Roclincourt, the line curved back to the point of junction with the 51st Division. The width of No Man's Land was in most places 100 to 150 yards, the exceptions being in St. Laurent and near Chantecler, where the distance separating the trenches was only about 50 yards. To the South of Arras the line bent back Westwards, so that the town and our positions lay in a salient, which was overlooked from the North by the Vimy Ridge, and from the South by the high ground at Beaurains.

The trench system taken over was of a complete order, much like that we had left at Bray, and the ground was also similar, *i.e.* clay and chalk. The weather had been fairly dry and fine, with the exception of the blizzard referred to, and, consequently, the trenches were generally in fair order, though some were in a very dilapidated state. Communication trenches led to the various sectors from the suburbs of St. Nicholas

and St. Catherine, all movements beyond the outskirts
of these places being visible to the enemy in daylight.
The Divisional Artillery took up positions among
the houses and in the gardens of Arras, or the suburbs,
and were thus enabled to obtain cover from observation,
and protection in the house cellars. The houses in
Arras, which at the nearest point was only some
thousand yards from the front line, afforded good
observation posts, the Réfugies and Séminaire being
popular resorts for Observation Officers of both Field
and Heavy Artillery.

The situation was generally quiet, and, with the
exception of one or two short periods, remained so
during our four months' stay in the area, which were
perhaps the happiest months of the whole War ; the
quietness of the front, the comforts of Arras, and a
fine Summer, all helped to this end. Although close
to the front, the town was rarely shelled by Heavy
Artillery, but there was a small daily ration of field-
gun fire. The areas which had suffered the most damage
in the early bombardments were the Station and
houses near by, the Hôtel de Ville and Petite Place,
both in ruins, and the Cathedral and Bishop's Palace,
both roofless shells. A few civilians remained in the
town, living mainly in their cellars, and a number of
shops were still open. The troops billeted in the
town lived for the most part in the cellars, which were
many and strong, and during the day the upper rooms
of the houses were used for messes and recreation.
The two Infantry Brigade Head-Quarters, Artillery
Group Head-Quarters, and Battalion Head-Quarters,
were very comfortably housed, some of the quarters
being quite luxurious.

In the event of a bombardment of the town there

was ample underground accommodation. In addition
to the cellars which nearly every house possessed, in
the region of the " Grande Place " there was a regular
underground labyrinth ; here there were as many as
four stories of cellars under the houses and the " Grande
Place " itself, and chalk caves from which, presumably,
stone had been taken to build the town. Further,
several miles of sewers had been cleared, and boards
laid, entrance being effected down manholes and other
laddered shafts. It is interesting to note that before
the opening of the offensive in this area in April 1917,
more than two Divisions were sheltered under the
town of Arras ; and the vaults under the Bishop's
Palace and the Cathedral were regularly used to
accommodate a Battalion while we were there. Many
of the gardens and orchards continued to bring forth
fruit and flowers ; in some of the Battery positions
strawberries, and asparagus even, grew among the gun
wheels, and, if our stay had been prolonged slightly,
there would have been a good supply of apples and
pears. A Divisional Officers' Club was later established
in the town, where a good dinner could be obtained
and a happy evening spent, whilst the " Whizz Bangs "
and other Concert Troupes paid occasional visits to
the Theatre. The Divisional Canteen, also, opened a
large establishment, so that all the advantages of
civilisation were available.

Mining was in progress at several points along the
line, but, as both sides had defensive galleries, most of
the activity was confined to No Man's Land. Trench-
mortars were also active along the whole front, and
it was in this area that we first met with the small
" Granatenwerfer," which, owing to its rapid rate of
fire and the fact that three or more guns were usually

used as a Battery, was a more dangerous weapon than the heavier type; the latter was much in evidence at Blangy, where its bursts had disastrous effects on the house walls. Our own armament of trench-mortars was rapidly improving, as, in addition to the 1½-inch and 2-inch trench-mortars (footballs), on 19th March we received the first of the Stokes 3-inch mortars; with its rapid rate of fire and excellent bursts this became a most valuable weapon to the Infantry, and deservedly popular.

It was at this time that trench-mortars were properly organised as a definite arm; after much discussion as to who should control them, it was finally decided by G.H.Q. that the Heavy and Medium trench-mortars should form part of the Divisional Artillery, while Light trench-mortars (3-inch Stokes) should be an Infantry weapon, organised into one Battery for each Infantry Brigade. This organisation was carried out; the 2-inch trench-mortars were formed into three Batteries under a Divisional Trench-Mortar Officer (D.T.M.O.), Captain Hewson, and the 13th, 95th, and 15th Light Trench-Mortar Batteries came into existence.

It may be of interest here to trace the gradual evolution of this arm, which played such an important part, especially in wire-cutting, and, in the case of Light trench-mortars, in dealing with machine-gun nests in attack, in the later stages of the War. When trench warfare was commenced the British Army had no trench-mortars, but the Germans almost immediately took them into use. To supply this want, in the Winter of 1914–15 several experimental mortars were made; amongst the earliest were the " Tobys," so called after Captain " Toby " Rawlinson (Lord Rawlinson's brother), who conceived the idea of utilising some old French 15 cm. cast-iron mortars of Crimean date, fired from a vent-hole; these threw a bomb containing ammonal, some 18 lb. in weight, about 400 yards, and developed "an important explosion," but they were not reliable, though better than nothing. The Indian Corps devised a contraption of wood bound with hoops of iron, not unlike the old leather Chinese guns, and the French actually experimented with a weapon which fired a projectile attached to a string, on which the desired range was measured; the projectile took the string out with it until the latter tautened, and thus stopped its flight. Next came the 4-inch howitzer, the first sent out from England, which threw a studded projectile, but, as the result was as often as not a premature burst, they were not popular, and met with an early demise. The 1½-inch and 2-inch mortars firing "footballs" were next on the scene, and were the first really satisfactory weapons. Like all early trench-mortars they were unpopular with the Infantry at first, as, when they were fired, they invariably drew retaliation from the enemy's Artillery, to which our own ammunition supply did not allow of an adequate response. The issue of the 3-inch Stokes mortar brought us on to level terms with the Germans, and from that date onwards we steadily gained superiority in this arm. Trench-mortar schools were established in various centres, and the trench-mortar was recognised as a valuable adjunct of war. About the end of 1916 the 9·45-inch trench-mortar was seen; this fired a bomb 4 feet long, the burst of which was devastating; but the mortar was very cumbersome, though it had its uses in destroying strong-points and dug-outs; its disadvantage was that frequently the bomb would fall very short indeed, in our own lines, and there explode with great éclat. At the end of 1917 came that most admirable weapon, the 6-inch Newton trench-mortar; this worked on the same principles as the 3-inch Stokes mortar, had a range of about 1100 yards, and could be fired so rapidly that it was possible to have four or five rounds in the air at the same time. One of the main difficulties in connection with trench-mortars was the question of their transport in moving warfare. In the case of the Stokes mortars, hand-carts were first used, but they were found too clumsy, and eventually limbers were used. Towards the end of the War the Artillery ingeniously devised means for rapidly transporting the 6-inch Newtons, and they often followed close in rear of the attacking Infantry, and were most useful in dealing with machine-gun nests and strongpoints.

To revert to the doings of the 5th Division. On 1st April Major-Gen. R. B. Stephens took over command of the Division from Major-Gen. Kavanagh, who had been promoted to command the Cavalry Corps.

During June, matters became more lively on the front; on the 4th the Germans, having bombarded our positions all day, in the evening exploded five mines simultaneously near the Arras-Bailleul road. In the confusion ensuing on this explosion they carried out a raid, and succeeded in penetrating into our line, but were quickly driven off, not, however, without our sustaining some loss; three of these mines formed huge craters just in front of our original front line, which were afterwards known as "Cuthbert," "Clarence," and "Claude," the names being taken from a song in vogue with the "Whizz Bangs" at the time. On the 19th another mine was exploded at the " Gridiron," 200 yards North of the Bailleul road, and, although little damage was done to our trenches, some of the men working in the mine galleries were lost.

We too had been active; many offensive patrols and raids had been carried out, and bombardments of the mining areas by the Field and Heavy Artillery had taken place. On one occasion a shoot was carried out by " Granny " (the 15-inch howitzer), who lived near Dainville, together with 12-inch, 8-inch, and 4·5 howitzers, against a part of the German front line distant only some 50 yards from ours. This operation caused much excitement among the Commanders of the various formations in the neighbourhood, and the shooting was observed with much interest by the gilded Staffs from the Army and Corps, who crowded the O.P.'s at the Réfugies and other buildings in Arras. Our front line had been cleared for safety in case of short rounds, but the shooting was accurate, the burst of the 15-inch and other heavy howitzers being most destructive ; the shoot was not crowned with complete success, however, owing to a breakdown of "Granny's " recuperating mechanism after two rounds had been fired.

We cannot pass without reference to the Battery of old French 220 mm. " mortiers," which assisted in bombardments on the Divisional Front, and lived among the trees near the Citadel of Arras. Their armament consisted of muzzle-loading mortars of ancient pattern, which were fired from the vent ; the French gunners, some of whom seemed almost as ancient as their guns, were provided with scales by which the requisite amount of charge was measured out according to the range, and, after this had been rammed home, the shell was inserted on the top, often with some cheery remark,

HÔTEL DE VILLE, ARRAS.

[To face p. 104.

such as, " Un cadeau pour Guillaume " ; in spite of this somewhat mediæval procedure, which precluded a rapid rate of fire, their shooting was most accurate, and the bursts of the projectiles were very effective, being accompanied by much noise and clouds of black smoke. About this time the organisation of the Divisional Artillery was slightly altered ; the 8th Howitzer Brigade was abolished, and the 37th and 65th Batteries were posted to the 27th and 28th Brigades respectively ; a new Battery for the 15th Brigade R.F.A. was formed by a section of each of these two Batteries, under the name of D/15.

During the latter part of our stay the Divisional Front was extended to include a new sector South of the Scarpe embracing the village of Blangy ; this necessitated the front being held by three Brigades, and a consequent re-adjustment of the dispositions.

About 25th June preparations were made for an attack with the 55th Division against the enemy's position South of Wailly ; this projected attack was usually known as the " Wailly stunt," and was planned to take place two days after the opening of the Somme Offensive. Positions were prepared, and vast quantities of trench-mortar and other ammunition collected in Wailly ; a Field Artillery Brigade was attached from the 35th Division, and the Batteries for wire-cutting took up their positions. When the preparations were almost completed, orders were received for a postponement ; subsequently the operation was cancelled, and the troops, who had been withdrawn to practise the attack, returned to their old positions near Arras. On 3rd July the Division was relieved, and marched to rest in the area around Le Cauroy, during which time the " Wailly stunt " came on again, and was again cancelled.

Our tour in the Arras area had been a happy one, and we left with regret ; both in the line and out of it the time had passed as pleasantly as could be expected. It was during this period that the first Divisional Horse Show was held, and achieved such success that it became an annual event.

The Somme Offensive had opened, after several postponements, on 1st July, and it was realised that our stay in the rest area was only until such time as the Division would be required to participate in that battle ; training was therefore proceeded with energetically, and many tactical exercises were carried out. The training, however, was not so strenuous that it did not allow of recreation, and time was found for polo—not, as may be expected, quite up to Hurlingham standard, but at the same time very enjoyable. The existence of a trout farm in the area proved a magnet for Mess Presidents, and strawberries too were plentiful. At this time the 1/6 Argyll and Sutherland Highlanders joined the Division as Pioneer Battalion ; they had been posted from the 51st Division to replace the 5th Cheshires whom we had left at Bray.

On the morning of 14th July orders were received for the expected move. The " Q " Staff, who had been issuing instructions for every conceivable kind of move by rail, were probably relieved to find that the move was to be by march route ; little time was allowed for preparation, as at noon the various units were scattered over the country on tactical exercises, and the move was to be commenced that evening. Everything had been kept in readiness, however, and in the evening the Division commenced to march Southwards towards the never-ending rumble of gun-fire on the Somme.

CHAPTER VI

THE SOMME—1916

(MAPS 10 AND 11)

A FTER three days' hard marching by way of Fren-
villers, Candas, Puchevillers, and Toutencourt,
over hot and dusty roads, the Division arrived on the
16th of July in the Lahoussoye-Bresle-Ribemont-Heilly
area. During the march, rumours came of a break
through by the Cavalry near Bazentin, and visions of
chasing a defeated foe over open country arose, only to
be shattered later by the news of the actual situation.

On the 19th, orders were received to move up
immediately to re-inforce the 7th Division, holding the
line between High Wood and Longueval. The move
was carried out in the afternoon, the 95th Brigade
going into position near Longueval, and the 13th
Brigade on their left to High Wood. The front line
ran along the road leading from the South corner of
High Wood to Longueval. The 15th Brigade moved
into position as Divisional Reserve in the captured
trenches on the Pommier Ridge, and the 15th Brigade
R.F.A. took up positions to support the Infantry in
Caterpillar Valley, the valley lying between Pommier
Ridge and Mametz Wood. During the afternoon the
position on the new Divisional Front was fairly quiet, but
to our right the battle for the possession of Longueval
and Delville Wood was raging with fierce intensity.

Before the relief was completed the 13th Brigade received a severe blow, the Brigade Major, Captain Wyllie, being killed by a stray shrapnel shell at the Brigade Head-Quarters near Montauban.

The area into which we had moved was a familiar one, as for six months we had overlooked it from our positions around Maricourt and Fricourt at the end of 1915. But what a change had come over the scene! The villages of Fricourt, Mametz, and Montauban were now only heaps of débris, with a mound of white stones marking the ruins of the Church in each place. Instead of a clearly defined system of trenches, with grass-land and trees in between, was a vast expanse of shell-torn ground, covered with deep, wide gashes, where trenches had once been, shattered stumps where once had been trees, and over all were scattered bombs, unexploded shells, arms, equipment, and all the other débris which marks the trail of modern battle.

Divisional Head-Quarters were located at " Rose Cottage," Fricourt. The peaceful beauty suggested by the name was not borne out in actuality, the name being applied to a field pitted with shell-holes, and covered with débris, the only cover in which consisted of a few tarpaulins stretched over poles, and a Nissen hut. The ruins of a red-brick cottage in one corner was the origin of the name, as, when in 1915 we had named the map, this had been a creeper-covered cottage with a fine rose-garden. Now it would have been impossible to find a rose or rose-tree anywhere in the locality.

The situation on 19th July was as follows : The XV. Corps (Lieut.-Gen. Sir H. S. Horne) held a line running from North of Bazentin-le-Petit to the Southern end of High Wood, and thence along the road leading to Longueval. From there the line was continued by

SOMME 1916.

Map 10.

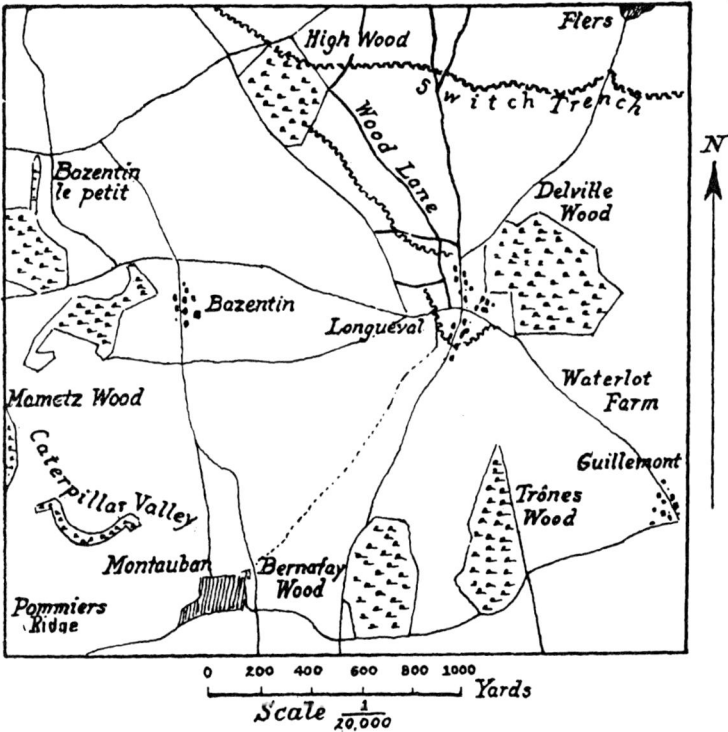

High Wood

Flers

Switch Trench

Wood Lane

Bazentin le petit

Delville Wood

Bazentin

Longueval

Mametz Wood

Waterlot Farm

Caterpillar Valley

Guillemont

Trônes Wood

Montauban

Bernafay Wood

Pommiers Ridge

```
0   200  400   600   800 1000
                          Yards
       Scale  1/20,000
```

N

[To face p. 108.

the XIII. Corps past the cross-roads and Church in the centre of the village, through the Southern portion of Delville Wood, and then due South, past Waterlot Farm, to the West side of Guillemont. Through the Northern portion of High Wood, and along the ridge North of Longueval, lay the German third line of defence, known as " Switch Trench," in which, on the left portion of Corps front, was the enemy front line; while from High Wood he held positions running approximately parallel to ours, through Longueval and Delville Wood.

Early on the morning of the 20th, at 3.30 a.m., an attack was launched by the 33rd, 7th, and 5th Divisions of the XV. Corps, against the enemy's position in High Wood and along Wood Lane, the sunken road leading from the East corner of High Wood to the South-East ; simultaneously the XIII. Corps attacked against Longueval and Delville Wood. The final objective was to be the Switch Trench, which necessitated a difficult change of direction for the 5th and 7th Divisions after the capture of Wood Lane, and this would be a particularly complicated manœuvre for the units of the 13th Brigade (K.O.S.B., and 14th Warwicks in support), who had not had an opportunity of studying the ground in daylight.

The attack on Wood Lane was met with very heavy machine-gun and rifle fire. The first objective was captured, and the advance continued to, and beyond, Wood Lane by the 2nd Gordons and 8th Devons of the 7th Division ; but eventually they had to fall back. On our left the 33rd Division met with determined opposition in High Wood, but yard by yard they worked their way forward, and by the evening had gained possession of practically the whole wood ; later they were shelled out of the Northern portion, but consolidated their position on the Southern half of the wood.

During the night the 95th Brigade Head-Quarters was blown in by a shell, and General Ballard received a wound which necessitated his evacuation ; his place was taken a few days later by Brig.-Gen. Lord E. C. Gordon-Lennox.

On the 20th the remainder of the Divisional Artillery came into action, taking up positions in Caterpillar Valley, and in the evening the troops of the 7th Division were withdrawn, except the Artillery, who remained in action under the command of the C.R.A. 5th Division.

Caterpillar Valley, in which the Artillery positions were, was a most " unhealthy " area. It was packed from end to end with guns of every sort, 9·2-inch, 8-inch, 6-inch, and 4·5 howitzers, 60-prs., anti-aircraft guns, and literally hundreds of 18-pr. guns, which kept up an almost continuous roar day and night. Overlooked by the German positions at Ginchy to the East, it was made the target of much Artillery fire. There was hardly any cover for the detachments, which were kept as small as possible in order to avoid losses, only holes dug in the ground covered with corrugated-iron and earth, which afforded little protection against the " Caterpillar Valley Barrage," which swept relentlessly down the Valley at intervals during the day and night. In addition to the gun positions, a number of units had formed horse-lines towards the Fricourt end of the Valley, and almost every square yard was occupied in some way or another.

The pronounced salient at Longueval was liable to enemy shell-fire from all directions, save from the South-West, a fact of which the Germans took every advantage. Apart from the shelling of the village and trenches, a barrage was frequently fired by the enemy on a line from the South edge of Delville Wood in a semicircle round the South of the village, to the windmill on the West side of it. This "Longueval Barrage" was so intense that it was practically impossible to reach the village through it. During the capture of the village on the 27th, communication was entirely cut off between the troops in this place and Brigade Head-Quarters for over twelve hours, as every man who attempted to pass through the barrage was either killed or wounded. As the line of approach for reliefs, or for ration and fatigue parties, lay across Caterpillar Valley and over the slopes South and South-West of Longueval, the difficulties which had to be faced may to some extent be realised.

The rest of the 20th and 21st passed without any renewed outbreak of fighting on the Divisional Front, except at 10 p.m. on the 21st, when a heavy bombardment was opened by the enemy along our front, and, although no attack took place against our line, assaults were made on High Wood and Longueval, on our flanks, without much success. At 2 a.m. another similar outburst occurred, but by daylight the position was again normal.

On the 22nd the danger of Caterpillar Valley as a site for horse-lines was brought home to those who had used it as such. In the afternoon the Germans opened a sudden concentrated fire on them, and, in order to prevent appalling loss, the horses were cut loose, and stampeded terrified down the valley towards Fricourt in a cloud of dust and shell smoke ; it was a work of some hours to collect them again, and by great good fortune not many were lost.

At 10 p.m., after a bombardment, the 13th Brigade advanced to the attack against Wood Lane, the West Kents attacking on the right, and the 14th Warwicks on the left. They were met with a heavy counter-barrage and streams of lead from numerous machine-guns, and, after suffering severe casualties, they were forced to retire to their jumping-off line. A further attack was then ordered for 1.30 a.m., the objectives being again Wood Lane, and afterwards Switch Trench. This attack was postponed till 3.30 a.m., and met with the same result as before. At the same time the 15th Brigade advanced on Longueval from the West, and, although they succeeded in penetrating some distance among the orchards and enclosures, their attack was broken up by machine-gun nests, and they had to withdraw, the Cheshires losing heavily.

The 23rd and 24th passed without any attacks on either side. On the latter day a message was received from a reconnoitring aeroplane that the Germans were massing in a trench between Delville Wood and Flers. All guns were immediately turned on to the trench, and shortly afterwards a message was dropped by the aeroplane, "No Germans left alive after our Artillery fire," a message which did much to cheer both the Artillery and the Infantry.

The 25th was another day of no attacks, though the usual "S.O.S. Longueval" was received during the evening and night. This message was regularly received by the Artillery every night of our stay in this area, often four or five times, and was due to the frequent barrages put down on that hapless village, any of which might have heralded an attack. How many times the prompt and effective reply of our guns prevented such an attack there is no means of knowing, but for the support thus given the Gunners earned the heartfelt gratitude of the sorely-tried Infantry.

During the night the Divisional Ammunition dump situated near Mametz, containing some 100,000 rounds of trench-mortar and Artillery ammunition, and large quantities of bombs and rifle ammunition, was set on fire by an enemy shell. Lieut. Traill of the D.A.C., in charge of the dump, and his Sergeant-Major made valiant efforts to extinguish the fire, but about half an hour after it had started it reached the trench-mortar bombs, and immediately the whole dump exploded with a tremendous detonation. Shells and bombs were hurled in all directions, and Lieut. Traill was blown about a hundred yards into the Cemetery. Luckily no one was killed, though several suffered from severe shock.

By the 26th we had extended our line to the right, the flank now resting on the ruins of the Church at Longueval; to our right the 2nd Division came up to replace the 3rd Division, and to the left were the 51st (Highland) Division. Preparations were now made for an attack on Longueval and Delville Wood from the South. To support this attack, 2-inch trench-mortars were brought up into the ruins of the houses in Longueval; whilst reconnoitring the positions, the D.T.M.O., Captain Clery, was killed, and when the trench-mortars had got into position they were buried by enemy shell-fire, and, in spite of all efforts, could not be got into action; they were not recovered from their positions until the capture of Flers on 14th September.

On the 27th, at 5.10 a.m., the bombardment of the enemy's position commenced, and continued for two hours. At 7.10 a.m. the attack was launched by the 15th Infantry Brigade, the Norfolks being in front,

8

supported by the Bedfords and 16th Warwicks ; and the 2nd Division on our right simultaneously assaulted Delville Wood.

In reply to our preliminary bombardment the enemy opened a terrific fire on the village, wood, and surroundings, and as a result the trenches occupied by the attacking troops were almost demolished. At zero hour many of the Norfolks were buried under the débris of trenches and houses, and the way in which they managed to extricate themselves and move forward to the attack was an exceedingly fine piece of work. It was in this attack that the " Creeping Barrage " was first employed ; it did not at this time, however, move forward with the Infantry advancing close behind at a steady pace, but moved in a series of leaps at fixed times, the Infantry following in rushes.

The attacking troops went forward steadily, and, starting from a point South of the cross-roads, captured most of the village. Towards the North end the German resistance stiffened ; parties of the enemy, armed with machine-guns, came up from cellars and dug-outs, and took up positions among the ruined buildings. The Norfolks, pressing forward, were checked, and the barrage went on in accordance with the time-table, leaving the Germans in the village free of shell-fire. The fight now developed into a struggle between the opposing Infantry amid the ruins of the village within a ring of Artillery fire. By a curious coincidence it was the 5th German Division opposed to us, and, man for man, they proved inferior to the British 5th. Gradually our men worked forward, bombing the cellars, rushing houses, and stalking machine-gun nests, until by late afternoon they had cleared the village. The final objective was a line

300 yards North of the village, necessitating the capture of a group of orchards and strong-points, but, bereft of the protection of the creeping barrage, our troops could not move beyond the outskirts of the village. The hardest part of the task was, nevertheless, completed, and the village of Longueval, for the possession of which fighting had been going on since 15th July, was completely in our hands.

On our right the 2nd Division had made good progress in Delville Wood, and at one time of the day had practically cleared it of Germans; later they were driven back from the Northern edge, but established a line some 200 yards inside the wood. Delville Wood, or, as it was known, " Devil's Wood," was at first a thick wood with almost impenetrable undergrowth, some 160 acres in extent. The battle had raged to and fro in it for a fortnight, and now it consisted of a confused mass of broken trees, barbed-wire, and hastily-dug trenches, among which were littered many of our own and the enemy dead. In the dark it was a veritable nightmare, the glare of bursting shells only serving to show more clearly its gaunt devastation.

From the opening of our attack a deluge of 5·9 and 8-inch shells was rained continuously by the Germans on the Southern portion of Longueval and Delville Wood. Owing to the barrage placed South of the village all communication with the rear was completely cut off, and for many hours no news could be got to Brigade or Divisional Head-Quarters, except a few messages from contact aeroplanes, and some messages through the 2nd Division on our right. Colonel P. V. Stone, commanding the Norfolks, took command of the operations on the spot, and carried them through to a successful conclusion. Even from his Head-Quarters in the village communication with the various units was most difficult owing to the intensity of the shell-fire, and two dug-outs, which he took up successively as his command-post, were blown in. One of them caught fire, and in the conflagration the two carrier-pigeons for communication with the Corps loft were killed; although a means of communication was thus lost, it is rumoured that the pigeons were a useful addition to the Mess. In the evening the enemy counter-attacked with great vigour, but was repulsed with heavy loss; and throughout the night he repeated these attacks, his greatest efforts being made against Delville Wood; but the line held firm. After dark the 15th Brigade regained touch with the 2nd Division in the wood on the right, which had been lost during the day.

All through the 28th, Artillery fire on both sides was continuous, and the scene of the fight was shrouded in a cloud of dust and smoke. The line was now consolidated and remained unchanged.

Since the commencement of the bombardment the Divisional Artillery had kept up a continuous fire for thirty hours, and on the 27th had fired an average of 520 rounds per gun. The support they gave to the Infantry, first in the creeping barrage, and, later, by the standing barrage beyond the village, was invaluable, and did much to prevent the formation of counter-attacks, and the advance of the enemy supports.

From prisoners captured it was learnt that the attack had been expected, and preparations made to defeat it, a fact which makes the capture of the village and wood all the more creditable a feat of arms.

On the night of the 29th the 13th Brigade relieved

the 15th Brigade, with orders to complete the capture of the orchards and posts North of the village.

At 3 a.m. on the 30th we attacked—the K.O.S.B. on the right and the 14th Warwicks on the left, the West Kents in support, and the 15th Warwicks in reserve. After severe fighting the objective was gained on the right, and a line was established well clear of the wood and village. On the left it was reported that the attack had failed to gain the objective, but that some progress had been made ; a line was then consolidated in these positions. Actually a machine-gun team of the K.O.S.B. had established themselves in the final objective on the left, and there, unknown to anyone, they remained gallantly for several days, subjected to our own Artillery fire, and beat off all enemy attacks upon them ; finally, receiving no support, and being short of food and water, they retired into the lines of the 17th Division after we had left the area.

On the night of 1st to 2nd August the exhausted Division was relieved by the 17th Division, and withdrew to the " Citadel " on the Bray-Fricourt road.

During these operations the R.E. had been utilised in preparing positions in and around Longueval ; and in the various attacks sections had been attached to, and advanced with, the Infantry, to whom they had been of the greatest support, not only in their capacity as sappers, but also as riflemen.

The 15th Field Ambulance had charge of the arrangements for evacuating casualties from the forward area, the A.D.S. being on the Mametz-Montauban road. Casualties among the bearers were heavy, but the clearing of the wounded was carried out gallantly and expeditiously.. On one day alone over

600 lying cases and 2000 walking cases were passed through the A.D.S. The 14th Field Ambulance was at Bécordel, and the 13th at Corbie, running the Corps Rest Station.

On withdrawing from the line we bade farewell to our Divisional Artillery, who remained in position covering the 17th Division ; it was the last time we were to have their valuable assistance for nearly three months, as, much to the disappointment of all, they did not again cover the Divisional Front in the Somme Battles, and did not rejoin until 13th October, when the Division was in the Béthune area.

Our first period of participation in the battle of the Somme was over, and a hard-earned battle honour had been added to the record of the old 5th Division ; Longueval will always be remembered by those who were there as the place where there was a more intense and continuous shell-fire than any other in the whole course of the War.

On 2nd–3rd August the Division entrained near Bray, and moved back to rest in the area round Avraines, and Belloy-St. Léonard, S.E. of Abbeville, where, after a few days' rest, training for future offensives was commenced. Tactical schemes were carried out, several with the assistance of low-flying aeroplanes, or "contact patrols," in order to accustom the Infantry to signalling their positions to the airmen. Contact patrols were a feature of the Somme fighting, it being the first operation of any magnitude in which they were employed, and the results fully justified their use.

A happy rest in this area was terminated by the receipt of orders for a return to the Somme, and on 24th August the Division moved by rail to the area

FALFEMONT AND MORVAL   Map 11.

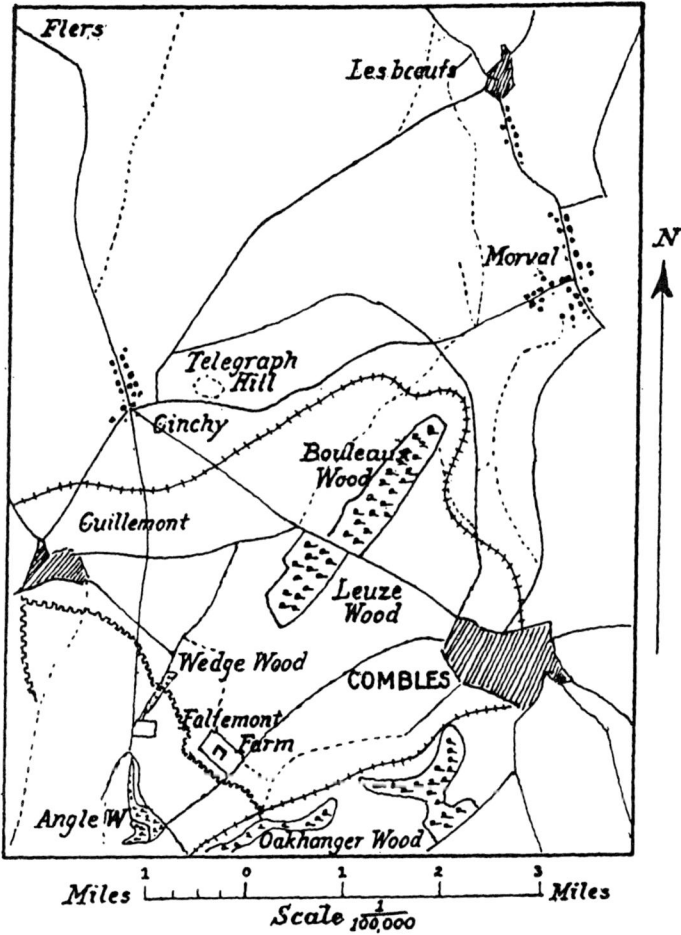

Flers

Les bœufs

Morval

N

Telegraph Hill

Ginchy

Bouleaux Wood

Guillemont

Leuze Wood

Wedge Wood

COMBLES

Falfemont Farm

Angle W

Oakhanger Wood

Miles ‖ 1 ‖ 0 ‖ 1 ‖ 2 ‖ 3 ‖ Miles

Scale $\frac{1}{100,000}$

[To face p. 118.

around Dernancourt, and joined the XIV. Corps (Lieut.-Gen. the Earl of Cavan).

During the night of 26th August the Division relieved the 35th (Bantam) Division on the Eastern slopes of the Maltz Horn Ridge, Divisional Head-Quarters being in dug-outs near Billon Farm. The front was held by two Brigades, 15th on the right and 95th on the left, the 13th Brigade being in reserve. On our immediate right were the French, who held the high ground East of Maurepas, and whose line joined with ours near Angle Wood; on our left was the 20th (Light) Division, holding a line half-way between Trônes Wood and Guillemont, the point of junction between the Divisions being the small plantation known as " Arrowhead Copse."

The Divisional position covered the whole of the Eastern slope of the ridge on which stood Maltz Horn Farm, the advanced posts on the right being in the valley which runs from Maurepas to Combles. Opposite the right Brigade front rose the end of the spur on which Leuze and Bouleaux woods are situated, and which ran North-East diagonally across the front of the Division; at the South-West point of this spur was situated the famous " Falfemont Farm."

On taking over, the situation was comparatively quiet, the battle having temporarily died down in this area, although our positions, especially in the valley near Angle Wood, were subjected to a good deal of shelling.

On 3rd September the Division attacked. Owing to the commanding position of Falfemont Farm it was decided that this place should be attacked some hours before the main battle, as, until it had been captured, the French would be unable to advance along the valley towards Combles. The French had undertaken the Artillery bombardment and barrage on this point.

At 9 a.m. the 13th Brigade attacked, the K.O.S.B. on the right being directed on the Farm, and the 14th Warwicks on the trenches between the Farm and Wedge Wood. The Infantry left their trenches and advanced towards the square enclosure of the Farm. Not a shell was falling, however, on that point, and the Germans were able to bring up numerous machine-guns from their deep dug-outs, and pour a murderous fire into the advancing line. Under this terrific deluge the attacking columns melted away, further advance against the undisturbed aim of the enemy's Gunners being a sheer impossibility. It subsequently transpired that the guns detailed for the barrage had been switched to meet a German counter-attack farther South, although we had no notification of this at the time. The remaining two Battalions of the 13th Brigade were then moved up, and preparations made to assault the Farm simultaneously with the main attack at 12.15 p.m.

At this hour the 95th Brigade, on the left, moved to the attack, while on their left the 20th Division, with the 47th Brigade of the 16th (Irish) Division attached, assaulted Guillemont. The advance went well. The 12th Gloucesters were on the right, and the D.C.L.I. on the left, and, keeping well up to the barrage, they carried all before them, and, two hours after zero, had gained their final objective, and had dug in along the line of the road from Ginchy to Maurepas, North of Wedge Wood. Their advance was magnificently executed, and, in spite of a withering machine-gun fire, the line never wavered for an instant ; but both Battalions suffered considerable casualties, the losses of the

Gloucesters being heavier on account of an almost
enfilade machine-gun fire from Falfemont Farm. To
their North, Guillemont, around which place the fight
had ebbed and flowed for more than a month, was
finally captured ; as a village it no longer existed;
in fact, except for the marking on the map, it would
have been impossible to tell that that shell-pitted
expanse of ground had ever been a peaceful agricultural
hamlet. Not one brick remained.

While events had gone well on the left, the attack
on Falfemont Farm did not progress so favourably.
The 13th Brigade had suffered severely, and the
Norfolks and the 16th Warwicks were sent up from
the Divisional Reserve to re-inforce them. During
the night the 13th Brigade was withdrawn, and the
15th Brigade took over the right sector.

On 5th September the attack was resumed, and
at 3.10 p.m. the 15th Brigade assaulted Falfemont
Farm and the German line thence towards Wedge
Wood. The Artillery preparation was terrific, but,
in spite of this, as soon as the Norfolks approached
the Farm the Germans could be seen mounting their
machine-guns on the parapet. It was impossible to
reach the Farm from the front over that open bullet-
swept zone, but, whilst the garrison's attention was
concentrated on the frontal attack, the Bedfords and
Cheshires reached the trench line to the North of it.
Quickly realising the position, Captain Barnett of the
Bedfords organised a bombing-party from men of the
two Battalions, which had by now become mixed, and
commenced bombing down the trenches towards the
Farm. This attack was magnificently carried out,
and gradually our troops worked their way, fighting
from traverse to traverse, into the corner of the en-

closure. Further, to assist in the flanking of the position, Colonel Onslow (O.C. Bedfords) led the remainder of the two Battalions up the slope towards " Lousy " Wood ; in doing so he risked our own barrage, which was due to recommence for the further advance in a short time, but his action was most valuable, as from the new position all approaches to the Farm were covered, and no supports could reach it. The movement was observed, and the barrage adjusted in time. A fierce hand-to-hand fight was now raging around the Farm buildings and enclosure, and gradually the garrison was reduced, and the numerous machine-guns destroyed or captured. By 5 p.m. the whole of the Farm position was in our hands, and German shells commenced to rain upon it, to ensure its complete destruction.

While this struggle was going on, the 95th Brigade advanced from their position on the Ginchy-Maurepas road, the Devons and East Surreys leading the way ; the Bedfords, Cheshires, and 16th Warwicks continued the line to the right, and, together, the attacking waves breasted the slope and disappeared into the dim recesses of " Lousy " Wood. Here opposition was encountered, but nothing could stop the advance, and by nightfall the whole of the Wood was in our hands, and the line of the final objective, the Ginchy-Combles road, was consolidated.

To our North the 16th (Irish) Division had assaulted Ginchy, but, meeting with a determined opposition, had failed to capture it, as also the Quadrilateral, a strong work between Ginchy and Leuze Wood. The left flank of the 5th Division was therefore very much " in the air," and to cover it the D.C.L.I. and Gloucesters of the 95th Brigade formed a defensive line along the North-West edge of Leuze Wood, and thus secured the position.

The positions gained were held against all counter-attacks, and the seal set on one of the finest exploits of the 5th Division during the War. In the attacks of 3rd and 5th September the 95th Brigade had advanced 3500 yards without a set-back of any kind, whilst the 13th and 15th Brigades had attacked and finally captured one of the strongest redoubts ever made by the engineering skill of the Germans.

The account of the battle would not be complete without a reference to the Artillery of the 35th and 56th Divisions, who covered the Divisional Front, and, by their bombardment and barrage fire, rendered possible the success achieved. Their gun positions in Chimpanzee Valley and the area South-East of Bernafay Wood were subjected to heavy bombardments and much gas shelling, but their support never faltered.

In Chimpanzee Valley were also located the two Brigade Head-Quarters. This valley, in which is the Bois Favière, lies to the West of the Maltz Horn Ridge, and was, during the stay of the Division in the area, subjected to frequent concentrations of gas shelling, which necessitated the wearing of gas helmets. The difficulties of command were much increased by the wearing of these encumbrances, and on one occasion a conference of the G.O.C. and the Brigadiers with regard to the operations was brought to an inglorious termination by a barrage of " green cross."

During these operations the Prince of Wales, at the time on the Staff of the XIV. Corps, was a frequent visitor to the Divisional and Brigade Head-Quarters, and was often seen both in the forward area and in the rest bivouacs and Transport lines.

On the night of 6th to 7th the 56th (London) Division relieved the Division in the line, and a composite Brigade, consisting of the 13th Brigade, Devons, East Surreys, 15th M.G. Company, and Argyll and Sutherland Highlanders, under Brig.-Gen. L. O. W. Jones, was left in the area under their command, the remainder of the Division withdrawing to the Morlancourt-Treux area. Fresh drafts arrived to make the units up to strength, and the time was spent in training there ; after a few days the 13th Brigade rejoined the Division.

On the 17th orders were received for a move back into the line to relieve the 6th Division, after the latter had completed the capture of the Quadrilateral. On the 18th the relief was carried out ; Ginchy and the Quadrilateral had now been taken, and the line ran some 1500 yards East of the village.

The 95th Brigade took over the right sector of the line, and the 13th the left sector. The Divisional Front extended some 2000 yards from the North edge of Bouleaux Wood, and lay on the Eastern slope of Ginchy-Telegraph Hill. The ground had only been captured the day previous to the relief, and the first efforts were therefore directed to the digging of trenches. The Germans had established posts on the near side of the valley, whilst dug-outs in the light railway embankment provided harbourage for a number of their troops and machine-guns.

For a week no move was made, but plans were prepared and arrangements made for a resumption of the offensive. On the night of the 24th and morning of the 25th our bombardment increased in severity. On the right of the Division the 56th Division were holding a line in Bouleaux Wood, and on the left the

6th Division held a short front ; beyond them were the Guards' Division. The 95th Brigade still held the right sector of the front, whilst the 15th Brigade had relieved the 13th in the left sector.

At 12.30 p.m. all the guns on the Divisional Front, and for some miles to the North, burst into a continuous roar of barrage fire. Simultaneously the Infantry leapt from their trenches, and once more advanced against the German lines. On the right the Devons and East Surreys formed the first line, supported by the Gloucesters and K.O.S.B. ; the 15th Brigade attacked with the Cheshires on the right and Norfolks on the left, the Bedfords and 16th Warwicks supporting them.

The Germans were holding the main trench line in force, and soon the 15th Brigade had collected numerous prisoners, many more of the enemy being killed by the fire from our rifles and Lewis guns. The advancing troops, closely following the barrage, swept irresistibly down the slope into the valley, but considerable opposition was met from the enemy on the railway embankment. The 56th Division on the right had been held up slightly farther back, and enfilade fire was brought to bear by German machine-guns on their front against the right of the 95th Brigade. Determined bombers moved out to deal with these, and soon the embankment was cleared, and the further advance rendered possible. After a short halt the line again advanced up the slope towards Morval, and assaulted the German trench line defending the village ; the enemy held this line in force, but the trench was rushed, and many prisoners were taken. After another halt the barrage again moved forward, and the attacking columns swept towards their final objectives. On the left the 15th Brigade carried the village of Morval with a rush ; a half-hearted opposition put up by the Germans still in the place was quickly overpowered, and, after mopping up the dug-outs and cellars in the village, the troops moved out into the open country East of the village.   Among the prisoners captured in the village was the German Town-Major, who remained faithful to his post, probably thinking that discretion, in the shape of a strong dug-out, was the better part of valour.

By nightfall the final objective running Southward from the " Moulin de Morval " had been consolidated. The whole attack had been carried through exactly to the plan and time-table, a truly remarkable feat.

A record of his impressions made by a French aviator flying above Combles gives a graphic description of the final phase of the attack.

" 5.30 P.M., 25TH SEPTEMBER,
800 METRES ABOVE COMBLES.

" A great calm falls on the battlefield.   The blue-coats have established themselves between Rancourt and Frégicourt, while more to the North, between Bouleaux Wood and Les Bœufs, a great line of khaki, harder to see, threatens the village of Morval.   Large shells here and there tear up the ground.   Looking from here one would say that after the hard struggles of the day the men had reached the limit of their endurance.   The fight is without doubt finished for the day.   Here and there an exhausted soldier is waiting for darkness to build up a small heap of earth to protect himself.

" But suddenly, just before 6 o'clock, the British Artillery opens a tornado of fire on the German lines. The enemy, unable to discover the threatened point

MAJ.-GEN. SIR R. B. STEPHENS, K.C.B., C.M.G.

[To face p. 126.

for this new attack, places a barrage at random behind
the British lines. Viewing the battlefield from my
lofty point of vantage it is possible for me to see at
which point in the bombarded line the English Artillery
wish to clear a way for their Infantry. It is at Morval;
for it is there that the fire of lighter shells is more
intense—it is there that the heavier shells are levelling
the obstacles—it is there, too, over Morval, that the
B.E.'s (the eyes of the Army) are circling.

" The rain of shells has continued for half an hour,
when suddenly, without anything to warn the enemy
of a change ‚in the situation, the Khaki Line swarms
forward as one man. Just as it reaches the curtain of
fire, the latter, as if actuated by a single mind, moves
forward in bounds, clears the village, and establishes
itself some hundred yards beyond it, forming a barrier
under cover of which the assaulting wave gains the
mastery of the village and its outskirts. A few German
signals of distress, a few bursting grenades around the
dug-outs, an attempt at defence rapidly overwhelmed,
and the Khaki Line, having gained almost a kilometre
of ground, reforms beyond the objective. Morval is
ours ! Combles will be ours to-night !

" But what gives me the greatest satisfaction, far
greater than the mere gain of ground, is that I can
affirm, once again, that our Allies, the British, not only
have glorious troops, but also have the knack of using
them, and I foresee that the Germans in the future will
be able to resist them no longer."

By the capture of Morval the fall of Combles was
assured. The French on our right had taken Frégicourt, while the 95th Brigade were working their way
Southward from Morval to join hands with them ; only

a narrow gap remained through which the enemy
garrison could escape, and all night long our Artillery
barraged this exit to catch the fleeing troops.

The attack on the 25th was the first occasion on
which the Division was allotted " Tanks " to co-operate
with the Infantry. Knowing the uncertainties of these
first experimental land-ships, it was wisely decided
that they should only be used to support the Infantry,
the attack being planned without absolute reliance on
their assistance. Well it was that this was so ; of the
three Tanks allotted, one failed to start ; the second
proceeded some distance, but " bellied " in the mud
in the vicinity of our jumping-off line by the sunken
road ; whilst the third, after various vicissitudes, arrived
some time after the Infantry on the South side of
Morval, but proved of considerable assistance to the
95th Brigade in dealing with a system of stubbornly
held trenches in that area. Though the Tanks may
have failed, their crews did not, and, dismounting
their machine-guns, they proceeded with the Infantry
in their attack.

Counter-attacks were driven off, and morning
found the Division holding the whole of the ground
captured. The Germans had been ousted from their
trench line, but were holding some old practice trenches
East of Morval, and sniping from these caused much
annoyance to the troops consolidating. This led to
an astonishing exploit : crawling out to one of these
trenches alone, Private Jones, of the Cheshires, captured single-handed 200 Germans, and led them in
triumph back to our lines, an act for which he was
awarded the V.C.

The way in which the Artillery of the 3rd Division,
covering the Divisional Front, had supported the

attack, and then moved forward their guns to cover the new positions, was worthy of the highest praise. Although in both this and the Leuze Wood attacks previously, the Artillery was strange to the Division, the utmost accord existed, and the Gunners could not have done more for their own Divisional troops than they did for us.

After a day of shelling, and a few alarms, the Division was relieved on the night of the 26th by the 20th Division, who, after holding that portion of the line for twenty-four hours, were in turn relieved by the French.

During the operations in September the arrangements for the evacuation of casualties were under the Corps, the Divisional R.A.M.C. units being at their disposal. As at Longueval, great gallantry was shown by the bearers and Medical Officers in dealing with the wounded ; the bearers had an especially hard task, with long carries over muddy ground swept by continual bursts of shell-fire, and they suffered somewhat severely.

On relief, the worn-out troops moved to the Citadel area, North of Bray, and there we had our first experience of night-bombing by aeroplanes. During the night a bomb dropped by a German aeroplane burst in one of the bivouac camps, and some men of the Bedfords, who had safely survived all the dangers of the Somme battles, were killed—truly a cruel stroke of luck ! On the 27th and 28th the Division moved back by train to the area around Hallencourt (South-East of Abbeville) on the banks of the Somme.

The 5th Divisional Artillery, whom we had left in the line near Fricourt at the beginning of August, and had not seen since, were still engaged in the battle. From 7th to 14th August they remained covering the

9

17th Division, and supported several minor attacks against the Germans who had regained a footing in the Eastern edge of Delville Wood, which, however, did not meet with much success. On the 14th, the 14th (Light) Division relieved the 17th Division, the Artillery still remaining in their positions. On 18th August an attack was launched along the whole Fourth Army Front, the objective of the 14th Division being the trenches North of Delville Wood. The attack was in the main successful, the 14th Division taking some 300 prisoners of the Saxon Corps, who surrendered freely. The Infantry in this attack were much pleased with the support given by our guns, and the G.O.C. Division, and 43rd Brigade, sent very complimentary letters to the Artillery, which were greatly appreciated.

On the 22nd the C.R.A. 7th Division took over the command of the Artillery on this front from General Hussey, and half of the weary Batteries of the 5th Division and the D.A.H.Q. were drawn out to rest at Bussy-les-Daours, near Amiens. The Batteries remaining in position first supported the 55th (East Lancs.) Division, and then the 14th Division, once again, in their successful assault on Switch Trench and the Flers Line on 15th September, while an attack supported by the first Tanks along the whole Army Front was launched, and resulted in the capture of Flers, Martinpuich, and Courcelette. These Batteries were then relieved by those who had been resting, and the latter took part in the great and successful attack on 25th September supporting the 21st Division when Geudecourt, Les Bœufs, and Morval were captured. On the 30th they were in turn relieved by the other half of the Batteries, who supported the 12th Division in the big attack on 8th October, when Le Sars was taken.

The guns remained in much the same positions, Caterpillar Valley, until 1st September, when they moved to Bernafay Wood to support the attacks on Ginchy and Guillemont, and afterwards to positions round Delville Wood for the Switch Trench and Geude- court attacks. On 1st October they again moved forward to positions in the vicinity of Switch Trench. Many guns were destroyed by hostile shell-fire and still more were rendered " hors de combat " by the failure of running-out springs ; at one time half the guns were out of action from these causes, but replacements were quickly forthcoming from a " pool " of guns kept by the Corps at the workshops. A vast quantity of ammunition had to be brought up to the Batteries each night, as, even when no attacks were in progress, there were daily barrages to be fired, night-harassing fire to be carried out, and frequent " S.O.S." calls to be answered. The Drivers bringing up the wagons in the dark had a very bad time, running the gauntlet of bursting shells, and threading their way through the ever-shifting maze of shell-craters ; many were killed or wounded ; and at the guns too there were many casualties.

" X " and " U " Batteries, R.H.A., were attached for a period, and both rendered yeoman service. On one occasion " X " Battery ran a section of guns forward into Delville Wood in order to enfilade a trench at a range of only 500 yards—a difficult job getting the guns up through the mass of tangled wire and broken branches.

Much of the registration of, and some observation for, the guns was done from Observation Balloons, of which large numbers were in use both by ourselves and the enemy throughout the Somme battle. These balloons also proved very useful for reporting on the general appearance of the barrage and " S.O.S." lines of fire, and also for spotting enemy Batteries and movements.

The Divisional Artillery from July to October supported at different times no fewer than five Divisions' Infantry, apart from their own. This mixing-up of Batteries, Commanders, and Infantry, which was a feature of the Somme fighting, was found to be inevitable, in order to concentrate the immense volume of fire necessary for the barraging. The Infantry were exhausted after two or three hard-fought battles and had to be withdrawn, whilst the guns remained in position. An attempt was made at the end of 1916 to avoid this splitting up of Commands by the withdrawal of an Artillery Brigade from each Division, and the formation of Army Field Artillery Brigades, which could be concentrated on any front where a mass of Artillery was needed. This did not entirely overcome the difficulty, however, as, at Ypres in 1917, the guns again remained in when the Infantry were withdrawn for rest.

The length of time the Batteries remained in action entailed a very great strain on the Officers and men, who were in some cases for as long as two months continuously in action, amid perpetual shelling, bombing, and gas bombardments, but they were rewarded by the knowledge that their efforts were appreciated, not only by the Infantry whom they supported, but also by the Higher Commands.

Bussy-les-Daours, to which the Batteries were withdrawn for periods, was a true haven of rest. The 28th Brigade, while there, managed to rout out an old brake and four-in-hand harness from the Château where they were billeted, and horses, which only a few days before had been bringing up ammunition through the hell of Caterpillar Valley, were seen proudly stepping into Amiens, six miles away, taking Officers in to dine at " Godeberts' " or the " Café des Huitres." Riding down partridges over the stubbles was also a popular sport, and when the Cavalry were in the same area waiting for the " G." in " GAP," hare drives by large numbers of mounted men took place.

No sooner had the Division, less Artillery, arrived in the back area than orders were received for an immediate move to take over the sector of line from Givenchy to Richebourg, in the XI. Corps (Lieut.-Gen. Sir R. B. Haking). By 1st October the move by rail had been completed, and the Division was on its new front. On 10th October the Divisional Artillery were concentrated at Bussy, and started to march to rejoin the Division ; after a pleasant march of four days through Molliens, Amplier, Orville, and the Canche Valley, they arrived on the 13th at Locon, where they were welcomed by the Division, and they immediately moved into action on the new front.

The casualties in the Division in the Somme fighting had been very heavy ; the total in killed, wounded, and missing from the 19th of July to the end of September was 559 Officers and 11,186 other ranks ; although our losses were so heavy, it was known that those of the enemy were equally so, and in all probability far greater.

The fighting in the Longueval area had not seemed to be entirely satisfactory, and raised questioning in some minds. The gain of ground had been slight, and at a heavy cost, although the advance had been a magnificent one considering the obstacles against which it was carried out. The reason for this is easy to be found in the fact that during this period of the operations attacks were being made on a small front ; the enemy was thus enabled to concentrate the whole of his Artillery which could be brought to bear, and, in the case of the salient at Longueval and Delville Wood, this was an enormous quantity. Subsequently, on 5th September, the advance carried out with the co-operation of other troops on a broad front had been a success, qualified only by the temporary difficulty at Falfemont Farm, which was gallantly overcome ; while on 25th September the Division had advanced, again as part of an attack on a broad front, to a depth of 2 miles, carrying all before it. We hoped that the lesson of these operations had been learnt.

The Division left the Somme Battle proud in their record of deeds achieved, and with high hopes for the future. In the words of the Army Commander, General Sir H. Rawlinson : " The heavy fighting in Delville Wood and Longueval, the attack and capture of the Falfemont Farm Line and Leuze Wood, and finally the storming of Morval, are feats of arms seldom equalled in the annals of the British Army. They constitute a record of unvarying success which it has been the lot of few Divisions to attain, and the gallantry, valour, and endurance of all ranks have been wholly admirable."

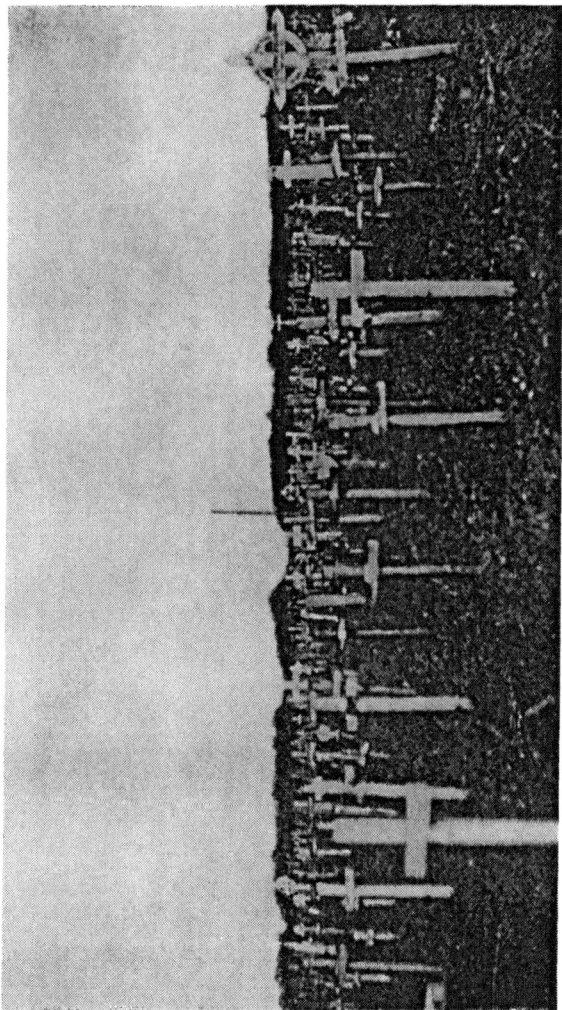

A SOMME CEMETERY.

[To face p. 134.

CHAPTER VII

THE BÉTHUNE FRONT

(MAP 4) [1]

THE Infantry Brigades detrained at Chocques and
Lillers, marched to Béthune, and took over the
Front from the La Bassée Canal to Richebourg L'Avoué
from the 31st Division. This was the theatre where
the Division had fought so magnificently in October
1914, but, alas ! there were now few left, either Officers
or men, who remembered it. The country and surroundings have already been described ; they had
altered little, for, with the exception of the German
attacks at Givenchy in January 1915, the Neuve
Chapelle battle in March, and the fighting near Festubert two months later, this front had been fairly quiet
for nearly two years. It was now to be the Division's
Winter quarters for six months.

At first the Canal was the Southern boundary, but
before they had been in a week the sector South of the
Canal was added to their Front, making a total extent
of nearly 7500 yards to be held. Several changes were
made during the Winter ; early in November there was
a side-slip to the North up to Neuve Chapelle, and in
December there was a side-slip back again. In February
the Division took over the Northern sector a second time,
and gave it up to the 56th Division in March, taking
over more ground again to the South of the Canal.

¹ See p. 34.

These shifts involved a good deal of work in connection with the defence schemes, which had to be re-written, and Batteries had generally to change their positions to cover the new ground.

The Front was divided up into three sectors, named Cuinchy, Givenchy, and Ferme-du-Bois, held respectively by the 95th Brigade (Brig.-Gen. Lord E. Gordon-Lennox) with Head-Quarters at Canal House, the 13th Brigade (Brig.-Gen. Jones) with Head-Quarters at Loisne, and the 15th Brigade (Brig.-Gen. Turner) with Head-Quarters at a farm called Cense-de-Raux. As a rule, two Battalions in each Brigade were put into the front line, one in support, and one in reserve, one of the reserve Battalions being held in Divisional Reserve ; but in December this arrangement was changed to keeping two Brigades in front and one in reserve at Béthune. Battalions relieved each other every four or five days. Division Head-Quarters were at Locon till the end of the year, when they moved into Béthune, which was more centrally situated.

On the right, by the Brickstacks, the line consisted of a number of sap-heads, mostly approached by wet tunnels about 200 yards long, and held by posts with machine-guns ; some of these sap-heads were only 20 or 30 yards from the Germans. In this sector they suffered a great deal from floods ; two powerful pumps on barges were established in the Canal, which succeeded in lowering the water there 2 feet or so, but after that, in spite of continued efforts, the nuisance did not abate, when it was discovered that the pumped water was running back again into the Canal higher up ! During the hard frost the barges presented an Arctic appearance covered with a mass of icicles formed by the dripping pumps.

In front of Givenchy, as a result of much mining, were many craters, the biggest of which was called " Red Dragon Crater." There was a great deal of activity here in this form of warfare ; it entailed an enormous amount of work on the tunnelling companies and fatigue parties carrying the spoil, but if one side began it the other side had perforce to play also ; each tried to get under the other's galleries and blow them up, which was called " defensive " mining, or to explode an undetected mine under the other's trenches, which was called " offensive " mining. At this time there were two schools of thought as to whether it was best to consolidate the near lip or the far lip of a mine crater ; " Near-Lipians " and " Far-Lipians " they were called, like the " Big-Endians " and " Little-Endians " in *Gulliver's Travels*.

On the right of the left sector the ground was so water-logged that continuous trenches were impossible ; the line therefore consisted of several islands held by posts of eight to ten men with machine-guns and Stokes mortars, the intervening ground being wired up ; on the left the trenches were more continuous ; the main garrison was some 200 yards to the rear in what was called the " Old British Line "—a line of breastworks with iron arch bomb - proof shelters. Proper dug-outs were of course out of the question in this spongy soil. This sector, too, was badly off for communication trenches, and there were none at all to the islands, which were only accessible by night. The other two sectors were better off in this respect, though in many of the trenches the water was six inches to a foot in depth, and some even had small fish swimming about in them ; but by this time the British Army were old hands at this kind of warfare, and no trench was complete without its duck-boards to walk on. In one communication trench in the right sector, called "Harley Street," one was reminded of a Tube exit in London, for, on emerging from the trench into the open air, one was met by small French "gamins" selling the *Daily Mail*, but this practice was soon stopped by the authorities, as it was thought unsafe for the boys to be so near the Front. Indeed, in this part of the line the inhabitants were still living fairly close up, between 3 or 4 miles from the front line, and one did not hear of many casualties to them, though their houses were often shelled.

The Artillery was normally divided into three Groups, covering the three sectors of the line, the Battery positions scattered about between Annequin, south of the Canal, to Richebourg-St. Vast, a distance of 5 miles. One Section was also far to the South at Vermelles, and another Section up North at Pont Logy, on the Éstaires road, sited in those places to enfilade the enemy trenches from the flanks. The gun emplacements and dug-outs were as a rule protected with elephant iron or corrugated-iron arches, covered with rubble, stones, etc., which made them fairly bomb-proof and watertight ; and very neat and tidy they were inside, embellished with tiles from ruined houses, paint borrowed (?) from the R.E., and artistic devices of sorts. Some Batteries, which were in the low-lying swampy woods near the Canal, were much bothered with water, and big drainage operations had to be undertaken. In one of these woods, where the 120th Battery was, lived a pheasant that eluded all the attentions of the personnel of the Battery, and used daily to crow his defiance at them. Some snipe and duck, too, were seen occasionally, and a few were shot. Each Battery had also to do caretaker to two alternative positions, into which they moved sometimes for "change of air," and there was no end to the O.P.'s, both building and projected, in Cuinchy, Givenchy, Le Plantin, Festubert, and Rue-du-Bois, so there was plenty of fatigue work to be done by the Gunners. These O.P.'s were generally strong, double-walled towers, built up inside the ruined houses. As long as they were not heavily bombarded it was all right, but if the outside walls were knocked down, the naked O.P.'s stood out advertising themselves as such, and speedily became very "unhealthy." In January our "oldest Allies," the Portuguese, sent up some Officers and men to be trained in the Batteries. They were fairly apt pupils, and appeared to enjoy their time with the British—when there was no shelling.

The Battery Wagon lines were in Béthune, or strung out in the villages and farms towards La Couture. This latter place went by the name of "Licatere," just as Le Cateau was called "Licatoo." Much trouble was taken to make these lines and those of the Infantry Transport comfortable for the men and horses ; cover was rigged up for the horses and harness, stable flooring was made of slag and broken bricks, dining-rooms were built with wood from the Maori saw-mills in the Forêt de Nieppe, and the men spent the winter in very tolerable comfort.

Before the Winter set in a curious rumour sprang up, to the effect that some of the old hard-fighting Divisions, of which the 5th was one, were to be sent for the Winter somewhere to the back of beyond, or even home, for an honourable rest, called "the King's Rest." Evidently the wish was father to the thought, and, needless to say, there was no foundation for it.

Fables such as this generally had their origin in the Transport and Wagon lines, the Signals, or the Train. In Béthune there was a Divisional School for lectures and theoretical instruction, the Brigades established bombing and bayonet-fighting practice grounds, and there were schools without number in the Corps and Army—Infantry schools, Artillery schools, Sniping schools, Trench-mortar schools, Lewis-gun schools, etc. In Béthune, too, there were the " Whizz-Bang " performances, the " Fancies " of the 6th Division, the " Pedlars " of the 31st Division, and in Christmas week there was an excellent pantomime done by the 56th Division in the Béthune Theatre. The town was seldom shelled; there was a bout of it about the beginning of January, which did a little damage, and the station was rather a favourite target, but, despite this, the nightly leave trains were never stopped running.

At the beginning of January a National Mission Campaign was inaugurated ; several meetings were held in the Béthune Theatre, which were well attended, and excellent addresses were delivered by the Army Commander (Sir Henry Horne), the Chaplain-General, the Rev. H. Blackburne, and others.

During the Winter the new gas-helmet, or box-respirator, was issued—a great improvement on the old one. Every one was practised in its use, and had to stay some minutes in a gas-chamber with it on him. Whenever the wind was at all from the East " gas alert " was ordered, which meant that all helmets were to be worn in the " ready " position, and various other precautions had to be taken. All entrances to dug-outs and shelters in the danger area were protected by double curtains of chemically treated blankets, for there was always a possibility of a cloud gas attack; gas shells, which the Division had had a taste of at the Somme, were little used, and the dastardly mustard-gas was not yet invented.

The greatest care was taken to prevent the enemy overhearing our telephone messages. All reliefs when completed were reported by some camouflaged message such as "Major Brown has arrived," and various codes were in use. One Battalion used the names of well-known actresses as a code, reporting a very good, good, or fair relief according to the attractiveness of the actress named. We too had our overhearing apparatus which went by the name of " IT," and bits of German messages were occasionally picked up. " IT " also acted as a sort of spy on any illicit conversations, which were at once reported, in order to bring the culprit to book.

In January and February there was a very hard frost, lasting for three weeks, and much snow; the men kept wonderfully fit and well, and there was less sickness then than in the damp, muggy weather. " Trench feet " was a common complaint, and to counteract this whale-oil was issued, but it is doubtful if it did much good; the main thing was to keep the feet dry and change if they got wet. Gum-boots, which were a trench store and handed over on relief, and skin coats, were also issued.

On arrival in this area the Battalions were very weak in men, having lost so many on the Somme, but drafts kept coming in, and the strengths were soon brought up to nearly a thousand; current wastage from sickness and casualties, which averaged between twenty and fifty a day in the Division, had to be made up too; one man from each Battalion also had to be found every week as a probationer for a commission, and it was not at all easy to find suitable candidates.

On the whole, this was a very quiet part of the front, and the enemy was nothing like so aggressive as we were. Sniping and trench-mortaring were the chief causes of annoyance and casualties. The Norfolk snipers, however, were one day successful in killing a German Officer who was looking over the parapet. It was ascertained afterwards from a prisoner that this Officer was none other than the Divisional General —a fact which made our own G.O.C. very apprehensive lest the enemy should retaliate on him during his visits to the trenches! But he was not deterred from his daily rounds.

In front at first was a Bavarian Division who had a severe hammering on the Somme. All they wanted was a peaceful time—but it was not to be so; the Higher Authorities ordained that all through the Winter the Germans were to be harassed in every possible way. Constant patrolling in No Man's Land and at least two raids in each Division every week was the order. The planning of these raids offered great scope for ingenuity and cunning; no two were exactly alike; some were dummy ones, some were subtle, silent ones, some were proclaimed by a previous bombardment, others were carried out with an Artillery box-barrage; but the most prolific ones were those in the nature of a surprise. Down South, for instance, the Canadians conceived the unusual idea of raiding the same place twice in one night, and the second one, being unexpected, was by far the most successful. It would take a volume to chronicle all the raids and patrol actions in which the Division took part during this Winter; two or three only are given as examples.

On the 31st of October the Bedfords carried out a big raid with four Platoons of twenty men each. Most careful preparations had been made beforehand, enlarged air-photographs had been issued, the ground had been staked out behind the lines, and the attack practised twice by day and twice by night till every man knew exactly what to do. On the raid night the men blacked their faces, which caused much hilarity among them. The right and left leading Platoons entered the German trenches where the wire was known to be weak, taking ammonal tubes with them in case they could not get through, only one of which was used, however. They then placed stops and bombed their way inwards ; the two rear Platoons then went through the stops and bombed inwards also, 100 yards ahead. There was a good deal of opposition with grenades and machine-guns, but the party overcame it, stayed there three-quarters of an hour, and returned with three prisoners, having killed a dozen Germans, while their casualties were two men killed and eighteen wounded. In this raid there was no Artillery preparation, but a barrage was put down on withdrawal, and a noisy demonstration was made 500 yards farther North.

The D.C.L.I. on the 5th of February organised a very successful raid South of the Canal near the La Bassée road. The raiding party, under Captain Taylor, was divided into four groups—right, centre, left, and a covering party. A few men carrying ammonal tubes to cut the wire preceded them. The right group, on entering the enemy trenches, formed a block ; the centre group then went through and turned to the North, bombing up the trench till they met the left group. Two prisoners were captured, six dug-outs

bombed and wrecked, and fifty Germans estimated to
be killed or wounded, as these dug-outs, according to
prisoners, were full of men. Captain Taylor had
meanwhile established a telephone in the German
front line, and was in communication with Battalion
Head-Quarters, and the covering Batteries, who kept
up an intense barrage the whole time they were in. At
zero + 20 the order was given to retire, which was
carried out successfully. Of the 114 raiders who went
over the top one Officer and one man died of wounds,
and fourteen others were wounded. The enemy
opposition was described as " futile."

On 16th March a party of twenty-four men of the
K.O.S.B., under Lieut. Aucott, visited the enemy trenches
in the Givenchy crater area. At 4.50 a.m. the Artillery
barrage opened; it then crept forward 300 yards and
formed a box round the area to be raided. The raid
was split up into three parties, which followed each
other closely ; the first party crossed No Man's Land
and leapt into the enemy sap, where they found three
men whom they made prisoners. The whole party
then advanced, bombed two dug-outs where five or six
of the enemy were killed, and six more prisoners taken.
In half an hour they were all safely back with only
three men wounded, while they estimated the enemy
casualties at about twenty. The Germans were evidently quite unprepared and taken by surprise, as there
was no Artillery reply nor machine-gun fire, only slight
rifle-fire which was very badly placed.

But by far the most famous raid was a daylight
one carried out by the West Kents at Givenchy on
10th February. The two Companies who were to
take part in it, commanded respectively by Captain
Cobb and Captain Scott, were trained for a fortnight

behind the line; No Man's Land was carefully reconnoitred by the selected leaders, and six crossings
were found among the maze of craters, so each Company was divided into three parties. Extra Batteries
were brought in, and their registration was spread
over several days so as not to give away the fact that
there was an increase of guns. Six Batteries took part
in the creeping barrage, three firing frontal and three
enfilade, while the rest of the 18-prs. and the 4·5
howitzers took on known machine-gun posts and soft
spots. The Corps Heavy Artillery arranged a neutral-
ising programme for firing on enemy Batteries, and
aeroplanes dropped bombs on suspected Head-Quarters
while the raid was in progress. Each man in the two
Companies carried six bombs, small black and yellow
flags were taken to mark the position, and the men, as
usual, removed all identification marks. The morning
was exceptionally quiet, except for a little desultory
shelling on our part to keep up the delusion that
nothing particular was on. At 3 p.m. the barrage
opened as one gun, and the two Companies advanced
on a front of half a mile with the utmost dash and
spirit; indeed, so keen were the men that some went
too quick and walked into our barrage, and there were
a few casualties this way. The surprise was complete;
about forty dug-outs were bombed or set on fire, four
mine-shafts and one bomb-store were blown up, this
being done by a party from the Tunnelling Company,
who unfortunately lost an Officer in the operation;
about 150 Germans were killed, and 1 Officer and
26 men were captured. In half an hour the two
Companies were back in their trenches, having lost
11 men killed and 59 wounded, half of the latter
only slightly; they were then relieved and went back

to a well-earned rest. The prisoners belonged to a Reserve Division which had lately come from the Russian Front, and they were not at all used to this sort of treatment; the Officer said that he thought the great British Spring Offensive had begun. Two days later the Commander-in-Chief came and congratulated the West Kents on their fine performance.

The Germans occasionally retaliated by raiding us, but they seemed to have no heart in this work, and our rifles, machine-guns, and Artillery generally frustrated their attempts. On one occasion they made an attempt on our trenches in the Ferme-du-Bois Sector. The Bedfords, who were holding the post, were alarmed one dark night by the bombing of their wire. They put up some Verey lights and saw some thirty or forty Germans stealing across No Man's Land in file. The machine-guns at once opened and scattered them, but one German Officer and six determined men got through the wire and started to bomb along the breastworks. Meanwhile the whole Company stood to arms ; a counter-bombing party, under Lieut. Millais, was organised, and a Lewis gun was mounted in position. Simultaneously another party of thirty or so was seen crossing No Man's Land, but they were at once dispersed by fire from the Lewis gun. Of the party who succeeded in getting in the Officer and three men were killed, and a number of bombs, some rifles, and knobbed sticks were left behind. The Bedford casualties were only one Sergeant killed and one man slightly wounded. On another occasion they raided the same sector with even less success, for they left two dead and a wounded prisoner in our hands, while our casualties were " nil."

During the Winter many " strafes " of the enemy trenches, the Brickstacks, the Railway Triangle, and offending "Minnies" and trench-mortars, took place, sometimes by the Divisional Artillery alone, sometimes combined with the Corps Heavy Artillery, who, in addition to their 9·2-inch, 8-inch, and 6-inch howitzers, had a 12-inch howitzer on the railway at Beuvry, and sometimes with the trench-mortars as well. The German trench-mortar positions were given names, such as " Carl," " Chris," " Bert," " Eric," and " Alec," so that, if any of them began to be obnoxious, there should be no delay in bringing down a swift retribution upon the sinner. For instance, the message " Bert active " would be replied to within two minutes by the covering guns. But " Carl & Co." were very peripatetic, and often were not at home in their usual quarters, in which case sometimes a trap was baited by sending over a few 2-inch trench-mortar bombs, so that they might disclose their position when replying. Certain retaliation schemes by the Artillery, which went by the names of "Hit," "Harass," "Hell," and " Hurricane," were also ready to be turned on at a moment's notice. Sometimes Batteries used to run up single guns or Sections into concealed positions close up to the front (which were called " positions of hate "), fire off twenty or thirty rounds during the night, and then withdraw home again. The 2-inch trench-mortars, under Captain Moreton, were kept very busy ; eight out of the twelve were generally in action about the support line, and there were two Heavies at Givenchy, but these latter were not popular, as they had a knack of dropping their " flying pigs " short, and the explosion, when it was not a " dud," was prodigious. The Germans were kind in informing us of any outside news ; for instance, on 7th December, a notice board was put up in their trenches saying that Bucharest had fallen.

As Christmas-time came on the Authorities were very anxious that there should be no fraternisation; our men had not the least inclination to hobnob with the enemy, but there was no knowing what the latter might do; in fact, on Christmas morning a patrol did approach our lines shouting, " Come over "—they were fired on furiously. During the whole of Christmas week a steady bombardment of the enemy trenches was carried on, sometimes slow and desultory, and sometimes bursting out into intense periods. The 2-inch trench-mortars, too, indulged in a big shoot, throwing over more than two thousand bombs in four days, thereby earning the congratulations of the Corps Commander. It was a big job to bring up all this amount of stuff up the winding communication trenches, as it could be only carried by hand, one man to one bomb, and it would have been impossible without the help of Infantry fatigue parties.

All these bombardments, raids, and patrol actions got on to the enemy's nerves, and towards the end he became very jumpy and apprehensive; frequent deserters came over. On one occasion a man was seen approaching the trenches of the East Surreys with his hands up. An Officer at once went forward to take his surrender, but he was just forestalled by an Officer of the West Kents; but, as neither party could speak the language, no information could be elicited from the prisoner. Nevertheless, his gesticulations caused it to be understood that he had come over because the Germans were just going to blow a mine. He was given something to eat, and an interpreter was sent for. With his good treatment the German recovered his composure, with the result that he denied all knowledge of any mine; but while he was still speaking the mine went up! History does not relate what happened to him.

The East Surreys too, on one occasion, varied the monotony of their trench life with the unusual task of treasure-hunting. The owner of Kingsclere, a ruined house near Cuinchy, who was weary of waiting for the end of the war, wished some valuables to be recovered from what was once his home. A plan was given to the Battalion, who succeeded in finding some damaged books, some silver, and some bonds, which were returned to the owner, much to his delight.

On 25th February came reports that the Germans were withdrawing from the Fronts of the Third and Fifth Armies, and it was thought that they might be contemplating a similar move here, so the patrolling in No Man's Land was conducted with extra vigilance, but no signs of withdrawal were to be seen. It was about this time that Germany notified the world that her submarines were going to sink every ship, whether neutral or belligerent, causing such intense indignation everywhere, especially in America. It seemed then like her last desperate effort, and certainly at the beginning of 1917 she was in very sore straits, and her fate was trembling in the balance.

In March the 66th Division arrived from England and sent up Platoons and Companies to be trained in the trenches. On the 18th they took over the Front, and the 5th Division marched away to the Bruay District for training, coming under the orders of the Canadian Corps, the 13th Brigade joining the 2nd Canadian Division in order to take part in the attack on Vimy Ridge. The Artillery was left in though for some days longer. There had been a scare about the safety of Givenchy ; it was thought likely that an attack would be made there, and, if that place fell, all the ground to the West as far as Béthune would be at the mercy of the enemy. A scheme was concocted in which every gun which could reach Givenchy should fire in case of need, and " S.O.S.GIV." was tested several times, but it was never required.

The 5th Division guns were at first to be relieved on the 20th, then the relief was cancelled, then again postponed. The men used to call the Corps Commander " Pharaoh," because " he would not let them go," and they badly wanted a rest before the arduous days which were in front of them. At last, on 26th March, the Artillery was relieved, leaving a few guns still in to re-inforce the Front, and marched South to join the 2nd Canadian Division, to whom they were to be attached for the attack on Vimy Ridge. A party of men had already been sent down there a month ago to prepare emplacements amid the ruins of Neuville-St.-Vast, and to bring up the vast quantity of ammunition required (1300 rounds per gun), and by the 7th of April all was in readiness for the Great Battle.

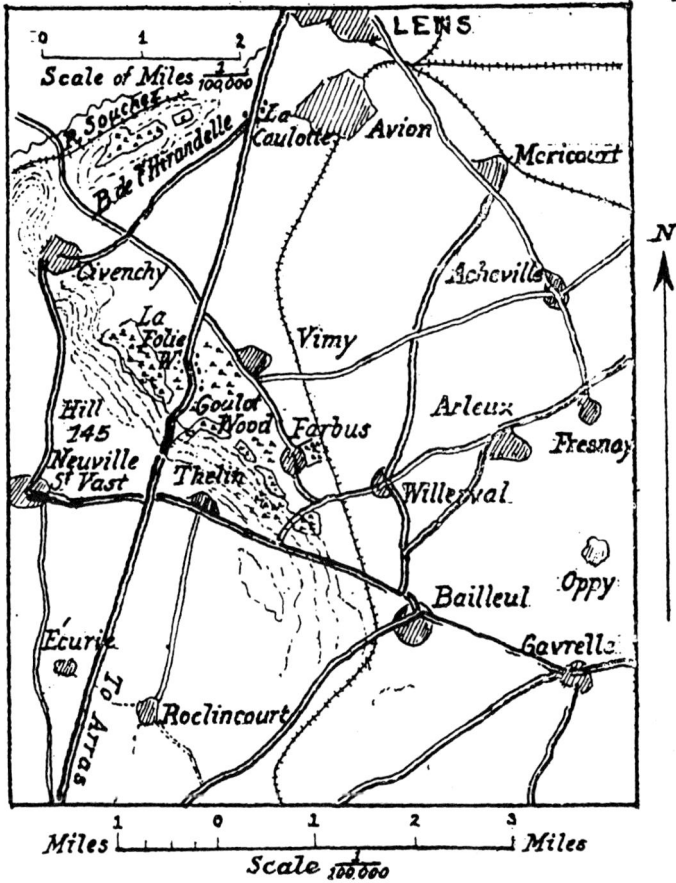

VIMY FRONT   Map 12.

LENS

0   1   2
Scale of Miles $\frac{1}{100,000}$

R. Souchez
B. de l'Hirondelle
La Caulotte
Avion
Mericourt

Givenchy
Acheville

La Folie W.
Vimy

Hill 145
Goulot Wood
Farbus
Arleux
Fresnoy

Neuville St Vast
Thelus
Willerval

Bailleul
Oppy

Ecurie
Gavrelle

To Arras
Roclincourt

N

Miles   1   0   1   2   3   Miles
Scale $\frac{1}{100,000}$

[To face p. 150.

CHAPTER VIII

VIMY RIDGE

(Maps 12 and 13)

THE glorious battle of Vimy Ridge, or, as its proper nomenclature is, the battle of Arras (for the attack extended through the Third Army right down to Arras and beyond) took place on Easter Monday, 9th April 1917. It ranks as one of the finest feats in the annals of the war, and the Canadian Corps, under Lieut.-Gen. the Hon. Sir Julian Byng, are justly proud of their magnificent achievement. Besides the moral effect it produced, the capture of the Ridge had far-reaching results, for it remained in our hands all through the great German push of 1918, forming an impregnable barrier to their advance, and it was the hinge upon which all future operations hung. The Ridge itself runs from the Souchez River, between Souchez village and Givenchy-en-Gohelle, in a South-East direction, gradually falling and losing itself in the undulating country North-East of Arras. The Western slope, on which Thélus is the only village, is very gradual, but from the summit the ground falls abruptly to the East through the Goulot and Farbus woods. The pretty little villages of Petit Vimy to the North, and Farbus to the South, lie closely nestling under the woods ; a little farther out is the bigger mining village of Vimy. From the top of the Ridge one gets a splendid view, from Douai, far away to the right, to Lens and its mining suburbs on the left. The open plain, dotted with the villages of Willerval, Oppy, Arleux, and Fresnoy, and, farther to the South, Bailleul and Gavrelle, lies spread out like a map at one's feet, and any movement except just in the villages is plainly visible to the naked eye.

The Head-Quarters of the 2nd Canadian Division, the 5th Division Artillery, and the Heavy Artillery were in a vast cave called " Aux Rietz," near Neuville-St.-Vast. This cave, like many others in the neighbourhood, had been used in former days for quarrying chalk for building purposes, and was about 80 feet deep. It was said to be capable of holding 5000 men— it certainly held thousands of rats, who made night hideous with their riotous conduct. In the vaulted kitchens the fires lighting up the stalactites and the cooks in their shirt-sleeves produced a weird and scenic effect. It was a cold, damp, and smelly place.

The preparations for the attack had been most carefully elaborated by the Canadian Corps ; every little detail had been thought of ; the barrage map, timing the Artillery tasks for eight hours and dovetailing in with that of the Third Army, was a work of art. The objectives were, first, the Black Line, some thousand yards from the Jumping-off Line; then the Red Line, 500 yards farther on ; the Blue Line, which included the village of Thélus ; and, finally, the Brown Line, on the Southern half of the attack. The Canadian line of battle was the 1st Division on the right, then the 2nd, 3rd, and 4th, and it was with the 2nd Division that the 13th Brigade and 5th Divisional Artillery were working. Daily bombardments, wire-cutting, and great aerial activity, in which the Germans seemed to

have the ascendancy, had been going on for the past fortnight, boiling up in intensity as " Z " day approached ;
so the Germans must have guessed something was on
—though, from prisoners' statements, they did not
expect the attack to come so soon.

The weather on the morning of the 9th was blus-
tering, with drizzle, and a few flakes of snow. Just
as the first streaks of dawn appeared, at 5.30, the
barrage burst forth. It was a grand pyrotechnic
display. From Arras to Lens the whole sky was lit
up by thousands of bursting shells, answered by the
red, green, and white rockets of the enemy calling for
help, and the Heavies kept up a continuous roar from
their guns. The valiant Canadian Infantry jumped off
to the second under the barrage, and took the Red
Line exactly on scheduled time, meeting with little
opposition. It was here, at the Red Line, that the
13th Brigade and 5th Division Artillery, whose positions
were so close up that they could not with safety fire
before, took up the battle.

For the past fortnight the 13th Brigade had been
strenuously practising the attack over taped trenches
on the ground near the Verdrel Woods, and were full
of dash and keenness. The plan was to attack the
Thélus trench frontally, and then swing round to the
South through the Goulot Wood, thus avoiding an
advance through the thick double belt of wire, which
ran from Count's Wood in a South-East direction.
The Battalions assembled during the night North of
Neuville-St.-Vast, and moved forward at 7.30 a.m.,
unfortunately losing some men from shell-fire in the
preliminary advance. The sodden ground over which
they had to move was pitted with shell-craters, making
it difficult going, but by nine o'clock they were deployed

in the Red Line ready to advance through the 5th Canadian Brigade as soon as the barrage started to move on. The West Kents were on the right, and the K.O.S.B. on the left, the 14th Warwicks in support, and the 15th Warwicks following up in reserve. The first thousand yards was plain sailing, until they reached the Thélus trench, where it was rather doubtful if the wire had been properly cut. Fortunately it was all right. The moment the barrage lifted off this trench the leading waves dashed in, bombed up the trench, and mopped up the garrison, many of whom were in dug-outs and refused to come out ; the rear waves then passed through and continued the advance, keeping close under the bursting shells. As they wheeled to the right a defensive flank was put up on the left, as the resistance was at right-angles to their line of advance. On they pushed, down through Goulot Wood, the K.O.S.B. capturing two 8-inch howitzers, and the West Kents three 5·9's, four 77's, and one 90 mm. gun, till they reached the final objective, where the reserves came up and took over the garrisoning of the line, the assaulting troops becoming the reserve. From the top of the Ridge many good targets offered themselves to our Lewis and machine-guns, and the captured machine-guns, too, were turned on to the fleeing enemy as they were seen bolting from their dug-outs and Batteries. The Gunner F.O.O.'s, also, had the time of their lives switching their Batteries on to retiring columns and guns. The Germans were completely demoralised, and fled in confusion from their guns and trenches. So hurried was their rout that one F.O.O. found a luncheon of stew and rice-pudding laid out for the Officers in a Battery dug-out, which he at once availed himself of.

Our casualties had not been heavy; at first the K.O.S.B. had lost some men from snipers firing from dug-outs in Bonval Wood on their left, and a defensive flank had to be put up until the snipers were mopped up by a bombing-party sent out from Captain Pringle's Company and by the 3rd Canadian Division advancing on their left. The total losses of the Brigade were 7 Officers and 280 other ranks. The 13th Brigade took no further part in the fighting, and rejoined the Division the next day, when they were placed in reserve.

By 2 p.m. the whole of the Ridge, with the exception of Hill 145 and a small hill called "The Pimple," where the 4th Canadian Division had been held up, was in our hands, and, farther South, the Third Army had been equally successful on their front. The total captures for the day amounted to nearly 15,000 prisoners and 200 guns, together with numbers of machine-guns and trench-mortars, and vast quantities of ammunition.

The night passed off without any counter-attacks, but there were many "S.O.S." calls—all false alarms. The Canadians next day pushed out patrols through Petit Vimy and Farbus to the railway, and in the course of the next fortnight advanced three to four miles, capturing the villages of Willerval, Arleux, and Fresnoy. At Vimy, two of our airmen, who had been captured a few days ago, were discovered; they spoke to the utter demoralisation of the enemy and their hurried flight.

The whole of this time the weather was vile; the roads were in an appalling state, and it was with the utmost difficulty that guns were pushed forward. Luckily there were many German guns, with stacks of ammunition, which could be used. The 8-inch howitzers in Goulot Wood, which the K.O.S.B. had captured, were often fired ; but the Germans, who of course knew their position to a nicety, could not stand this indignity, and soon put a stop to it, pounding them unmercifully whenever they opened their mouths. The R.E. worked indefatigably at making plank roads over the quagmire of shell-holes, and bridging the larger craters ; some Heavy Batteries managed to get to Thélus, and by 16th April the 5th Division Batteries were all in position along the railway, just East of Farbus, where they had a miserable time, what with the wretched weather, the gas, and the shells. The Germans had the exact range of the railway, the men had practically no cover except what the embankment afforded, and the Batteries suffered more casualties here than at any period during the whole War, except at Le Cateau. On one occasion a shell struck the Mess shelter of the 120th Battery, and killed four Officers, including the C.O., Major McBride ; and a similar disaster to the 121st Battery resulted in the death of two Officers. Eventually deeper dug-outs were made, with the help of Lieutenant Oliver and a section of R.E., and casualties were reduced. There were constant " S.O.S." calls, which the Gunners never failed to answer, despite the heavy shelling, and barrages to be fired to help the Canadians in their further attacks. All ammunition had to be supplied by pack-horses, which could only cross the Ridge by night, the load being eight 18-pr shells or four 4·5 shells to one animal ; many horses succumbed to shell-fire or were drowned in the shell-holes. In May positions were changed, some Batteries remaining about the railway and Farbus, others being in Willerval and on the top of the Ridge.

Dumps of ammunition were constantly being blown up by shell-fire, or air-bombs, leaving great cauliflower-shaped clouds floating about in the sky. An enormous one went up at Arras, and another with 10,000 60-pr. shells at Thélus. One joy was to make dummy ones of tarpaulins and boxes, for the pleasure of seeing the enemy wasting their ammunition ; one of these, near Thélus, was so realistic that the Corps " Q," on seeing it, raised strong objections to a dump being there.

While this fighting was going on, the 5th Division had been kept back in reserve, ready, on the 9th, to move at two hours' notice, in case they should be wanted by the Canadians. Head-Quarters moved from Bruay to Château D'Acq', when the latter place was vacated by the 2nd Canadian Division, and, later, to Château de la Haie, the troops being bivouacked in the woods between Château D'Acq' and St. Eloi. On 13th April the Division relieved the 4th Canadian Division, who had captured " The Pimple " on the 12th, and Givenchy on the 13th, and had begun to advance towards Avion. The 15th and 95th Brigades relieved the Canadians while the movement was taking place, and continued the advance ; but on the 14th they were held up in front of a strongly-wired entrenched position running from the Electricity Works South of the Cité du Bois Moyen, through La Coulotte, to Acheville. The left flank of our position rested on the Souchez River, and the right on the Arras-Lens road ; immediately South of the Souchez River, in the left Brigade area, was the wooded spur of the Bois de l'Hirondelle, a locality subjected to very severe shelling by the enemy's Artillery. With the exception of this, the ground behind our lines was open and practically flat for a space of 2000 yards, to the point where the Vimy heights rose from the plain.

The German position was formidable, protected with three deep belts of barbed-wire entanglement ; opposite the 95th Brigade was a strongly-fortified railway embankment and the buildings of the Electricity Works, transformed by concrete and steel into a veritable fortress, whilst opposite the 15th Brigade were the mine buildings, factory, and houses of La Coulotte, similarly strengthened and fortified. Between the two ran a double trench-line, with numerous shell-proof dug-outs and machine-gun emplacements.

The Artillery covering the front was the Reserve Division Artillery (late Lahore Division Artillery), consisting of four Brigades, and with them six or eight Batteries of Siege and Heavy Artillery.

At 4.45 a.m., on the 23rd April, the two Brigades were launched to the attack of this stronghold ; on the right, in the 15th Brigade, the Norfolks and Bedfords, and on the left, in the 95th Brigade, the Devons and D.C.L.I. Each Battalion attacked with two Companies in front and two in support ; the 16th Warwicks were echeloned in support of the right centre, and the rest of the Division was held in reserve. The leading waves jumped off behind an excellent creeping barrage, but they had not gone far before they ran up against uncut wire. As the barrage rolled off the enemy's front line, they made gallant efforts to reach the defenders, many of whom were holding up their hands ready to surrender ; but at this juncture the German machine-guns opened, and the attackers were obliged to seek shelter in shell-holes, where many men remained until it was dark, exposed to bombs and trench-mortar fire. A few Platoons of the Norfolks and

LA COULOTTE.

Map.13

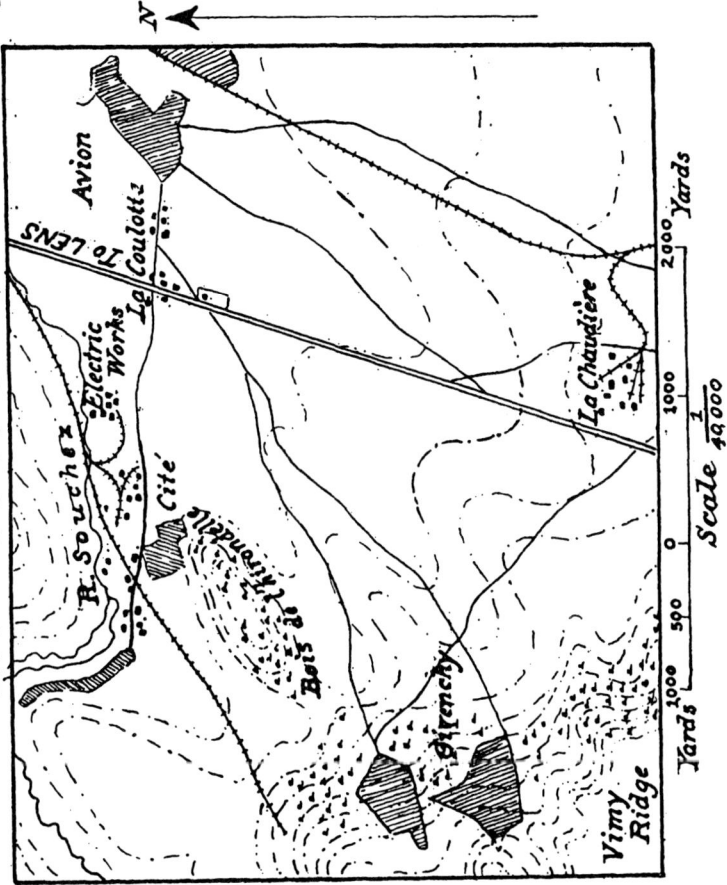

N

Avion

To LENS

La Coulotte

Electric Works

R. Souchez

Cité

La Chaudière

Bois de Hirondelle

Givenchy

Vimy Ridge

Yards 1000 500 0 1000 2000 Yards

Scale $\frac{1}{40000}$

[To face p. 158.

Bedfords managed to move to a flank, and to pass through gaps in the wire, and some of the D.C.L.I. on the left were holding on to the railway; but further advance by such small parties was impracticable, though at one time it looked as if they were going to achieve the impossible. · Bombing-parties were organised, and were successful in clearing some lengths of the enemy trenches, until they were arrested by the concrete emplacements. At 10 a.m. the hostile barrage became very intense, and all the efforts of our counter-Batteries were of no avail. The isolated parties could hardly hold out any longer, and any attempt to re-inforce them, or to replenish their bombs, was impossible. The enemy, when they saw our difficulties, regained confidence, and fought stubbornly, and our troops were slowly forced back, sternly contesting every inch of ground. By 3 p.m. our last men were compelled reluctantly to give up the possession of the German trenches after 10 hours' hard fighting, but this was not done before a gallant counter-attack with the bayonet, initiated by a Sergeant of the Norfolks, had been delivered. At length, overwhelmed by weight of numbers, the troops had to fall back. The failure of the attack was undoubtedly due to, in the first instance, the uncut wire, and, secondly, the lack of a thorough previous bombardment; it must be remembered, too, that owing to the French failures farther South, and the necessity of maintaining the offensive in these parts by constant hammering at the enemy, the attack had been much hurried on. The casualties were very heavy: the 15th Brigade lost, in killed and wounded, 36 Officers and 709 other ranks; and the 95th Brigade 30 Officers and 850 other ranks.

The work of the R.A.M.C. in this operation, under

most difficult and dangerous circumstances, is worthy of the highest praise. Lieut.-Col. Bradley, 15th Field Ambulance, was in charge of the arrangements of the forward area, and had under his command the whole of the Bearer personnel of the Division. It was an extremely long and difficult carry for them, either over the Ridge or along the Souchez Valley, to the main A.D.S. in Zouave Valley. Both these routes were heavily shelled, and there were many casualties, but, thanks to the excellent organisation and the gallantry of the bearers, all the wounded were brought back expeditiously, and were sent on in the evening in the motor-ambulances through Angres to the main Dressing-Station.

After this the Division handed back the front to the 4th Canadians, and, on 3rd May, relieved the 1st Canadians and part of the 2nd British Division on the front from Fresnoy inclusive down to Oppy. We now belonged to the XIII. Corps (Lieut.-Gen. Sir R. Congreve, V.C.), together with the 2nd, 31st, and 63rd (Royal Naval) Divisions ; later, when Sir R. Congreve was wounded and lost his hand, Lieut.-Gen. McCracken took over command of the Corps. The 5th Division was on the left of the Corps front, working in and out with the 2nd Division, the 31st and 63rd being alternately on the right ; and this was the arrangement all through the ensuing Summer. The Artillery of all four Divisions was in the line the whole time, and came under the command of the respective C.R.A.'s of the Divisions holding the front for the time being. 5th Division Head-Quarters were in dug-outs and huts at Roclincourt (2 miles North of Arras), which place was also the home of the Brigade in reserve.

On taking over the front, the left was assigned to the 95th Brigade and the right to the 13th. The Artillery, which remained in their present positions, returned to the fold on the 7th of May, having been away just a month with the Canadians.

Our stay on this front started badly, for in the first week Fresnoy was lost. This village formed a bulge in the line, and the 95th had at first to throw back a defensive flank on their right, though the line was straightened out a bit in the first two or three days. Early on the 8th of May, as dawn appeared, the Germans delivered a strong attack on the village, but three times within the space of two hours was it beaten off by the machine-guns and rifles of the Gloucesters and East Surreys. The enemy fire then quietened down, and it appeared as if he had given up the attempt to capture the village, when, at 6.30 a.m., an intense bombardment burst on the whole of the left and part of the 13th Brigade fronts, followed by an Infantry assault. It was raining heavily at the time, and owing to the thick mist the " S.O.S." signals were not seen by our Gunners. The Gloucesters, on the left, had their entire line blotted out, and, though the D.C.L.I. made a vigorous counter-attack, the enemy pressed on, and forced back the Gloucesters out of the village, together with the Canadians on their left. A little later the East Surreys, on the right of the 95th Brigade, were attacked, and, their left flank being exposed, were compelled to fall back to the trenches East of Arleux, and the K.O.S.B. on their right conformed. The Norfolks were sent up from reserve, but by this time the Germans were firmly established in the village. A counter-attack was then arranged for in conjunction with the 2nd Canadians,

II

to take place at 7 p.m., but the enemy's fire interfered with the orders reaching the units, and it was postponed till next morning. In the evening a further attack was frustrated by the enemy in mass being caught by the " S.O.S." barrage, and he was driven back.

At 2 a.m. the next day the counter-attack was launched by the Devons, Norfolks, and 15th Warwicks ; but only small bodies could penetrate into the woods round Fresnoy, and all attempts to recapture the village failed. The 19th Canadian Regiment, which was to have joined on the left, could only send forward one Company, as the runners carrying the orders to the other Companies had been killed and all wires had been cut by shell-fire. A party of the Devons alone advanced to and captured a trench just North of the village, and bravely maintained their ground, until they were withdrawn as soon as it was dark. The action of this little party is about as gallant a piece of work as was ever performed in the whole War. The two attacking Companies, under Captain Hallé and Lieut. Wonnacott respectively, reached their objectives in pitch dark through a heavy hostile barrage, which considerably thinned their ranks ; and, after taking stock, the party was found to have dwindled down to four Officers and forty other ranks, at least half of whom were N.C.O.'s, with two Lewis guns (one of which was Canadian), and a few Mills bombs. Their position here, in about a hundred yards of the enemy trench, was a very precarious one, for both their flanks were in the air, the Norfolks on the right, and the Canadians on the left, having failed to reach their objectives. It was a question whether they should hang on or retire, but, with the hope that the advance of the flanks had only been delayed, it was decided to stick to it. On the left the enemy attacked with bombs, but were driven off with the bayonet, while on the right Fresnoy Park was packed with Germans, seemingly massing for attack, and machine-guns opened from there. Thus they remained until 4 p.m., when bombing started on the right, and some German machine-guns, mounted on the left, began raking them in enfilade. The position appeared hopeless; they were running short of ammunition, and were out of touch with their comrades in the rear, who were powerless to give them any assistance. A German prisoner they had with them, who spoke English, begged them to signal to the wood, saying they would surrender; but still they held on. Suddenly, about 5 p.m., there was a terrific scream overhead, and Fresnoy Park was deluged with our shells for twenty minutes; what the German casualties were would be difficult to say, but not another shot was fired from the wood. As darkness came on, the gallant band withdrew to their own lines, taking their wounded with them. Captain Mason and Lieuts. Bush, Wonnacott, Hardwick, Bazalgette, and Grigson were killed, and half the men. The following afternoon the Army Commander arrived, and for the second time in less than a fortnight congratulated the Battalion on the fine show it had put up; but it was a sad little crowd which turned out on this second occasion. Only the 1st Battalion of the Devonshire Regiment can fully appreciate what the simple name "Devon Trench" means on the map.

By 4 a.m. on the 10th the troops of both Brigades were disposed to cover Arleux village and the ground North and South of it, and no further attacks took place.

After this the alarums and excitement gradually died down, though the enemy continued for some time his shelling both on the front trenches and also on the back areas. Batteries came in for a good deal of it, and during one week in May they had nearly a quarter of their guns knocked out by shell-fire. By the end of May, with the exception of a few outbursts of "hate," and, on our part, some barrages to make the Germans believe we still meant business in these parts, the front settled down to comparative calm. Many heavy and siege guns and extra Field Batteries were drawn out and moved up North in anticipation of the Messines attack on 7th June, and, later, for the offensive at Ypres on 31st July. The old 28th Brigade, R.F.A., which had become Army Field Artillery in January, now left the Division for good, to every one's regret, not to be seen again for the rest of the War.

The outstanding feature of the Division's stay on this front was the very successful attack on Oppy Wood on 28th June, combined with an attack of the 31st Division on the trenches South of the wood. This wood, which was only an acre or so in extent, had long stared us in the face, and was the home of many enemy O.P.'s, machine-guns, and trench-mortars—a very desirable spot to annex to our territory. The 15th Brigade carried out the operation with all four Battalions, disposed as follows : 16th Warwicks on the right, Cheshires right centre, Norfolks left centre, and Bedfords on the left, all of whom had had a week's previous training behind the line. The preliminary task of the Artillery was to completely destroy all wire, but not to blot out the trenches, so that our men, after the capture, should find some shelter. This was done to the entire satisfaction of the Infantry. The weather

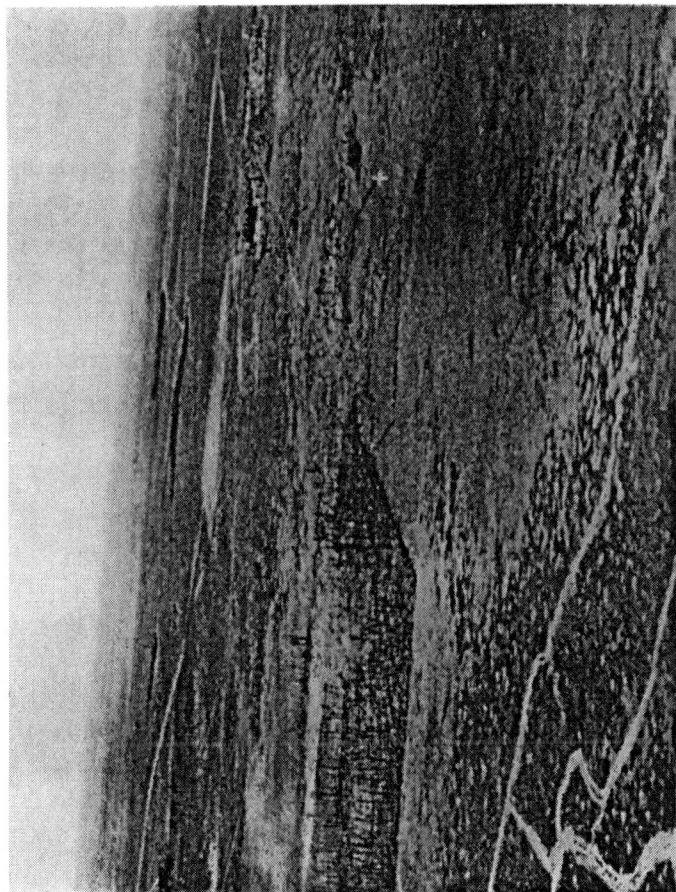

OPPY WOOD.

[To face p. 164.

during the day was sultry, culminating in a thunder-
storm and a heavy downpour of rain in the evening ;
the daily Artillery fire went on as usual with no notice-
able increase, though the enemy may have suspected
something, as he put down a heavy bombardment for
a few minutes on the assembly trenches, causing a
few casualties; but the 15th Brigade were undismayed
by it.

Suddenly, at 7.10 p.m., the thunder of the Heavy
Artillery Counter-Batteries and the intense barrage of
the Field Artillery broke forth with a crash ; at the
same time the howitzers put up a thick smoke screen
on the North, to cover the left flank from observation.
Our troops advanced rapidly, keeping close under the
barrage, in which they had the greatest confidence,
charged the trenches, and carried the front line at 7.15,
before the enemy had time to man his machine-guns.
The attack was a complete success ; the enemy trenches
were strongly held, but only on the left, where the
objective was deeper than on the rest of the front,
was there any opposition. The German reply was
feeble and disjointed ; it was six or eight minutes
before a definite barrage was formed, and, by that
time, the position had been won, and a large batch of
prisoners had been sent back. By 9 p.m. all Battalions
were busy digging and consolidating the line, and R.E.
and Pioneers had been sent across to help them. The
captures amounted to 2 Officers and 141 other ranks,
besides a number of machine-guns and trench-mortars ;
and the 31st Division, who had been equally successful,
took about the same number. Our casualties in killed
and wounded were 10 Officers and 342 other ranks.
The morale of the Brigade, always good, attained a
standard of perfection after this success ; their only

regret had been that they were not allowed to advance farther and pursue the enemy.

There were no counter-attacks; the Germans seemed to take their defeat lying down; no doubt they were expecting a further attack at Fresnoy, which had been treated with burning oil during the day, and his Artillery attention was confined to that place.

This projection of burning oil was a new form of " hate," an answer to the German " flammenwerfer frightfulness," but in our case it was carried out by the Special Companies, R.E., who had lately come into existence. The method was as follows : A large number of cylinders of oil (often as many as 200 or 300) were discharged electrically and projected from mortars into the enemy trenches. On impact with the ground they were ignited by a fuse, and produced a most terrifying effect. Machine-gun and shrapnel fire was generally added, by way of pepper, to enhance the result, and sometimes gas was substituted for oil. This form of war was resorted to several times on the front with good results, Fresnoy Wood and Park generally being the scene of action.

Some raids were also carried out, the most notable ones being one done by the 15th Warwicks on 15th July, and another by the East Surreys two days later.

In the former, a party of twenty-six men, under 2nd Lieut. Coldicott, captured one prisoner and killed some eight or ten Germans. The party was divided up into three groups, the first to move North on reaching the enemy's trenches, the second to move South, and the third to form a block at the point of entry. The wire had been well cut by the Heavy Artillery, whose F.O.O. gallantly established himself with a telephone in a forward shell-hole in No Man's Land, for the better

observation of his fire; but the trench was reduced by
the bombardment to a line of shell-holes, which upset
the original plan of a bombing attack, the result being
a bayonet and revolver fight. The party remained
twenty minutes in the enemy lines, and returned at
3 a.m. with only three men wounded.

On the 17th, two Companies of the East Surreys
captured another prisoner and killed at least thirty
Germans in a raid at Fresnoy Park. The right party
was held up by uncut wire, but Lieut. Fyson, with a
bombing section, fought his way through, and up to
the parapet, where he joined hands with the rest of his
Company under Captain Mason. The left Company,
under Lieut. Jones, met with no difficulties; they found
an entrance to a dug-out, which they bombed, smoking
out the occupants, who were all shot down like rabbits
as they were seen escaping through the park gates.
In twenty minutes they were back in their own trenches,
but they had sustained over fifty casualties. Fresnoy
Park was again " oiled " when all the raiders were in.

On another occasion there was a dummy raid with
only Artillery fire. A two-minute barrage of H.E. and
shrapnel was opened on the trenches near Oppy, with
regular lifts to make the enemy believe an assault was
intended and man his parapet, when the 4·5 howitzers
suddenly dowsed him with gas, with the result, it was
hoped, of many being killed.

The morale of the Germans opposite us was not
good ; several deserters came over, among them some
Poles, and all spoke to the enemy's being thoroughly
sick of the war. In fact, in July there were strong in-
dications that they were about to retire to the Drocourt-
Quéant line (that famous line which was afterwards,
in September 1918, broken by the First Army).

Detailed plans were worked out for a pursuit by bounds, in case this should happen, but the Germans did not move.

There was great activity in the air all this time; large British bombing squadrons were often seen flying over, and there were many aerial fights; some very aggressive Red Scouts brought down several of our aeroplanes, and attacked our observation balloons. The latter were also shelled by long-range guns using a clock-work fuse. On one occasion a balloon was set adrift, and floated gaily away towards the East, rising higher and higher till it became a mere speck in the sky. The occupant had escaped by parachute, and our " Archies " made vain endeavours to bring it down, and even one of our aeroplanes attacked it, but on it went, unscathed, till eventually it must have come down in German territory. Low-flying enemy aircraft also were very persistent in firing their machine-guns on our trenches, and always managed to get away safely.

July and August were very hot months, and many a weary walk there was to the trenches along " Tired " and " Tommy " Alleys—winding, stuffy communication trenches, which started at the top of the Ridge, and seemed to have no ending. A certain Brigadier was one day so much overcome by the heat while walking up one of these trenches, that he had to strip off everything except his trousers ! From the top of the Ridge back to Roclincourt, a distance of 1½ mile, a service of trams on the Decauville track was instituted, and one talked of catching the 3.45 Express back to Division Head-Quarters. The Vimy glacis, through which this track ran, which in April was a shot-ridden sea of brown mud, was now a waving mass of flowers, mostly poppies, daisies, and cornflowers—the colours of the Tricolor.

There were crowds of butterflies, too, chiefly Red Admiral and Painted Ladies, and the G.O.C., who was an ardent entomologist, was seen one day chasing a Swallowtail, which he captured with his tin hat. Mixed up among the flowers was an amazing amount of rubbish and material—shell-cases, bandoliers, rifles, great-coats, and every sort of equipment, all of which had to be salved. G.H.Q. had opened a rigorous and very necessary campaign against WASTE, and had established great depôts at Boulogne for dealing with every kind of salvage. Nothing came amiss: old boots, rusty buckles, clothing of all sorts, were all put to some use or other. Lorries were seen on the road with the query on them, " What have *you* salved to-day ? " and the same remark was painted up on conspicuous walls and buildings. Weekly returns of shell-cases, equipment, and material salved were sent in by Regiments and Batteries, and there was a healthy rivalry as to who should head the list; the Infantry used to accuse the Artillery of including in their returns the cases of the shells they had just fired !

In the way of relaxation polo was started on a flat bit of ground near Écurie, where the shell-holes were filled in, and a rustic pavilion was erected by the R.E. Any animal from a 16-hand Battery wheeler to a 13-hand pony took part in the game, and many a good match was played there, the opening match being one between the Artillery and the Division Staff, in which the former were victorious.

Sports and Horse-Shows (Divisional, Corps, and Army) were held, producing keen competition among Battalions and Batteries. The British Army at this time might well be proud of their horsemastership; horses were shown in the pink of condition, and the turn-outs of the Infantry Transport and the Artillery Teams rivalled anything ever seen at Aldershot. The heavy-draft horses of the Train, which carried off most of the prizes at the First Army Horse-Show, were a marvel of fitness and grooming, and were quite fit to take their place in any Agricultural Hall Show.

Arras, which the Division knew so well in 1916, was now six or seven miles behind the front, and a very pleasant little Officers' Club had been built in the " Jardins," almost on the spot of one of our old gun emplacements. Here one could enjoy an excellent dinner on off-days, after a roam about the old battered town. The next year, though, the Club had to be hastily evacuated when the great German Push came, and the " Jardins " reverted to a shell-torn wilderness.

At the end of August, Roclincourt was one night shaken to its foundations by a prodigious explosion. A vast heap of derelict trench-mortar ammunition, British and German, was struck by either a shell or bomb, resulting in the whole lot going up. A great crater 25 yards across was formed, but there were strangely few casualties. Some men of the 63rd Division, who were sleeping near, were injured, and some of their Head-Quarter huts were destroyed ; otherwise no damage was done.

Other items of interest were a visit of H.M. the King to the Front on 11th July, when the troops paraded and cheered him *en route*; and a Church Service, held on 5th August at the First Army Head-Quarters in the beautiful grounds of Ranchicourt Château, to mark the fourth anniversary of the Declaration of War. It was attended by 6000 troops, who sang the hymns with a verve and earnestness befitting the occasion, and the solemn and impressive

Service was fittingly conducted by the Padrés of every denomination. After some stirring addresses, the troops marched past the Army Commander, and were conveyed back to their quarters in lorries and wagons. Near the Division Head-Quarters at Roclincourt lived the Area-Commandant, a post generally held by a dug-out Officer, whose duty it was to superintend the billeting, sanitation, and locations of camps in the area. The Corps were anxious to start an Officers' Club, and sent for this Officer to inquire if he were willing to undertake the running of the accounts. When asked if he had had any previous experience in finance, he replied that he was not entirely ignorant of such matters, as he was a Governor of the Bank of England. His questioner must have felt somewhat foolish !

In the outside world, on the Eastern Front, tremendous events were happening : the seeds of Bolshevism were being insidiously sown by the Germans, and the Russian Armies were in mutiny ; by the end of September the whole country was seething with revolution, and German troops were beginning to pour back to the Western Front. Italy, too, was affected by Bolshevist propaganda—there were perilous times for the Allies ahead.

The Division had now been on this front since April, with only one short rest from 23rd May to 15th June. On 7th September they were relieved, and handed over the line to the 31st and 63rd (Royal Naval) Divisions, and the Brigades marched away to the Le Couroy and Rullecourt areas for training and rest, and a few days later the Artillery were drawn out and moved to Habarq, where a successful little race-meeting was held.

While the Division was in this area there was a

Platoon Competition, instituted by the G.O.C., which was won by Lieut. Littleboy's Platoon of the 16th Warwicks. A Cricket Match was played also between the Division and the VII. Corps, the latter winning; in the Division Team four Generals were playing. The Battalions had some practice with contact aeroplanes, and there was an attack-exercise with smokescreens, arranged by Colonel Worrall, commanding the Bedfords, who was the keen champion of the smoke theory; perhaps he remembered how, as a subaltern in the Devons in the fighting on the La Bassée Canal in October 1914, he had succeeded in getting his men away under cover of the smoke of some burning haystacks.

On 18th September orders were received to entrain and proceed to an area North-West of St. Omer, near the Éperlecques Forest, where the Division came temporarily into the Fifth Army, in G.H.Q. Reserve.

A matter which much worried all Commanding Officers at the time of moves and marches was the lack of sufficient transport. The ridiculously small scale allowed to units was quite inadequate to carry the Winter clothing, the masses of correspondence, maps, and impedimenta, which had to accompany them. The result was that nearly every Head-Quarters, Battalion, and Battery had either looted, salved, or acquired in some manner UNAUTHORISED TRANSPORT. Prior to a move, this question was always raised by the Authorities, but by the time the correspondence had reached a climax and peremptory orders were received for the disbandment of the vehicles, the Division was well away on the march, and the matter was shelved until the next move. The Artillery were perhaps the worst sinners in this respect; one

Battery had a delightful little home-made forge on wheels, another had a useful German travelling-oven " scrounged " at some captured dump ; when they were on the march " Q " obligingly had a blind eye, and allowed the vehicles to pass without molestation, and at inspections they could always be temporarily put out of the way.

During the three weeks the Division was in rest they were fortunate enough to enjoy glorious weather, and what with training and recreation, Officers and men were quite ready and fit at the end of the time to undergo the hardships and tremendous fighting which were in front of them.

CHAPTER IX

THIRD BATTLE OF YPRES

(MAP 6) [1]

THE third battle of Ypres commenced on 31st July 1917 ; since that date two wide attacks had been made by the Second and Fifth Armies on 15th August and 20th September, resulting in large captures and considerable gains of ground. The British line at the Salient now ran from Hollebeke in the South—West of Gheluvelt—just East of Polygon Wood—through Zonnebeke—West of the Gravenstafel Ridge—to just East of Langemarck.

Immediately on arrival in the Éperlecques area the Division received orders for one Brigade to be sent up as a reserve for the V. Corps in the attack taking place on 26th September. The 13th Brigade were moved up West of Ypres, and, although not called upon to take part in the fighting, suffered losses from aeroplane bombing, the West Kents being particularly unfortunate in losing several of their Officers.

On the 29th the remainder of the Division marched to the area East of Hazebrouck, and, on the 30th, to near Méteren and Berthen. Here the 13th Brigade rejoined, and the complete Division came under the orders of the X. Corps (Lieut.-Gen. Sir T. L. Morland).

On 1st October the Division moved forward, the

[1] See p. 58.

Battalions ordered to take over the front line going by bus, and the remainder by march-route. During the night the troops of the 23rd Division were relieved on the line from the Menin road to Polygon Wood, and on the morning of the 2nd, General Stephens took command of the front.

The line, which ran from a point approximately of 1000 yards West of Gheluvelt on the Menin road Northwards to Polygon Wood, was held by two Brigades, the 13th Brigade (Brig.-Gen. Jones) on the right and 95th Brigade (Brig.-Gen. Lord E. Gordon-Lennox) on the left, the 15th Brigade (Brig.-Gen. Turner) being in Divisional Reserve near Ridge Wood, East of Dickebusch Lake. Divisional Head-Quarters was in huts near Burgomaster Farm, on the West side of Dickebusch Lake. On this Lake, which was covered with coots, there was a floating target for our aeroplanes to practise at with their machine-guns, as they flew to and from the front. It was a pretty sight to see them swooping down close to the water from a height of 1500 feet or so ; but unfortunately on three occasions they were too bold and struck the water, resulting in the death of the airmen. After these accidents the stunts were stopped.

The Divisional Artillery relieved the Batteries of the Anzac Corps in positions around "Hill 60," Sanctuary Wood, and Hooge, in most cases exchanging guns *in situ,* as it was difficult to move them in the mud.

The elements seemed determined to put a spoke in the wheel of the British ; wet and stormy weather had dogged their advance during the past month, and rain commenced again on the 3rd, and was continuing, so that the ground, at the best wet and low-lying, and intersected by many streams and ditches, was now a morass. The intensity of the shell-fire had destroyed everything, and the whole country was a vast wilderness of mud, water-logged shell-holes, and lakes, with here and there the shattered stumps of trees marking where once had been woods. No vestige of a building remained anywhere. The roads had been destroyed, and in place of them plank roads had been made across country, by which the transport and guns could move forward. Once off these roads vehicles sank up to the axles in mud, and the work of getting Batteries into position was stupendous. For the movement of dismounted troops " duck-board " tracks had been laid for miles across country. These tracks were narrow, and movement among them in the dark was difficult, especially as, when two bodies of troops met, one had to leave the track and flounder in the mud at the side. Enormous water-filled craters were everywhere, and into these many men fell. At the best this meant a ducking in the filthy water, but in some cases men, weighed down by their equipment, were drowned.

The 23rd and 33rd Divisional Artillery and 242nd Army Field Artillery Brigade were attached to the Divisional Artillery to support the attack, making a total of 108 18-prs. and 36 4·5 howitzers ; in addition, of course, there was a large amount of Heavy Artillery under control of the Corps. To assist in the barrage two groups of machine-guns were formed, the right consisting of 24 guns of the 205th and the 13th Machine-Gun Companies, and the left of 16 guns of the 15th and 95th Machine-Gun Companies. The machine-gun barrages conformed to that of the Field Artillery, each machine-gun covering a front of 50 yards. Six machine-guns were detailed to accompany the 13th Brigade, and four the 95th Brigade in the attack.

The Germans had now adopted a new method of defence. Finding that the clearly defined trench systems, in which they had previously put their trust, formed good targets for the enormous weight of Artillery now wielded by the Allies and served by an incomparable Air Force, were quickly turned into death-traps, they had organised a defence in depth. The forward area was held by an irregular line of fortified and garrisoned shell-holes, supported by concrete strong-points. This " Mebus," or, as it was generally known, " Pill-box," was a rectangular " dug-out " of anything up to 20 feet square, built of re-inforced concrete 3 feet or more in thickness, and proof against direct hits of shells of 6-inch or even larger calibre. In each of these forts was a garrison armed with one or more machine-guns fired through long, narrow loopholes. They were sited irregularly in the position, so as to cover all the ground with their fire and so break up the lines of our attacking Infantry. Being invulnerable to rifle and machine-gun fire, except through the loopholes, the only way in which they could be reduced was for the loopholes to be kept under fire, while a party armed with bombs crept forward, surrounded the " Pill-box," and either killed the garrison or forced them to surrender by bombing through the loopholes or doorway ; if the garrison tried to escape they were dealt with by the party at the door. In some cases it was found that the shock caused by the detonation of heavy shells on the outside had killed the occupants.

At 6 o'clock on the dark and tempestuous morning of 4th September the Second and Fifth Armies advanced to the attack. On the left of the 5th Division was the 21st Division of the same Corps, whilst on the right was the 37th Division of the IX. Corps. The attack

12

was carried out by the West Kents (Lieut.-Col. Johnstone) and the K.O.S.B. (Lieut.-Col. Furber) on the 13th Brigade front, and the Devons (Major Anderson Morshead) and the D.C.L.I. (Lieut.-Col. Norton) on the 95th Brigade front. The Devons had just lost their C.O. (Lieut.-Col. Blunt) and their Adjutant (Captain Sir B. R. Williams), who were both killed on the 3rd on their way up to the front.

The attack started well, and by 7 a.m. our troops had reported the capture of the first objective and many prisoners. Under the creeping barrage they pushed on, forcing their way through the mud and water, and clearing the enemy from the many " Pill-boxes " on their way. But the attack on Gheluvelt had not succeeded, and the West Kents on the right were subjected to a heavy fire from that place when advancing to the North of it along the valley of the Scherriabeek. Their right was held up, but the left continued to advance in touch with the K.O.S.B., who had with difficulty pushed on into the park of Polder-hoek Château. The Château is situated on the top of a rise which falls on the North to the stream of the Reutelbeek, and to the South to the valley of the Scherriabeek ; it had been strengthened with concrete by the Germans and turned into a veritable fortress, packed with machine-guns which covered the ground on all sides. Numerous " Pill-boxes " had been erected in the grounds, and the position was one of enormous strength. The K.O.S.B. on entering the park were met with machine-gun fire, which checked them. Gallantly they set to work to capture the various " Pill-boxes," each one being the focus of a separate attack ; one Tank also managed to reach thus far, and gave much assistance. Gradually these strongholds were reduced by bombing, Lieuts. Aucott and Cappy doing particularly good work, and the Château itself was approached. But it proved too strong, and the line came to a stand in front of it.

On the left, in the meantime, the 95th Brigade had been going well. On the right of their line the Reutelbeek proved to be an impassable bog, but, moving along the North of it, the Devons captured Cameron Cover. The D.C.L.I. reached the village of Reutel, but, being unsupported on the left, they had to withdraw their line to the West of that place.

Later on in the day and during the night numerous violent counter-attacks took place, seven in quick succession being directed against our lines at Polder-hoek and Reutel. The attacks were carried out by masses of the enemy supported by intense Artillery fire. Their losses were heavy, but our men were forced to give way in places, and, by the morning of the 5th, the line ran along the Western edge of Polder-hoek Park and West of Reutel.

The attack on 4th October had, however, been a success, as, although on the Divisional Front the final objective had not been captured, a considerable advance had been made, many prisoners had been taken, and severe losses had been inflicted on the Germans. On the whole front of the British attack 138 Officers and 5200 men had been captured, and the Gravenstafel Ridge and Broodseinde had passed into our hands. It was ascertained from prisoners that a German attack had been planned to take place almost at the same hour as our advance commenced ; this concentration of troops added greatly to the number killed by our bombardment and barrage fire, as well as to the number of prisoners taken.

For a few days the situation remained unchanged, and no attacks took place. Both we and the enemy were recovering from the exhaustion of the battle, and attempting to construct defences in the sodden ground. The 15th Infantry Brigade were moved up to replace the 13th Brigade, who had suffered much in the stubborn fighting at Polderhoek.

While in this area, it was impossible for troops to obtain proper rest anywhere. The accommodation for units withdrawn and for the " dumped " personnel of the Battalions and Transports was most inadequate. Some huts and dug-outs were available in Ridge Wood, but the majority of the troops lived in bivouacs or tents which gave poor protection against the continuous rain. Very little had been done to organise the back area, and some time elapsed before we could get timber to build huts. To add to these physical discomforts, on every night when the weather conditions allowed, which were unfortunately many, the back areas were bombed by enemy aeroplanes. Considering that most of the ground was occupied by encampments of one kind or another, it is extraordinary that we did not suffer more severely ; except for some casualties to the Machine-Gunners and Argylls near Ridge Wood, and to the Divisional Head-Quarters, very little loss was sustained. On one night all the horses of the 95th Machine-Gun Company were killed or wounded by two bombs falling in their lines, and, although the men were sleeping all round and the tent occupied by the Transport Officer was riddled, nobody was hurt. The large dumps and rail-heads in the area were generally their objectives. In order to lessen the danger to the masses of Transport and Wagon lines, horses were scattered about in small groups and pro-

tected by " parados," or long mounds of earth, which
proved very effective.

The difficulties of supply to the forward troops were
very great. Some of the Artillery ammunition was
taken forward by light railway, which was always being
broken up by shells, but most of it and the Infantry
supplies were sent up on pack mules or horses. It was
possible for Transport to be got fairly far forward in
some places on the plank roads, but as these were
constantly under shell-fire, and frequently smashed up,
wagons rarely made the journey without becoming
bogged at one point or another—with consequent delay.
The two main channels of approach were along the
Menin road, past Hell Fire Corner, Hooge, and Stirling
Castle (an area associated with the gallant deeds of the
15th Brigade in November 1914), or by Zillebeke and
Observatory Ridge (ground well known to those who
fought in " Hill 60 " in 1915). From these arteries
branched off the plank roads, the most important
one in the Divisional area being " Plumer's Drive."
Throughout our stay here, the Divisional Engineers
and Pioneers worked night and day in repairing and
improving this and the other roads, overcoming
tremendous difficulties in the way of mud, and generally under shell-fire ; and their work in maintaining
tracks in the forward area (in doing which they had
numerous casualties) in a great measure rendered
success in the front line possible. To them must
be given a large share of the honours of the
battle.

After a wet and stormy night, the Offensive was
continued at 5.20 a.m. on the 9th October. The main
attack by the Anzac Corps, the Fifth Army, and the
French lay to our North, towards the Forest of

Houthulst and Passchendaele, and on the Divisional Front it was limited to an attack on Polderhoek.

The assault was carried out by the 15th Infantry Brigade, led by the Norfolks and 16th Warwicks. Under a creeping barrage of Artillery and machine-gun fire the Battalions went forward and entered the Château grounds. Here they were met with the usual machine-gun fire' from the " Pill-boxes " and the Château, and the line was checked. The battle now became a series of actions against the various strong-points, but, after some success, the intensity of the bullets, and the appalling mud, rendered further progress impossible, and, despite desperate efforts, the troops were forced back to their original positions.

Preparations were then made for a further attack the same night, but this was cancelled, and the line remained in the same position until the night of the 10th to 11th, when the 14th Division took over the front. On relief, the Division, less Artillery, moved back into camps in the La Clytte-Westoutre district. The Gunners remained in the line covering the 14th Division front.

The whole of the back area behind the Salient was crammed with troops, withdrawn from, or about to be engaged in, the battle, and consequently accommodation was somewhat cramped. In spite of this, a fairly happy ten days was spent, during which very welcome baths, new clothing, and other necessaries were obtained, and an opportunity given to scrape off a good deal of the all-pervading mud of Ypres. The " Whizz Bangs " gave performances in a theatre at Reninghelst, and Bailleul and Poperinghe also proved attractions.

On the night of 23rd October the Division again took over its old front from the 14th Division, and

POLDERHOEK CHÂTEAU, BEFORE.

POLDERHOEK CHÂTEAU, AFTER.

[*To face p.* 182.

preparations were commenced for a resumption of
the Offensive on the 26th. The rain had continued
almost unceasingly since 3rd October, and the mud
was now indescribable.

In conjunction with an attack farther North, the
5th and 7th Divisions of the X. Corps attacked respectively Polderhoek and Gheluvelt at 5.20 a.m. on the
26th. The 13th Brigade carried out the operation on
a three-Battalion front, West Kents on the right, 15th
Warwicks centre, and 14th Warwicks left. In addition
to the usual Artillery barrage the machine-gun barrage
had been thickened to one gun for every 10 yards of
front. The attack of the 7th Division on the right was
held up West of Gheluvelt, chiefly by the men getting
bogged, though some few of them forced their way up
to the place. The West Kents, once again attacking
down the valley of the Scherriabeek, found it an almost
impassable morass. They valiantly attempted to
struggle on, but their rifles and machine-guns became
clogged, and they were raked by fire from Gheluvelt.
Advance over this awful ground was impossible.

In the centre the attack went well, and the 15th
Warwicks cleared the Park and took the stronghold of
Polderhoek Château. In the cellars of the Château
they found and captured a German Battalion Commander, an Artillery Liaison Officer, a hundred men, and
many machine-guns. On the left the 14th Warwicks
were held up along the Reutelbeek, but their right had
gone forward in touch with the 15th Warwicks.

Along the whole of the line most of the rifles had
been choked by the mud during the advance, and could
not be used. Finding himself much in advance of the
rest of the line, and fearing what the results of a
counter-attack on such a position would be with so

many rifles out of action, the Company Commander at Polderhoek Château decided to withdraw his line, in order to conform to that on his flanks. The decision was unfortunate, as the Germans quickly re-occupied their stronghold, from which they swept the ground to the West with machine-gun fire and counter-attacked with such effect that by nightfall our troops had been pushed back to their original line.

The enemy had large quantities of Artillery, both heavy and light, hardly less than that of the Allies attacking him ; with this he deluged not only the forward positions and Batteries, but also the tracks and roads leading East of Ypres, whilst with longer range H.V. guns he fired on rail-heads, dumps, and camps West of the Salient. Every day he put down " area shoots " at intervals behind our front ; the areas plastered by these bombardments did not vary much, and, consequently, it was soon possible to mark them on a plan and to make tracks to avoid the worst spots. Another factor which made the barrages less effective was the depth of the mud. Ordinary percussion shells buried themselves before exploding, and, though they threw up volcanoes of mud, the main effect of the fragmentation was lost—this of course applied equally to our own shells fired against the German position. Shells fitted with the " 106 " instantaneous fuse were better in this respect, though even they did not burst with their full effect. After a short stay in the line the Division was again relieved by the 14th Division, and, on the 28th, moved back to the Reninghelst-West-outre district. This proved to be a rest of very few days, as the night of the 1st to 2nd saw us once more taking over the Polderhoek front. The Artillery had remained in the line, firing daily Corps and

Army barrages, counter-preparations, and "S.O.S."
calls.

The 13th and 15th Brigades (the latter now under
Brig.-Gen. Oldman) took over the line from right to left.
The front must not be imagined as being a clearly
defined trench line, such as is usually implied by the
word ; the state of the ground made any attempt at
digging or maintaining such a trench an impossibility ;
consequently the forward troops made the best defences
they could by preparing shell-holes for defence and
linking them up one to another. The task of carrying
out reliefs in such a line was most difficult ; practically all landmarks had been obliterated, and any
one shell-hole was much like the next. Further, the
line was not continuous, and the possibility of finding
that the next shell-hole was full of Germans was always
present, as the " trenches " were close together in many
places. Apart from the shells and bullets, the lot of
the soldier who had to be continually on the alert to
prevent himself slipping down the crater side into the
slimy water, full of unsavoury things at the bottom,
was an exceedingly trying one.

Looking at the battle as a whole, the Allied Army
was now approaching the goal it had set out to gain—
the high ground of the Passchendaele Ridge, which
overlooked the Ypres Salient from the North-East.
On the British Front, on 9th April and subsequent
days, the high ground South-East of Arras and the
Vimy Ridge had passed into our hands ; on 7th June
the Messines Ridge had fallen, and now preparations
were made to oust the enemy from the last of his
commanding positions in the North by an attack on
6th November.

At 6 a.m. on that date the attack was launched.

The main operations were undertaken by the Canadian Corps, some miles to the North, but it had been decided once more to make a bid for that hotly-contested position, Polderhoek. The assault was entrusted to the 95th Brigade, who carried it out with the Devons on the right and the D.C.L.I. on the left. The Artillery barrage had been thickened to a density of one 18-pr. to every 9 yards of front, some firing shrapnel and some H.E. with instantaneous fuse, and the Heavies poured in their H.E. projectiles—but a " Pill-box " is a small target, and the Germans in them were in the main protected from the rain of shells. As soon as our Infantry appeared following up the barrage the machine-guns again began their deadly work, and once more the attack was broken up and reduced to confused fighting in the Château grounds. Backwards and forwards the struggle raged in fierce intensity, but the approach to the Château proved too strong, although at one time our troops reached to within 70 yards of the ruin. The end of the day saw only a small advance consolidated, the D.C.L.I. having captured a largish " Pill-box " in the South-West corner of the grounds, whence they frustrated all efforts to dislodge them.

In the North the Canadians captured the village of Passchendaele, and established themselves on the high ground, so that the main objective of the day had been successfully obtained.

This was the last attack here by the Division, as, on the night of the 11th, the 39th Division took over the front. The Château of Polderhoek, which had been in our possession for a short time on 26th October, resisted all subsequent attempts at capture, and remained in the hands of the Germans until August 1918, when it was given up in their final retreat from Belgium.

The Divisional Artillery had remained in action continuously since 4th October, and still remained. At first they and the Artillery of the 23rd and 33rd Divisions were organised into three Groups, Right, Centre, and Left. For a short time a fourth Group was formed, but, later, when the 23rd and 33rd Artilleries were withdrawn, two Groups were formed under Lieut.-Cols. Hawkes and Berkley, with Head-Quarters in a damp and unhealthy dug-out near Zillebeke, called "Half-way House." The Batteries remained in much the same positions the whole time, though some had to move owing to severe bombardments. Cover here, as elsewhere, was practically non-existent, and, except for a short period in October, when some of the personnel were withdrawn for a few days' rest to the wagon lines, they remained for the whole six weeks continuously in action, subjected daily to heavy "area shoots" by 8-inch and 5·9 howitzers and bombardments by gas shell. In addition to the barrages for attacks, Army and Corps barrages were fired almost daily, and the expenditure of ammunition was colossal. On 4th October, and during each of the three attacks on Polderhoek, the Batteries had fired without cessation for over twenty-four hours. An average of 1000 rounds per 18-pr. gun and 700 rounds per 4·5 howitzer was kept at the Battery positions, and the maintenance of this supply entailed a great strain on the drivers and horses, who had to bring the bulk of it up by pack. Casualties among the personnel were fairly heavy, but they performed their duties with that high standard of gallantry and determination which distinguished them throughout the War.

For all the operations in this area the Advance Collecting Station for wounded was at Clapham Junc-

preparations were commenced for a resumption of
the Offensive on the 26th. The rain had continued
almost unceasingly since 3rd October, and the mud
was now indescribable.

In conjunction with an attack farther North, the
5th and 7th Divisions of the X. Corps attacked respectively Polderhoek and Gheluvelt at 5.20 a.m. on the
26th. The 13th Brigade carried out the operation on
a three-Battalion front, West Kents on the right, 15th
Warwicks centre, and 14th Warwicks left. In addition
to the usual Artillery barrage the machine-gun barrage
had been thickened to one gun for every 10 yards of
front. The attack of the 7th Division on the right was
held up West of Gheluvelt, chiefly by the men getting
bogged, though some few of them forced their way up
to the place. The West Kents, once again attacking
down the valley of the Scherriabeek, found it an almost
impassable morass. They valiantly attempted to
struggle on, but their rifles and machine-guns became
clogged, and they were raked by fire from Gheluvelt.
Advance over this awful ground was impossible.

In the centre the attack went well, and the 15th
Warwicks cleared the Park and took the stronghold of
Polderhoek Château. In the cellars of the Château
they found and captured a German Battalion Commander, an Artillery Liaison Officer, a hundred men, and
many machine-guns. On the left the 14th Warwicks
were held up along the Reutelbeek, but their right had
gone forward in touch with the 15th Warwicks.

Along the whole of the line most of the rifles had
been choked by the mud during the advance, and could
not be used. Finding himself much in advance of the
rest of the line, and fearing what the results of a
counter-attack on such a position would be with so

Service, who gallantly went out at all times and under all conditions to repair the broken wires, in order that the touch between units and formations, so essential to the success of operations, might be maintained. Many miles of armoured cable had been buried previous to the attacks, and more was laid down nightly, but these precautions will not suffice against the intensity of a barrage in modern war, and it is only by the action of " THE MAN " who takes his life in his hand, and goes out with wire and pliers to repair the breakages, that communication by telephone and telegraph is rendered possible. Of the many " immediate rewards " given throughout the War, a large percentage was earned by " Linesmen." Pigeons proved invaluable as a means of communication. In the bad weather of the first attack (4th October) the birds took two to twelve hours to get back, but in the later attacks they worked very well, the average being thirty-five minutes. Much use was also made of visual signalling with Lucas Daylight Lamps, but the most reliable of all were the brave " Runners " who carried their messages back to Battalion Head-Quarters across the fire-swept zone with a superb devotion to duty. Many were killed.

On relief the Division withdrew to the Westoutre area, and, on the 15th, moved thence by rail to the district round Nielles-Les-Blequin, between Lumbres and Boulogne.

On the 16th the Divisional Artillery was relieved from the front. A number of their guns had been destroyed by shell-fire, and it was impossible to get the others out of their positions through the quagmire without the most stupendous efforts and the risk of losing more in the attempt. They were therefore left in position and handed over to the relieving units, an

equivalent number being taken over at the wagon lines.
On the 18th they rejoined the Division in the rest area.

Thus ended the participation of the 5th Division
in the Third Battle of Ypres. The remaining impression
is MUD! MUD! MUD! and shell-fire. The advance
in ground had measured at its deepest 2000 yards,
but the Division had borne an honourable part, under ·
the most appalling difficulties which had ever faced
an Army. It must be remembered also that the
Division was in each case acting on the flank of a big
attack—always a difficult position.

Our casualties from 1st October to 11th November
were :

13th Infantry Brigade.	{ 77 Officers. { 2220 Other Ranks.
15th Infantry Brigade.	{ 57 Officers. { 1486 Other Ranks.
95th Infantry Brigade.	{ 83 Officers. { 2221 Other Ranks.
R.A. .	{ 18 Officers. { 288 Other Ranks.
R.A.M.C. .	{ 6 Officers. { 155 Other Ranks.
R.E. and Pioneers	{ 7 Officers. { 165 Other Ranks.
Divisional Troops	{ 8 Officers. { 90 Other Ranks.
Total	{ 256 Officers. { 6625 Other Ranks.

The time in the Nielles area was spent in rest,
refitting, and training, for which there was much
suitable ground available. The billets were good,
and the country pleasant ; and the full enjoyment of
rest was only marred by the prospect of an early
return to the mud-bath of the Salient.

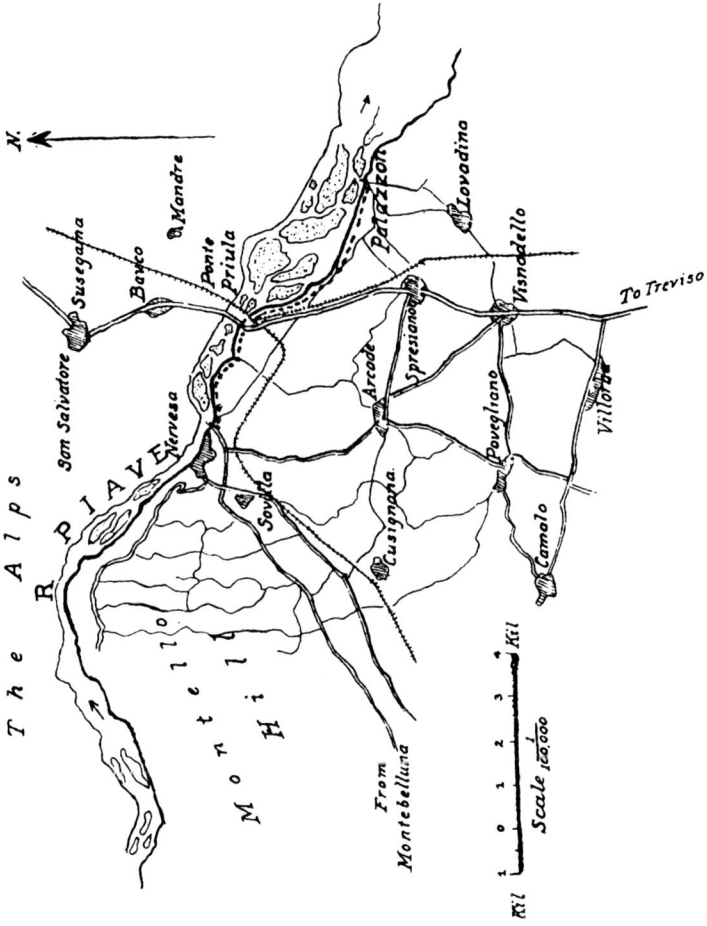

PIAVE FRONT

Map 14.

N.

The Alps

R. PIAVE

San Salvatore

Sussegana

Banco

Mandre

Ponte Priula

Palazzon

Lovadina

Nervesa

Arcade

Spresianoo

Visnadello

Soverta

Povegliano

To Treviso

Cusignana

Villorba

Camolo

Montello Hill

From Montebelluna

Kil 1 0 1 2 3 4 Kil

Scale 1/120,000

[To face p. 190.

CHAPTER X

ITALY

(Map 14)

THE rumours of Italy which had been going round the Division the last few days grew stronger. Officers and men were recalled from leave and courses, warm clothing was issued, worn-out horses were exchanged, re-inforcements put in an appearance, and new guns arrived for the Artillery to replace those which were still stuck in the mud at Ypres. At first it was explained that all these preparations were " normal," and that there was no foundation for supposing that the Division was bound for Italy—even when a reserve of nine days' rations and forage was issued, it was declared to be for " normal reasons." At length orders came to entrain, commencing on 27th November, and it was then known definitely that *Italy* was the destination.

During November the Italian Armies, whose morale had been weakened and undermined by insidious propaganda, had been pushed back from the Isonzo Front ; a complete rot had set in, and they had retired across the Tagliamento River (where it was hoped they might have made a stand) to the Piave River. In the mountains about Asiago and M. Grappa they were standing firmer, but were still being pressed hard there by the combined Austro - German forces. Twelve Divisions — seven French and five British — were hastily dispatched from the Western Front to their assistance, and the 5th was one of the five. The prospect of a change to this new theatre of war was viewed by the Division with mixed feelings ; some felt that it was only a side-show, and that we should be missing the main and important operations in France, others looked forward to the clear skies and comparative ease we should enjoy in Italy. Anyway it was an end to the mud, the shells, and the discomforts of Flanders.

The Artillery were the first to leave, entraining at Ligny and Tincques in twenty-five trains, and they were followed by the three Infantry Brigadiers with their Staffs, and one Battalion in each Brigade. The Third Army in France had on the 20th November carried out a highly successful attack with tanks South-West of Cambrai, but a week later they had been violently counter-attacked and driven back. The railway lines were congested by the sending up of re-inforcements, the move of the rest of the 5th Division was held up, and a composite Brigade was formed of the Battalions left behind, under Lieut.-Col. Norton.

Meanwhile the Artillery and some Battalions were already on their way to Italy. The journey took five days, and was full of interest, and by no means uncomfortable, though the Artillery Head-Quarters had to travel the first few hours packed in a horse-truck, with the usual legend on it " 8 chevaux 40 hommes." Soon after starting they noticed, after several bumps, that half the train was missing, and investigation showed that the coupling of the Officers' coach was broken, so the carriage had to be left behind and the journey continued in a truck. The journey the first two days, past Troyes, Dijon, and Lyons, to Marseilles, was uneventful, but after that it was one continuous scene of novelty and interest. The train crawled along in a leisurely fashion, paying no heed to the scheduled halts where one was supposed to water the horses, make tea, etc. ; on the other hand, there were plenty of unauthorised halts, sometimes for hours at a time ; for instance, in one of the Infantry trains there was break-fast at one end of a short tunnel and lunch at the other end. The men had to take these opportunities for performing their ablutions and watering the horses ; and the engine-driver seemed to take a malicious pleasure in suddenly starting the train off without any notice, leaving Officers and men to sprint after it. Sometimes they caught it up, and sometimes they didn't, in which case they boarded the next train that was following. The troops were cautioned to be very careful when going through the tunnels, as it was said that some men of the 48th Division, which had pre-ceded us, had been electrocuted by touching the live wires. The only accident heard of, though, was that of a man of the D.C.L.I., who was kicked off the train by a refractory mule ; he was picked up on the line much shaken and bruised, and had to be taken to hos-pital. All along the Riviera the weather was glorious, and by night the Mediterranean with the soft moon-beams scintillating on its placid waters presented a picture of indescribable beauty ; the scenery, the palms, the flowers, and the bright sunshine delighted every one. When the frontier was crossed the people all along the line were wild with delight, and at the halts the ladies, a good proportion of whom were British, plied the troops with chocolate, apples, and flowers. At Genoa, where a stop of an hour was made, a great crowd had assembled on the platform ready to welcome the British heroes ; they decked the Officers and men out with

13

flags and roses, whilst coffee and cigarettes were provided by the Italian Red Cross ladies. The whole scene reminded those who had seen it of the first landing in France in 1914. In one of the Infantry trains there was a band which discoursed music while standing on an empty flat as the train was moving, to the great delight of the cheering crowd. On the fifth day this triumphal journey came to an end at Legnago, where the troops detrained, and marched to billets in the neighbourhood. Two or three of the Division Staff had preceded the Artillery, and met them here, but there was no news yet of the rest of the Staff or Infantry; nor were there any orders—there seemed to be no one to give any, for the Corps had not yet started to function. So the troops were left to their own devices for the next week or so, and wandered about billeting in different villages as best they could, making themselves understood by signs and " Trench " French; fortunately supplies had been arranged for, so there were no difficulties in that line. In another week the rest of the Division began to dribble in, detraining at Legnago and Montegnana; most of them had travelled by the same route and met with the same acclamation everywhere. A few trains had gone by the Mont Cenis route, and in one of these, in which the 6th Argylls were travelling, an episode occurred greatly to their credit. Near Modane a French leave train took charge down a steep gradient, ending up in a tremendous smash; the Argylls were at once on the scene, and worked heroically, saving lives and tending the injured.

On the 17th December the Division Head-Quarters arrived, and established themselves at Vaccarino; by the 20th the Brigades had all detrained, and the Division was more or less concentrated East of the

ASIAGO PLATEAU.

[To face p. 194.

Brenta River, not far from Padua, the 13th Brigade near San Giorgio-in-Bosco, the 15th at Arsego, the 95th at Villa-del-Conte, and the Artillery at Levada. The XI. Corps (commanded by Lieut.-Gen. Sir R. B. Haking), to which the Division belonged, was at Campo Sampieri, the other Division of the Corps being the 48th. The second British Corps, the XIV., commanded by Lieut.-Gen. the Earl of Cavan, consisted of the 7th, 23rd, and 41st Divisions. General Sir H. Plumer was the Commander-in-Chief, until the middle of March, when he returned to France and Lord Cavan took over the supreme command.

The first instructions received were that, owing to the constant pressure of the enemy against the Italian troops on M. Grappa and Asiago, and the continued absence of snow, certain groups were to be organised to meet the situation in the event of a hostile success between the Rivers Piave and Astico, to the West. The XI. Corps, together with the French XII. Corps and an Italian Corps, were to form one of these groups under General Maistre, commanding the Tenth French Army, whose rôle would be to prevent the enemy debouching into the plain between the Brenta and Astico Rivers, to cover the withdrawal of the Italians, and to counter-attack. The 5th Division would be in Corps Reserve, and would be prepared to act as the occasion demanded—either to re-inforce or to counter-attack.

Thereupon orders were issued for reconnaissances to be made in the mountains ; Alpenstocks and " grapines " (iron spikes fixed to the boots) were issued, and many interesting and strenuous expeditions were carried out through Bassano and Marostica up to Rubio, Conco, and M. Alto, up the Brenta Valley, and in the foot-hills West of Bassano. These excursions meant a long motor-drive of 20 miles or more, and then some desperate climbing up the mule- or goat-tracks, 6000 feet up into the snow. One mode of ascent was to seize hold of the tail of a mule and be towed up, and it was possible, too, to motor up as far as Rubio, but it was a long way round, and the British cars had difficulties in turning the hairpin corners, which the Italian Fiat cars negotiated quite easily. The Italians had good back defence lines on the successive knife-edge ridges, with trenches 7 or 8 feet deep blasted out of the solid rock and extraordinarily neatly finished, and machine-gun emplacements ready sited and prepared. The difficulty would be getting guns up these steep narrow tracks ; some of the Batteries made the attempt with mules, with a certain amount of success. After a time a reconnaissance camp was established close to the foot-hills at Palazzo Michieli, near Valrovina, where Officers could stay for three or four days and carry out their duties, thus avoiding the necessity of the long cold drives to and fro. It was hot, thirsty work climbing about the mountains, and often bitterly cold on the top ; luckily there were " albergi " (Anglicè, " pubs ") strategically placed at the top of the mule-tracks, where excellent " vino rosso " could be procured at a ridiculously low price.

While this work was going on in the mountains the troops in the plain below were not idle ; the flat ground, planted with rows of mulberry-trees with interlacing vines, and the few open fields provided ample opportunities for practising open warfare and for technical training. The R.E. built bridges on the Brenta, over which all three Brigades crossed while carrying out a route-march ; the Artillery started training horses and

mules with a view to pack-work in the mountains ; the
Infantry were exercised in manning back lines of defence, crossing rivers in Berthon boats, and other
operations of war, and schemes for all arms were worked
out in the foot-hills.

Billets were comfortable, in barns or houses, horses
were mostly under cover, rations were good and could
always be supplemented with local supplies in the way
of eggs, spaghetti, polenta, etc. At first the villagers
viewed us with a certain amount of suspicion, but when
they found that we always paid for the goods they
became quite friendly, and promptly put up the prices
50 per cent. The seductive " vino rosso " was very
popular, but was found to be considerably more potent
than the " vin ordinaire " of France, and there was
some villainous local cognac which was the source of
some trouble ; at first there was a good deal of drunken-
ness, due partly to these causes, and partly to the men
going a bit large after the strain of the last two months.
The men soon picked up a smattering of the language,
the negative " niente " being the first word they learnt,
like " napoo " in France, or " ikona " in South Africa ;
and in a short time, what with a mixture of English,
French, Italian, and signs, they could carry on quite a
fluent conversation with the village maidens.

Christmas Day was kept in good old-fashioned style,
every unit got a donation from the Divisional Canteen
funds—enough to buy pigs, poultry, puddings, and
fruit for all—the N.A.C.B. provided beer, the rooms
were decorated, and the Officers went round and exchanged compliments, as in home life in Barracks.

The weather in December and January was as a
rule fine—clear and cold. Soon after the Division
arrived there was some snow, followed by a hard

frost—snow was what the Italians prayed for, as it would stop all offensive in the mountains. The roads at this time became very slippery and dangerous, and as most of them had a high camber, and generally deep ditches on each side, many of our clumsy 3-ton lorries came to grief. When the thaw came a fortnight later, the roads became a pudding, and were absolutely impassable for any sort of wheeled traffic.

Italy was short of fuel at this time; many of the olive trees had to be cut down, and there were great stacks of this wood in the amphitheatre at Verona. Though coal was issued in doles as a ration, it was as much as one could do to keep warm, especially on the stone and marble floors of the villas in which the Officers were generally billeted. The Artillery Head-Quarters at Levada was a particularly cold spot. Here there dwelt a very fat and amiable Count. One day a complaint was made to him that the Mess-room fire smoked badly, and that his pictures were being spoilt. He said he would soon put that right, and sent a small boy from the village up the chimney; the small boy was not seen again, and the fire smoked worse than ever! This Count, by the way, sent in an enormous bill for " dégats " when the Head-Quarters left, one of the items being the wearing-out of the marble staircase up which the Officers (five in number) went to their bedrooms! It was not paid.

Leave was granted pretty freely to Venice and Rome, and Padua was a great shopping centre. This place was continually bombed by a German air-squadron attached to the Austrian Army—it was not surprising, as it was the British Army Head-Quarters, which in consequence had to be moved a few miles out of the town. Considerable damage was done in

the town : one of the churches and part of the Head-
Quarters were reduced to ruins, but the famous Giotto
frescoes, which had been carefully protected with rope
mantlets and sandbags, luckily escaped injury. During
one of these bombing bouts two Officers of the Devons
were unfortunately killed in the streets. Treviso and
Castel-Franco were also favourite targets for their
Airmen ; in the latter place the French Army Artillery
General, General Liset, was killed, and there was a
big funeral, attended by the Prince of Wales and most
of the Allied Generals.

Football and boxing tournaments, sports, cross-
country runs, and competitions were held, and thus,
what with moderate work and a good deal of play, six
weeks were very happily, though uneventfully, passed.

Then in the middle of January came the orders
that the Division was to go into the line, not, as was
expected after all the reconnaissances and preparations,
in the mountains, but on the Piave River. Parties
were sent off to reconnoitre the new front, guides being
provided by the Italians. On 27th January the
Division took over the trenches from the 48th and
58th Italian Divisions, and the G.O.C. assumed command, after much health-drinking and clinking of
glasses between the British and Italian Staffs.

The Piave, after emerging from the mountains and
rounding the Montello Hill, flows generally in a South-
Easterly direction. It varied in breadth, on the front
taken over, from 400 yards on the left flank to $1\frac{1}{4}$ mile
on the right. At this time of year the water flows
with a swift current through several channels, most of
them being fordable, leaving many islands of shingle
and sand, some of which are sparsely covered with
coarse grass. Perhaps two or three times in the year,

in the Autumn and early Summer, there is a flood, when the islands shift their positions; consequently the existing maps were quite unreliable and had to be corrected from air-photographs. On either side the country is dead flat; close to the river the soil is shingly; farther away there are a few villas and farms, with vineyards, open fields, and acacia trees. The leaves of the acacia, by the way, were said to be very poisonous for horses, and all mounted troops were accordingly warned not to picket their horses anywhere near the hedges or trees. No horses, however, were lost from this cause, and the poison theory was probably a myth.

In France we were forbidden to tether the horses in the orchards, as, according to the Army Order, they would be " sure to bark and destroy the trees ! " Many of the G.H.Q. and Army Orders often had a distinct touch of humour in them. One, on the subject of complaints about the quality of the pork-and-beans rations, ran something as follows : " Soldiers on opening a tin of pork-and-beans must not be disappointed if they find no pork ; the pork has been absorbed into the beans." Somebody, on reading this, wrote and asked whether it was safe to pack pork-and-beans and bully-beef in the same lorry, or whether the bully-beef would not be absorbed in like manner ! In a certain Corps Intelligence Summary one read at the bottom of the page that " a strange-looking enemy aeroplane was seen flying over our lines backwards " ; it was not till one turned over the page and read the words " and forwards " that this astonishing exploit was satisfactorily explained.

To turn to Italy again, after these digressions.

About the centre of the front, and a mile or two

back from the Piave, are the villages of Spresiano and Arcade, both a good deal knocked about and uninhabited. Farther back are Visnadello and Povegliano. On the extreme left, and close to the river, is the village of Nervesa, which was held by the British Division of the XIV. Corps on our left. Here the ground rises in an isolated hill, seven or eight miles in length by three or four in width, called the Montello Hill. This was the only high ground on our side of the river, and was the sole place, except for a few houses near the river, where O.P.'s could be found. On the left bank the Austrians were better off in this respect, as the foothills to the North, about San Salvatore and Susegana, completely dominated our lines and back areas, though they were some way off; but in the clear atmosphere no doubt the enemy could see much that went on. On this account many of the roads had to be screened, either with sacking or palisades of rushes. Almost exactly in the centre of the line were two bridges—a road bridge called Ponte Priula, and a railway bridge; both had been destroyed, but on our side three or four piers in each were left intact.

The extent of front taken over was about 8000 yards—from Nervesa on the left to Palazzon (2 miles below the bridges) on the right, where the Division joined hands with an Italian Division. It was divided into two sectors, the dividing line being a little below the bridges; each sector was allocated to a Brigade, two Battalions of each being in the front line; the respective Brigade Head-Quarters were at Casa Pin on the left, and near Spresiano on the right. The Brigade in reserve was located at Povegliano, and the Division Head-Quarters were first at Visnadello, and afterwards, when that place was shelled, at Villorba.

The trenches were in fair order, those taken over from the 48th Italian Division on the right being far better found and cleaner than those of the 58th on the left. Owing to the shingly soil there was a good deal of revetting to be done, and there were many dug-outs to be completed, which kept the R.E. busy. In some parts the front line consisted of a number of T heads, with M.G. posts run forward into the retaining wall of the river ; behind this wall there was good protection and cover from view. A complete system of back lines existed, and there were lines upon lines of wire-entanglement, both parallel and at right angles to the front. The policy of defence was to divide the ground up into a number of compartments, or pockets, so that, in the event of a break through, the attack could be localised and time gained for launching a counter-attack.

The Divisional Artillery, to whom had been added the 76th Army Field Artillery Brigade, were comfortably off in the positions taken over ; some of these positions, though, were very much exposed to view, and had to be changed ; others had to be screened to hide the flashes. Dug-outs were fair, but the Officers and men mostly lived in the farms and cottages close to their Batteries.

The 13th and 95th Brigades were the first to be put in, on the right and left sectors respectively ; for the first week or so the sentries wore Italian helmets, so that the enemy should not be aware of the relief, and prisoners, captured later, expressed great astonishment at finding the British opposite to them.

The Austrian Artillery did not bother us much ; whenever a Battery was more than usually obnoxious it was hunted unmercifully by our Corps Counter-

Batteries. On one occasion the air-photographs showed a hostile Battery as having moved its position three times after being dealt with in three destructive shoots. It did not move again, as it no longer existed after the fourth lesson.

But what did worry us considerably was the bombing, especially that by night. The trenches were bombed, the roads were bombed, and the villages were bombed, not only on moonlight nights, but on any clear nights as well ; extraordinarily little damage was done, but it was very nerve-racking and kept one awake. Behind Visnadello, and close to the Artillery Head-Quarters at Palazzo Venturali, was an old disused Italian aerodrome, which had a peculiar attraction for the enemy aeroplanes. Night after night they used to visit it and drop their eggs ; it was a good thing to encourage them in the belief that it was an important spot, as no one lived there and consequently no damage could be done. The Hippodrome ground—a large open space South of Visnadello, where training and football were carried on—also received attention. The Airmen had an uncomfortable habit, too, of machine-gunning the roads at night ; there was a report on one occasion of a machine-gun Company, belonging to the XIV. Corps, being caught in column-of-route and almost annihilated. The Airman flew up and down the straight white road, firing his machine-gun at them, and the unfortunate Company was helpless, being unable to scatter, as there was a deep ditch on either side of the road, and the whole thing was over before they could do anything in the way of reply. Artillery wagons and Transport, when moving on the roads at night, had to keep their eyes and ears open ; but the surest safety lay in using tracks off the roads, under cover of hedges or buildings. Several Gothas were brought down, and about Christmas-time our Airmen made a great bag, killing 5½ brace of birds in one day. The story was that the enemy Airmen had been suddenly ordered out on a bombing excursion after a convivial evening, and were not altogether *compos mentis*.

No Man's Land was so wide that the men in the trenches were immune from sniping or ordinary machine-gun fire. The Infantry managed to carry out a good deal of patrolling in the Islands, where they sometimes met Austrian patrols and had a miniature battle. These patrolling expeditions had to be conducted with great caution, as it was difficult to walk noiselessly on the shingle ; the men generally wore canvas shoes, and the 15th Warwicks went out one night clad in blotched and dirty sheets, making themselves quite invisible against the light background when they stood still. Several prisoners were captured, but no big raids were ever attempted.

At the end of February preparations were commenced for an operation to be carried out early in March, in order to help the Third Italian Army in an attempt to recover the lost ground between the old and new Piave Rivers near Venice. With a view to drawing off the enemy's attention from that place, and pinning his reserves down, the 5th Division were to send a Brigade across the Piave on the day of the Italian attack, establish a bridge-head, and hold the ground for forty-eight hours, after which they would withdraw to their own side. The ground selected was that between Nervesa and the bridges, and the 15th Brigade was designated for the operation. General Oldman's plan was as follows : On the left a Battalion

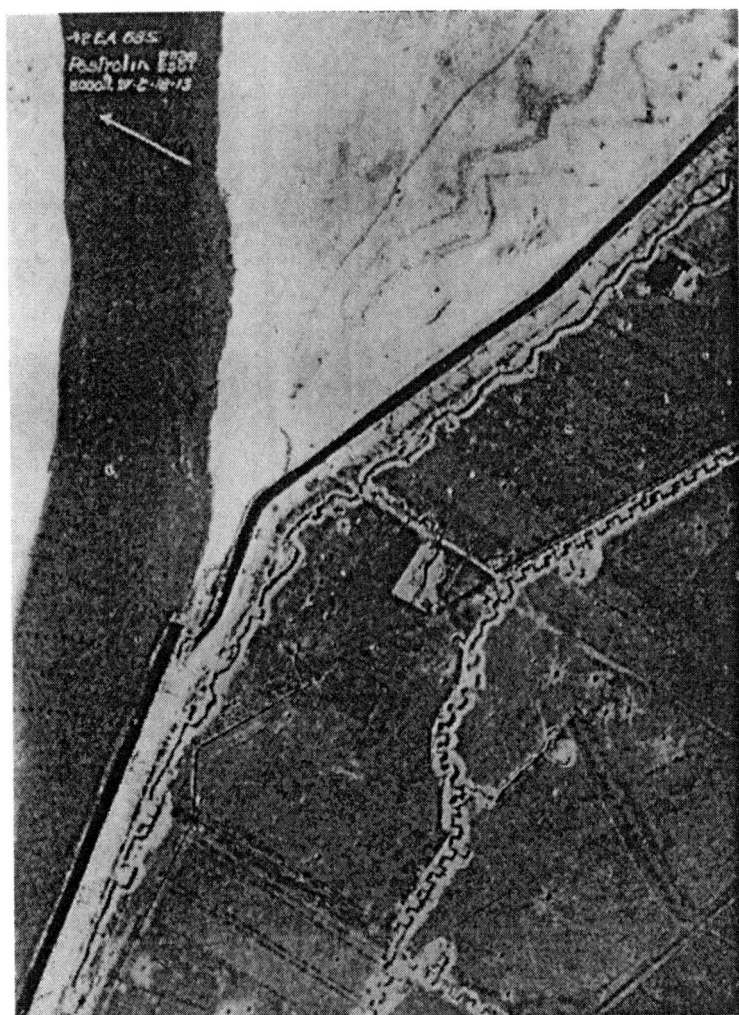

BRIDGE ON RIVER PIAVE.

[*To face p.* 204.

was either to ford or to be ferried across the channels, and establish a footing on the left bank ; under cover of this, two more Battalions were to cross, deploy to the right, and, under a creeping barrage, to extend the bridge-head so as to include the two bridges. Simultaneously with the first attack, the 4th Battalion were somehow to send a small party across at the bridges, " some on boards, some on broken pieces " (after the manner of St. Paul's shipwreck at Malta), and so to get a footing on the other bank, when the remainder of the Battalion were to cross and join hands with the main body. At the same time the 13th Brigade were to make a demonstration, with the help of lines of dummies, lower down the river, and, if they met with success, to cross over and raid the Austrians on the other side. The troops were practised in aquatics, a Company being sent down to Treviso for that purpose, and a party of bluejackets from H.M.S. *The Earl of Peterborough*, with boats, and some gondoliers from Venice arrived to help in the crossing.

A large force of Artillery was collected, and the C.R.A. had under his command 26 18-pr. Batteries and 11 4·5 Howitzer Batteries, exclusive of the Corps Heavy Artillery ; and opposite the bridges there was a great array of trench-mortars, 6-inch Newton and 3-inch Stokes ; nearly 250,000 rounds of ammunition were brought up into the gun positions and stacks of trench-mortar bombs. The barrage map went by the name of " Tiger," from its resemblance to that animal in a couchant attitude. By night the R.E. drove in piles on the site of the bridges, but, to every one's horror, as secrecy was of course imperative, the air-photographs showed these up plainly, though they were well below the surface of the water.

By 1st March all was in readiness, but on the 3rd and following days there was heavy rain ; the Piave rose 18 inches, and the operation was postponed ; then the Italians asked for a modified scheme, then they only wanted a bombardment, and finally the whole thing was cancelled. After all the preparations and training it was a very great disappointment to every one, though there was a certain tinge of relief, as, though initial success was fairly certain, the Brigade might not have been able to get back if the Piave rose in the meanwhile. The re-inforcing Batteries were sent back, and the vast piles of shells had to be returned to store—a job which took several days.

Directly after this, orders came for the handing back of the front to the Italian 48th Division, and on 18th March the 5th Division left the Piave and marched to the back areas near Padua. It was understood that the Division was to move to the foot-hills North of Vicenza, and undergo further training in mountain warfare, and the prospect of spending the Spring among the valleys and hills of the Lower Alps was very pleasing. The Division Head-Quarters were first at the fat Count's villa at Levada, afterwards at Montegalda, in a picturesque castle named " Castello Grimiani," situated on an isolated hill and surrounded with grand old cypress trees ; it was said to belong to the Mayor of Venice. Here Easter Sunday was spent, and, on the Saturday before, a Polo Match was arranged, to which many Italian Officers and the rank and fashion of the neighbourhood came ; band and tea were provided, and the scene was reminiscent of the piping times of peace.

Just at this time dark news came from France, where the Germans were beginning their supreme

effort for victory and the British and French Armies
were fighting with their backs to the wall. Day after
day telegrams arrived with the gloomy news of further
retreats and more captures of prisoners and guns ;
and we learnt the then incredible news that Paris had
been shelled at a range of 60 miles. The fighting spirit
of the 5th Division arose and asserted itself, and all
and every one prayed that they might be sent back
to rejoin the ranks of our hard-pressed comrades in
France. One Division, the 41st, had already left, Sir
Herbert Plumer had gone, and the XI. Corps also ; at
length on 24th March the welcome orders came to
commence entraining on 1st April.

During the week of waiting some experiments and
demonstrations with the new 6-inch Newton mortar
were carried out at the Trench-mortar School, before a
cosmopolitan assembly of French, Italian, and British
Officers. The ground chosen was some hilly ground
with deep gullies, where the spring flowers were just
beginning to peep out, and the demonstration included
wire-cutting, barrages, and bombardments. For the
latter there was a small cottage on the steep side of a
gully, and the owner of it sat with a broad grin on his
face, watching his home being reduced to ruins—he had
evidently been well paid for its destruction.

On 1st April the entrainment commenced at the
stations of Padua, Vicenza, Poiana, and Campo Sampieri, and sixty trains conveyed the 5th Division back
to the scenes of their former triumphs. Thus ended a
very happy interlude in their experiences of the Great
War.

CHAPTER XI

FORÊT DE NIEPPE

(MAP 15)

THE return journey was very different from what the Division had experienced on arrival in Italy; the inhabitants seemed rather to scowl at us, imagining no doubt that we were leaving them in the lurch; in addition, too, instead of the bright sunny weather, it was dismal, cold, and wet. Some of the trains went by the Riviera and up the Rhone Valley, others by the Mont Cénis route, and Frévent, Mondicourt, and Doullens were reached on 7th April. The Germans were within 10 miles of Amiens, so in passing that place the trains were diverted to the West of the town; a few H.V. rounds came over, and one of the D.C.L.I. trains was almost hit, a shell exploding within 10 yards of the track and causing four casualties. The Division detrained in pouring rain, and the Head-Quarters settled themselves in the picturesque village of Lucheux, the Artillery at Occoches, and the Brigades at Sus-St. Leger, Neuvillette, and Ivergny. The orders were to relieve the 2nd Canadians, South of Arras, on the Basseux-Wailly front, and, accordingly, after the usual reconnaissances, the troops moved up on the 10th to take over the line. They had nearly reached their destination when dispatch-riders hurriedly arrived with orders to cancel the relief, to return to billets, and to be

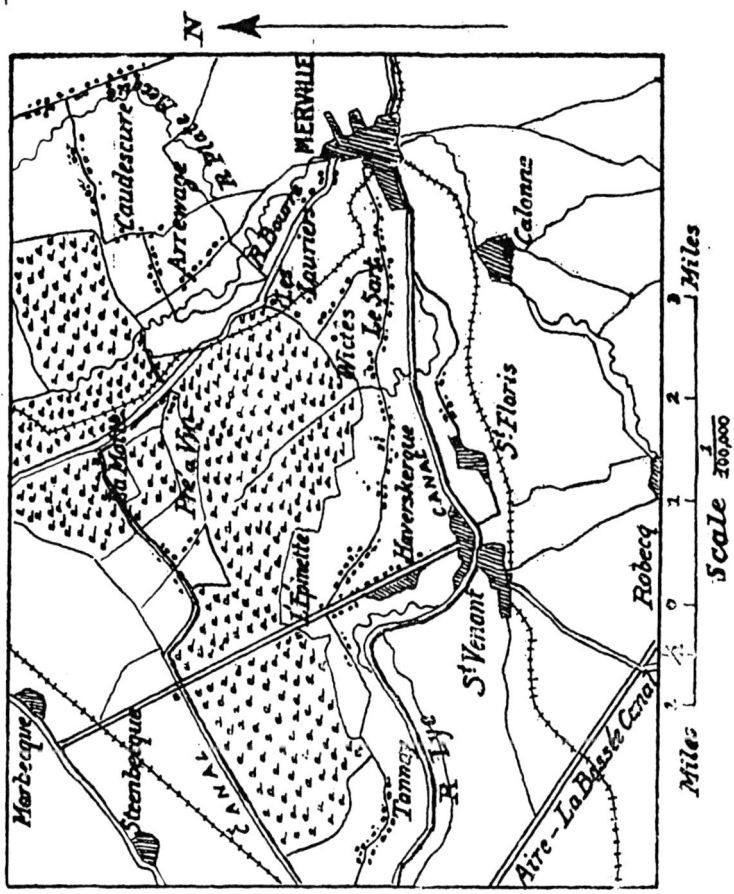

BOIS DE NIEPPE.

Map 15.

MERVILLE

Calonne

Laudescure

Artemage

R.Plat

R.Bourre

Les Iaurnes

Le Sart

Wittes

Haverskerque CANAL

St Floris

St Venant

Robecq

La Motte

Pt a W.

Epinette

CANAL

Morbecque

Stembecque

Tannay

R. Lys

Aire - La Bassée Canal

N

Miles

Scale $\frac{1}{100,000}$

0   1   2   3 Miles

prepared to move North at once—the Infantry to go by tactical trains the same evening, and the Artillery and Transport of the Division to march next morning. Then came the news that the Germans had made another big attack on a wide front on the First Army between the La Bassée Canal and Armentières, that they had driven in the Portuguese opposite Neuve Chapelle, and were threatening the Forêt de Nieppe and Hazebrouck; Armentières had been captured, and it was reported that Messines was in German hands.

The Infantry entrained at Monlicourt and Soulty, and proceeded viâ Doullens, St. Pol, and Chocques, arriving at Thiennes and Aire on the night of the 11th–12th; portions of the line on the way up showed signs of war, for in one place a train had been cut in two by a shell, and Chocques station was badly knocked about. General Stephens, with his Staff, preceded the Infantry by car on the.11th, in order to ascertain the situation, which was very obscure; it was then fairly well established that the 61st Division had taken up a line South of the Lys Canal and were holding on with difficulty, that there were only a few remnants of the 50th Division left, and that the 4th Guards Brigade were between Merville and Hazebrouck, with some Lewis guns of a Tank Battalion near Le Sart. That night, therefore, as soon as the Infantry had detrained, the 15th and 95th Brigades were ordered to put out an outpost line between Aire and the Forêt de Nieppe, and East of the steel-works at Isbergues, which they did.

At 9.40 a.m. on the 12th the G.O.C. met the Brigadiers at Thiennes station, and explained to them the state of affairs; Merville had been occupied by the enemy, and the Corps had ordered the 5th Division to re-take it. He directed the 13th Brigade to move South

14

of the Forest *viâ* Tannay, and the 95th Brigade North of the Forest *viâ* Prè-a-Vin and La Motte—to join hands on the Eastern side, and to make good the line Wictes-Les Lauriers-Arrewage before continuing the advance on Merville. This would be a difficult and rather risky operation, as there was no communication through the Forest between the two Brigades. The 15th Brigade was ordered to move in reserve on Haverskerque *viâ* St. Venant. Artillery support was to be arranged for, but how, no one quite knew, as the Divisional Artillery was not yet up, and nothing was known of any other Batteries in the neighbourhood. The C.R.A., consequently, went to La Motte Château (the old Cavalry Corps Head-Quarters) in the middle of the Forest, to see what could be done. On arrival there, he found a scene of great confusion ; the Head-Quarters of three Divisions were there temporarily, with their lorries and baggage-wagons jostled up together in front of the house. All was chaos—no one knew what was happening, or where any troops were. It was lucky the place was not shelled.

About two hours later the XI. Corps (to which the Division now belonged for the third time) sent a message cancelling the attack on Merville and ordering a line to be taken up, and to be held at all costs, from Robecq in the South, through the Forest, to La Motte Château.

By this time the two Brigades had started—the 13th with the 15th Warwicks on the right, the 14th Warwicks on the left, the K.O.S.B. in support, and the West Kents in reserve, and the 95th with the Devons and D.C.L.I. in front, and the Gloucesters and East Surreys respectively in support and reserve. The troops pressed on through and on either side of the Forest, meeting with only a few stragglers of the 50th

Division, reached the Eastern edge, and established themselves 100 to 200 yards outside. The Devons, on the right of the 95th Brigade, pushed forward to the lock and bridge over the Bourre stream, where they stopped any further advance of the Germans.

General Stephens now urged the advantage the line at present held would have over that through the Forest, and obtained the sanction of the Corps Commander (Sir R. B. Haking) to consolidate the position there.

Meanwhile the Artillery, who had received their orders at midnight, had started on their march on the early morning of the 11th, and were nearing the scene of action ; the Batteries were diverted from the line of march, positions were reconnoitred on the South of the Forest and in some open ground in the middle, and, by the evening, the guns were all in action covering the Infantry, with a large amount of ammunition. They had made a fine march of 65 miles in two days, and were ready to open fire at 8.30 p.m. on the second day.

Up to this point the Infantry had met with little opposition, except on the extreme right, where the 15th Warwicks successfully attacked the Brickfields, and, later, repulsed a counter-attack, losing, however, nearly a hundred men in the engagement. In the evening the 61st Division, South of the Canal, under strong pressure began to yield ground, and a defensive flank was formed on the right by the K.O.S.B. By the evening our line was firmly established, the right in touch with the 61st Division, and the left with the Guards. It was ascertained afterwards that the enemy had been engaged in ransacking the cellars in Merville, and so had not pressed their advantage home at once as they might have done.

The night was fairly quiet ; but next morning, the

13th, the furious attacks began. Commencing with a heavy bombardment, the enemy launched an assault at 10 a.m. on the left, and a party of the Guards, who were holding a very extended front and were much weakened by repeated attacks, was cut off at Le Cornet Perdu. The Coldstream and Irish Guards quickly put up a defensive flank, but there was a gap between them and the D.C.L.I.; the latter counter-attacked with their support Company, thus giving time for the Guards to reform. Both eventually fell back a short way in good order, and touch was gained with the Australians on the left; the Gloucesters, too, were sent up, and the position was held firm. Three other attacks were delivered on this front in the course of the day, but the fire from the trenches and the Artillery barrage kept the enemy off every time.

In the right sector, in the afternoon, an attack developed against the 14th Warwicks, who repulsed it, except at Le Vertbois Farm, into which the enemy penetrated; during the night they retook this farm, unfortunately losing their C.O., Colonel Quarry, who was gallantly leading his men; but later they evacuated it, as it formed a too exposed salient in the line.

During the day there were urgent demands for tools and barbed wire for use in the front line; the Transport, other than the tactical which accompanied the units, was still on the march from the South, and in it were all the tools of the Division. Search was made in the back area, and a dump of tools and wire was found at the Inland Water Transport Depôt at Aire, and also two lorries. The whole lot was commandeered and taken up to the front line, while ammunition was obtained from an old Army dump near Aire, and sent forward. On this date the enormous amount of 2¼ million rounds of S.A.A. was sent up to replace expenditure.

Early on the 14th a very determined attack again developed on the left of the Division in the vicinity of Arrewage ; it continued without intermission for five hours, and again it was completely stopped. On the right the 15th Warwicks and the Artillery barrage prevented any advance at the Brickfields. The 14th Warwicks were also involved in an attack, necessitating a slight withdrawal ; but the support Company of the Devons immediately counter-attacked, and the situation was promptly restored. Several times during the day concentrations and mounted detachments were seen, and as soon scattered by the intense barrage of our Artillery and machine-guns, and the assaults were neutralised. All these attacks were preceded and accompanied by bombardments, and it was extremely difficult to move up any re-inforcements through the belt of fire. The task of breaking them up devolved upon the Infantry and machine-guns in the front line, who had been there from the beginning, and who stolidly stood their ground with the utmost gallantry and steadiness.

On the 15th the Germans were again seen massing for attack several times, but in every case were dispersed by the Artillery and machine-gun fire, and no attacks materialised. The Australian Division on the left was firmly established, securing that flank, and the presence of the 2nd Cavalry Division, who were in bivouac in the wood, made the situation very much happier.

By the 16th the Germans had expended their strength, and began to dig and wire their front ; the dead lay thick in the fields in front, and stretcher-bearers were constantly seen at work ; the lull in the fighting gave the opportunity for the tired front-line troops to be relieved, and the 15th Brigade took over the left front from the 95th, who had stood the brunt of the fighting. The casualties had been severe; the 13th Brigade in April lost 81 Officers and 500 other ranks, and the 95th Brigade 40 Officers and 650 other ranks. The 95th Brigade, too, had lost their Brigadier, Lord E. Gordon-Lennox, who was severely wounded on the 14th by a direct hit on his Head-Quarters at Prè-a-Vin, his Brigade-Major, Captain Gotto, and 8 signallers being also wounded. Lord E. Gordon-Lennox was succeeded by Lieut.-Col. Norton of the D.C.L.I.

In these three days the 5th Division had saved the situation on this part of the Western Front, and had stopped the German thrust on the important town of Hazebrouck. The Infantry, fresh from their four months in Italy, had gone into the attack with a marvellous dash and spirit, and their steadfastness in withstanding the furious and continuous onslaughts of the enemy was magnificent. The Artillery, too, deserve some praise for their rapid march and quickness in getting into action ; during all these attacks they had fired almost continuously throughout the day and night. The devoted action of the 80th Battery, under Major Smith, on the 13th, deserves a special mention ; during one of the enemy attacks the Battery had kept up its rate of fire the whole time, though it was being heavily shelled by 8-inch and 11-inch—seeing the place afterwards, it was a marvel how the Battery was not annihilated. To General Stephens himself also is the highest credit due for his insistence in taking up the forward line East of the Forest. One shudders to think what the fate of the Division would have been during the ensuing four months when the Forest was drenched with gas, had the line been taken up through the middle of it as at first ordered.

A message was received from General Haking: "Well done, 5th Division! The Corps Commander congratulates all ranks on their steadiness and gallantry "; and the Army Commander sent his congratulations in the following words: "I wish to express my appreciation of the great bravery and endurance with which all ranks have fought and held out during the past five days against overwhelming numbers. It has been necessary to call for great exertions, and more still must be asked for, but I am confident that in this critical period, when the existence of the British Empire is at stake, all ranks of the First Army will do their best."

For the next few days it was quiet, at times ominously so, and we fully expected more attacks, but the enemy showed no desire to go on dashing his head against this front, and turned his attention to the North and South. On the North he captured Bailleul and Kemmel, and there was bitter fighting about Méteren and Locre, which latter changed hands two or three times. On the South, Givenchy was his objective, but the redoubtable 55th Division repulsed all the attacks and stood firm. Prisoners captured said that the intention was to pinch out the Forest by attacks North and South of it, while the Forest itself was to be gassed; and on the 22nd there was a gas bombardment—the first of many that the Division was to undergo.

Energies were now directed to improving and strengthening the front, and forming back lines of defence. A Decauville railway was built in a marvellously short time by the 7th Canadian Railway

Troops, concrete " pill-boxes " were made by the R.E. for Head-Quarters, wire was put out in front of the trenches, and cellars of houses re-inforced. An extra Brigade of Artillery (the 84th) was allotted to the Division, Siege and Heavy Guns were brought into position, the Corps Counter-Batteries were organised, and trench-mortars were posted on the edge of the wood—in fact, it became trench war over again.

The Forest, which consisted of low oaks and horn-beams and in places thick undergrowth, extended for nearly 5 miles to the rear. It had the advantage of concealing all movement or concentrations of troops, but, on the other hand, there were no com-munications through it from West to East, except paths and the Decauville railway. This railway, with its radiating branches built afterwards by the Divisional R.E., was of enormous value for bringing up reliefs, ammunition, and stores of all sorts ; many times it was broken up by shell-fire, but the R.E. invariably had it going again in a few hours. The ground avail-able for gun positions was very limited ; in the centre of the Forest there was an open space South and South-West of La Motte Château, where many Batteries were collected, and in some of the less dense parts of the wood room could be found for howitzers. The ground was dead flat, with many farms, hedges, and rows of trees which interfered much with observation. The Rivers Bourre and Plate Becque, slow, sluggish streams with muddy bottoms, traversed the ground from the North to the River Lys, the Bourre flowing part of the way through the Forest. It was difficult to fix up suitable sites for the Infantry Brigade and Artillery Group Head-Quarters and Dressing-Stations ; farms and estaminets were used, and later camps were established in the Forest, but they were hunted about a good deal by gas and shells, and had to be shifted on several occasions. There were many tree-trunks lying about, and great stacks of fascines, which could be used for strengthening shelters, and even the stacks themselves were used as living-quarters.

The first operation undertaken by the Division was one against two farms, a few hundred yards outside the Forest, on 25th April, with a view of advancing the line 300 yards or so on a front of 2000 yards. The attack took place at 9.30 p.m. under a strong creeping barrage, the Gloucesters on the right being directed against Le Vertbois Farm and buildings, and the Bedfords on the left against a farm South-East of the ruined Les Lauriers Château. In the right attack one Company and a Platoon of the Gloucesters advanced with great pluck and determination and gained all their objectives by 10 p.m., meeting with considerable resistance at the farm, where they killed or captured the whole garrison. In the left attack the Bedfords were equally successful, and quickly established themselves in the new position, unfortunately losing some men from our barrage. A total of fifty prisoners and four machine-guns were captured, and the farms were christened " Gloucester " and " Bedford " Farms respectively. The new positions were counter-attacked on the 27th, the enemy advancing to within 100 yards of our line, where they came under such heavy fire from machine-guns and rifles that the attack was completely broken up.

At Gloucester Farm there was a pathetic tale about an old Frenchwoman who was found there. She had been wounded in the leg, probably by our fire, but she stoutly refused to leave her home. While it was in

German hands she had been living in the cellar, and, on our capturing the place, she still refused to leave. Eventually the Doctors injected morphia, and took her away to hospital.

May and June passed without any further offensive developing on our front, though one was constantly expected. Prince Rupprecht of Bavaria, who had made an abortive attempt on Ypres on 29th April, still had a large reserve of 29 Divisions, and it was not known where his next blow would fall. Early in May the " wind " blew very strong on our front, and again about 20th June. Every preparation was made to meet the expected attacks; all isolated bodies in rear, Head-Quarters, Transport-lines, etc., prepared schemes for local defence in case of a break-through, and " Man Battle Stations " was practised several times; plans were cut and dried for rushing up the reserves by De-cauville, and Batteries had " battle positions " ready for occupation, as, in previous attacks, the Germans had begun their offensive by obliterating all known Batteries in their existing sites; and whenever an attack appeared imminent, " counter-preparation," consisting of a bombardment of suspected assembly-places and Head-Quarters, was put down.

At the end of May and beginning of June the Germans made their colossal effort on Paris, crossing the Marne and reaching Château Thierry, 45 miles from the Capital—the aspect appeared very dark—but the time was not yet ripe for Foch's great counter-stroke. And in Italy the Austrians attacked across the Piave on the well-known front, only to be driven back again with tremendous losses ten days later. On our front there was still comparative calm, mingled with expectancy. There was a great deal of shelling, mostly from 8-inch

and 5·9 howitzers, and some night-bombing, most of
which fell on Aire and the iron-foundry works near.
Thiennes was shelled at the beginning of June, and the
Division Head-Quarters shifted to a small rustic hamlet
a mile to the West, where they lived in tents, farm-
buildings, and huts, and where the Artillery shared
their office with some calves, poultry, and a family of
pink pigs.

There were a good many pigs, live stock, and poultry
about the vacated farms near the Forest when the
Division first arrived. It was strictly forbidden to
kill the pigs, and on one occasion a man was caught in
the act of shooting one—his excuse was that he thought
it was going to attack him ! Which reminds one of a
story of the South African War when, contrary to orders,
a man, with the lust of slaughter on him, was busily
engaged in bayoneting some sheep that had been ·
rounded up. On looking up he saw a Staff Officer
approaching. " I'll larn yer to bite," said he, at the
same time plunging his bayonet into another unfortunate animal.

The worst enemy the Division had to encounter was
the gas shelling.[1] In the Summer and Autumn of 1917
the chemical struggle between the belligerents became
very intense. In July of that year a big surprise was
sprung upon the British at Ypres by the use of a new
gas, which for a time eluded our gas discipline. This
mustard-gas was a distinctly new departure. With
very little odour, and no immediate signs of any dis-
comfort or danger, it was very persistent, penetrating
the dug-outs and remaining on the ground for several
days, and ca sing huge casualties. It produced
temporary blindness and affected the throat and lungs,

and even burnt the skin through the clothes. The surest panacea was to evacuate the shelled area at once, and not approach it again until the shell-holes had been sprinkled with chloride of lime and filled in with earth, as the sun's rays brought out the noxious fumes, even when there appeared no trace of the gas about. Other gases, the " Blue " and " Green Cross," producing violent nausea and intense pain, were also used, but it was the " Yellow Cross " mustard-gas with which the Forest was being continually drenched during these months. It was no uncommon thing for an entire Head-Quarters, or nearly the whole personnel of a Battery, to have to be sent down to the Field Ambulance affected by this disgusting and cruel weapon of war. The Allies, in self-defence, were obliged to resort to the same weapon, and when these bombardments took place, our guns invariably retaliated in like manner, firing shells containing " P.N.," described as a " lethal and persistent " gas, or " V.N.," which was " lethal and volatile."

As a precaution against gas in the Forest a " gas patrol " was organised by the R.A.M.C. The duties of this patrol were to locate the areas in which mustard-gas shells had fallen, to warn troops against passing through these areas, and to fill in the shell-holes. They covered all the area of the Forest East of the St. Venant road, and, thanks to the thorough way in which they carried out their duties and closed tracks and roads when gas was about, many casualties were saved.

The Gunners at this time revelled in the plentiful supply of ammunition, which was practically unlimited. Unfortunately there was a good deal of short shooting caused by defective ammunition and shells being of different weights ; it was most difficult to get to the

LORD RAWLINSON'S CHÂTEAU.

[*To face p.* 220.

bottom of it, and it was a great source of annoyance to the Gunners, and more so, of course, to the Infantry, who suffered some casualties thereby. The enemy's roads and tracks were harassed unmercifully every night by our guns, and on one occasion, when a relief was known to be going to take place, every bridge and road was barraged continuously for two nights in succession, thereby (as was heard afterwards) stopping the enemy Division being taken out and sent up North for an attack.

A word must be said for that mysterious person " Meteor," who apparently lived somewhere up in the clouds at G.H.Q. His weather prognostications were never wrong, and four or five times a day his cryptic messages were flashed all along the British Front; the Gunners understood them, and from them worked out their corrections for elevation and deflection, thereby improving their shooting enormously.

Poor ruined Merville was daily shelled by our guns, and the fine church tower, which was used by the Germans as an O.P., had to be demolished by the Heavy Artillery. Another favourite target was the villa occupied by Lord Rawlinson in 1914–15, which was known now to be a German Regimental Head-Quarters. It was here that H.M. the King met the President (M. Poincaré) and General Joffre in December 1914, and where a little later a well-known Society Lady, not unknown to literary fame, paid an unexpected visit to the IV. Corps. From being a comfortable modern château in those days, it is now a mere heap of stones and rubbish.

During this time the 34th Division Artillery, and during July, the 59th, were attached to the 5th Division. Both these Divisions had suffered much in the Retreat,

and were practically non-existent, so their floating
Artilleries were used to re-inforce any front where they
might be required.

The plight of the enemy in the front line was not
enviable; he lived in cubby-holes in the ground with
a thin line of wire in front, and often had to go ration-
less, as the ration parties could not approach the front
line through the machine-gun and Artillery fire; daily
his morale was getting lower. Hardly a night passed
without a raid being carried out by our Infantry, or
prisoners being captured by a patrol, or deserters
coming in.

The most notable raids in May were one carried
out by the Norfolks on the night of the 11th and one
by the East Surreys on the 20th.

In the former, one Platoon, under Lieut. Howe,
and a Lewis gun Section, under Lieut. West, tackled
some houses on the Canal bank in the right sector.
The Lewis gun was taken forward on the left flank,
while the rest of the party followed up the Canal to
where a hedge jutted out, behind which were seen
some steel helmets. The houses, after being bombed,
were found to be empty, the occupants having hastily
decamped, but the Germans in the trench were
rounded up, and the result was six prisoners and one
machine-gun captured, with only three casualties to
the Norfolks.

In the latter raid three Companies took part, the
scene being on the left of the Division Front. Wire-
cutting had been going on on the two preceding days,
but was not completed, and there was also a thick hedge
in front; so a party went out at night with wire-cutters
and bill-hooks to clear the way. At 4 p.m. the word
" Cheerio " was sent, meaning that all three Companies

were in position and ready, and at 4.20 the barrage opened. The left Company, under Lieut. Niven, attacked with two Platoons, and met with no opposition or difficulties except on the right, where they had to negotiate some hedges and work round an orchard before they could get to grips with the enemy. The centre Company, under Captain Sutton, also successfully reached their objective ; in one place the enemy were seen pushing a machine-gun through a hedge, but a brave Sergeant seized it by the barrel and dragged it out of their hands. Four machine-guns were captured by this Company. The right Company, under Captain Crouch, met with more opposition from some houses, which were full of Germans, but the bombers did some fine work, overcame the resistance, and captured 15 prisoners. The total bag was 24 prisoners and 8 machine-guns, besides abandoned rifles and equipment. The prisoners stated that owing to their failure in April their Division was no longer classified as an " Assault Division," and that they were all very tired and demoralised.

Again, on 17th June, a neat little patrol action was executed in the right sector by Lieut. Cubitt and one other man of the Norfolk Regiment. The two crawled out by night through the long grass in No Man's Land up to the corner of an orchard, then along a ditch until they came to the enemy's wire and parapet. Having got through the wire, they proceeded quietly to pull down some of the parapet, and dropped into the trench. Coughing was then heard a little farther on, and four pairs of boots were seen sticking out of a shelter under a blanket. As it was impossible to capture these men and bring them back all the way in the dark, they crept forward and threw in a bomb, killing the four men. They then made off at a trot, hopped out of the trench, and regained their lines in safety.

Hitherto the Division had had its back close up against the Forest—an uncomfortable situation ; and, with a view of improving it, and to enable an outpost line and main line of resistance to be formed well clear of the Forest, a big attack was carried out on 28th June on a front of 3 miles to a depth of 1 mile (see Map 16). This was the anniversary of the famous attack on Oppy in 1917, and oddly enough the same two Divisions carried out the operation, for the 31st Division, which was the right Division of the XV. Corps on the left, also took part in it. It was lent to the XI. Corps for the time being. The 28th June has consequently been chosen as the date of the Annual Divisional Dinner in London. The operation, which was camouflaged by the name of " Borderland," was carefully thought out by the Staff, and rehearsed with the help of a model of the ground by the troops taking part in it. These were, from right to left, Cheshires (2 Platoons), 15th Warwicks, West Kents, K.O.S.B., D.C.L.I., and Gloucesters. At 6 a.m. the Artillery, who had been re-inforced with two Brigades, and the trench-mortars, opened an intense bombardment lasting for four minutes ; the barrage then lifted, and the Infantry advanced under it, passages through our own wire having been cut overnight. The men displayed the greatest eagerness to come to grips with the enemy, and, though at first there was some opposition from machine-guns, these were quickly disposed of either with bombs or the bayonet, and the objectives were all gained up to time.

Immediately the attacking troops had reached their final goal, strong patrols were pushed forward

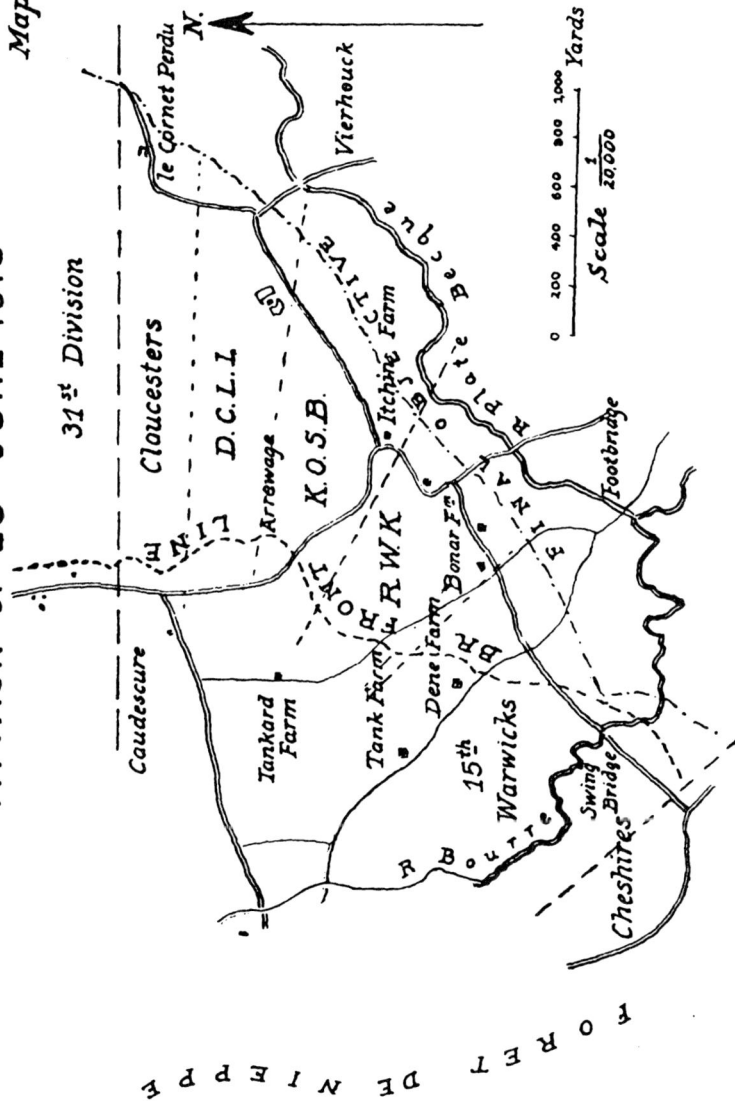

ATTACK of 28TH JUNE 1918

Map 16

31st Division

Caudescure
Le Cornet Perdu
Cloucesters
D.C.L.I.
Arrewage
N 17
K.O.S.B.
Itchine Farm
R.W.K.
FRONT
Tank Farm
Bonar F.
Dene Farm
BRITI—
Tankard Farm
15th
Warwicks
R Bourre
Swing Bridge
Cheshires
Footbridge
Vierhouck
PLATE BECQUE
RIVER
N.

FORET DE NIEPPE

0   200   400   600   800   1000
Scale 1/20,000   Yards

[To face p. 224.

with Lewis guns, and brought most effective fire on
the demoralised enemy, while the R.E., under cover
of darkness, destroyed the bridges over the Plate
Becque. A great number of the enemy were killed
in this attack ; in front of Itchen and Bonar Farms
alone were 200 dead, and in one place 37 Germans
were found heaped together, all of whom had been
bayoneted. It is significant that the 32nd (Saxon)
Division, which had suffered our attack, was withdrawn
immediately and sent to a peaceful sector at Verdun.
The total number of captures by the two Divisions
amounted to 500 prisoners, 50 machine-guns, 5 trench-
mortars, and 3 field guns, of which the 5th Division
took more than half. Our casualties were 29 Officers
and 890 other ranks.

The Division was greatly elated by this victory,
which was the first successful operation of any size
undertaken by the British since the Retreat, and
congratulations poured in. Almost immediately after
this, General Stephens left the Division on promotion
to the command of the X. Corps ; it was an appropriate
send-off to the beloved Commander who had led them
to so many triumphs on previous occasions. He was
succeeded by Major-Gen. J. Ponsonby of the Coldstream Guards.

July was an uneventful month. Early in the
month there was recrudescence of " wind up " in
High Places ; an attack on the Bailleul-Ypres front
seemed probable, and an offensive on this front had
to be reckoned with as long as Prince Rupprecht had
his reserve of 29 Divisions in hand. On the 15th the
blow fell on the French between Épernay and Chalons,
opposite Reims, but three days later Foch opened his
great counter-stroke towards Soissons, which com-

15

pletely changed the situation farther North. The German reserves would be required there, and the enemy was unlikely to attempt anything in this area on a large scale, though he might possibly strike at once in order to raise his falling morale by an initial success.

The Division, however, was kept quite busy, and the enemy, unable to attack, wreaked their vengeance in deluging the Forest with gas and making himself generally unpleasant with his guns and howitzers. Brigade Head-Quarters, Batteries, Reserve Camps, all suffered, and one Artillery Group, which had just pitched a camp in the wood, had to send down that night all their Officers and personnel gassed. The enemy trench-mortars, too, kept things lively in front; they were given Judaic names—"Esau," "Isaac," "Aaron," and "Joseph"—while the machine-guns were alluded to in gentler terms, "Gertie," "Elsie," etc.

The country all round the Forest was thick with corn, peas, beans, and flax, just beginning to ripen; it was sad to see these fine crops blackened with gas and going to rack and ruin. Possibly the French peasants may have been able to save some two months later when they came into their own again, and the Corps made some laudable efforts at harvesting the back areas, detailing special Agricultural Officers for the purpose; the Transport and Artillery horses meanwhile revelled in the green food in front, which was only being wasted.

Patrolling in No Man's Land, and beyond, was easy. Prisoners were picked up like plums out of a cake; on one night alone the Australians on the left, who excelled at this work, accounted for 110. Some interesting documents found on captured men came to light, testifying to the utter demoralisation of the Germans opposite. One such said, " Cases of soldiers openly refusing to obey orders are increasing to an alarming extent " ; and another, signed by Ludendorf, regarding information given by prisoners, " The soldier who refuses to speak does honour to himself, keeps a clear conscience in his own eyes, and in the eyes of his countrymen and of his superiors, and ends by winning the respect of the enemy " ; and there is no doubt a good deal of information was obtained in this way.

All July the weather was very hot. The Forest grew insufferably stuffy, and mosquitoes added to the discomforts ; but life there had its pleasant moments : the early mornings were fresh and often quite quiet; one heard nightingales singing, and saw a few pheasants close up to the front. There were even some roe-deer, too, which escaped the gas and the British " shikaris " ; poor beasts ! they had nowhere else to go to. Though there was no malaria, which might have been expected owing to the swamps and mosquitoes, there was a good deal of mild fever about, called " P.U.O." ; and, from what was heard, the enemy suffered from it too—they called it " Merville fever."

At the end of July another operation, surnamed " Partridge," was in course of preparation, when, on 7th August, the 61st Division took over the front together with " Partridge," and the Division retired to back areas for rest, for the first week in the vicinity of Aire, Division Head-Quarters being at Wardrecques. While they were in this area His Majesty again visited the Front, the troops, as before, lining the roads in groups and cheering as he passed, and the Staff and Commanding Officers had the honour of being presented to him.

On the 14th the Division entrained at St. Omer and Wizernes for the Frévent area, East of St. Pol, being held in G.H.Q. reserve. It was generally thought that the ultimate destination would be to the South. But was it to be for attack or defence ? No one quite knew, but the weight of opinion was in favour of the former, for already, on 8th August, the Australians, Canadians, and two French Corps had attacked on a broad front in the Somme country and had progressed well, making large captures. On the front we had just quitted, also, the Germans had begun to retire, and patrols had been pushed out nearly a mile.

On 15th August there was a conference at the VI. Corps Head-Quarters at Lucheux, when it was learnt that the Division was shortly to take part in an offensive on that front, but no sooner had the Staff returned to their quarters when these orders were cancelled. Then followed three days of calm ; polo, football, and boxing competitions were talked of, when, on the 18th, the G.S.O. 1 and the C.R.A. were suddenly summoned to the IV. Corps Head-Quarters at Marieux, where definite orders were received for an attack on the 21st. On returning in the evening they found the troops already in motion, and the G.O.C. (General Ponsonby) entertaining a large party at dinner at the Head-Quarters at Rebreuve, to be followed by a performance of the " Whizz Bangs " ; the Divisional Conference on the coming battle was not held till that was over. This dinner, almost on the eve of the tremendous events which followed, was known afterwards in the Division as " The Waterloo Dinner."

Farmhouse
Farm

ATTACK OF 28TH JUNE 1918.

CHAPTER XII

FINAL OPERATIONS

(MAP AT END OF BOOK)

ON the night of 18th August the Division moved to the Authie-Doullens area, with the 13th Brigade around Bouquemaison. Great secrecy was observed. During the day no moves were permitted; fortunately the sky was overcast, and no hostile aeroplanes could report the concentration in progress.

The next night a further move was made to near Couin and Coigneux. After dark on the 20th the march to the assembly trenches, averaging 8 or 9 miles over totally unknown country, was successfully carried out. There was little hostile shelling, but the night was misty, and it was not easy to keep direction. The 15th and 27th Artillery Brigades, who were to accompany the advance of the 5th and 63rd Divisions respectively, moved up to positions of readiness between Hannescamps and Essarts, some 4000 yards from the front.

The IV. Corps, consisting of the 5th, 37th, 63rd (R.N.) (replaced later by the 42nd), and the New Zealand Divisions, under Lieut.-Gen. Sir G. Harper, held the line on the Western side of Bucquoy, the N.Z. Division being on the right, and the 37th on the left. The plan of attack was for the 5th Division, with the 95th Brigade (Brig.-Gen. Norton) on the right and the 15th Brigade (Brig.-Gen. Oldman) on the left, to pass through the right Brigade of the 37th Division after the latter had captured the first objective (the high ground East of Bucquoy), and continue the advance. On the left the 63rd Division was to pass through the left Brigade of the 37th Division, and on our right the New Zealanders were to carry the attack right through.

During the night the mist thickened, and by zero hour—4.55 a.m.—on the 21st a dense shroud covered the ground. Ninety minutes after zero our troops passed through the 37th Division, the attacking Battalions from right to left being the Devons, East Surreys, 16th Warwicks, and Cheshires, accompanied by two Companies of the Machine-Gun Battalion. By 7.40 a.m. a line West of Achiet-le-Petit, representing the first objective of the Division, and an advance of about 2000 yards, had been made good with very few casualties. This attack was supported by 12 Mark IV. Tanks and a creeping barrage from the 37th Division Batteries in their original position; to support the further attack the 15th Brigade R.F.A. (Lieut.-Col. Hawkes) advanced at zero hour, and, after encountering many difficulties in the way of wire, fog, and hostile shelling, got into position East of Bucquoy by 8 a.m.

The fog was now thicker than ever, and in the second advance, supported by Mark IV. and Whippet Tanks, it was almost impossible to keep direction; units became much mixed, the Infantry could not keep close to the Tanks, and on several occasions narrowly missed being fired at by them.

On the left, the Cheshires (Lieut.-Col. Roddy), having the Bucquoy-Achiet road to guide them, advanced through Achiet-le-Petit, where a stiff fight with rifles and machine-guns took place. Leaving a Company to mop up the village, they rushed the line of the railway South-East of the village, and, after much opposition, got a footing on the ridge beyond, which was the final objective. On their right the 16th Warwicks, moving on a compass bearing, crossed the railway and also reached their goal. On crossing the railway a Battery of 5·9 howitzers was found firing into the advancing line of the 95th Brigade; Lieut.-Col. Deakin, accompanied by a few men, himself shot down the gunners.

The 63rd Division had been held up, and our flank was in the air. About 9.30 a.m. the enemy counter-attacked, and got right behind the Cheshires, at one time threatening to cut them off completely; the latter, however, fell back, counter-attacked in their turn, and regained the trench-line North of the railway.

The 95th Brigade also had a hard fight near the railway. When the situation was eventually straightened out, the line ran along a trench about 200 yards short of the railway, with a defensive flank thrown back on the right to join up with the New Zealanders.

The Division had advanced more than two miles, and had captured over 500 prisoners, a Battery of 77 mm. guns, and one of 5·9 howitzers, a large number of machine-guns, rifles, and trench-mortars, and much other material. The conduct of the troops had been magnificent, hampered as they were by the thick fog, the performance of the 16th Warwicks, who, counting their march to the assembly positions, had covered over 15 miles in 16 hours and reached their final objective, being particularly meritorious. Our casualties were extraordinarily light. The Tanks which had supported the attack had not got farther than the railway; many lost direction in the fog, and a good number were destroyed by the German anti-Tank guns which covered all the railway-crossings.

The night and the following day were spent in consolidating the positions gained. During the morning Lance-Corporal Onions and Private Eades of the Devons, when on a patrol, captured over 250 Germans by manœuvring them into an old trench, opening fire, and thus compelling them to surrender. Later, also, a patrol of the 12th Gloucesters captured a party of 100 of the enemy.

Late on the 22nd orders were received for the attack to be continued next day. The objectives were Irles and the ridge South of the railway, a portion of which had been captured on the 21st by the 15th Brigade, but from which they had been ejected. At 11 a.m. the assault was launched by the 95th and 15th Brigades, the Battalions from right to left being the 12th Gloucesters, East Surreys, 16th Warwicks, and Bedfords. The position attacked was one of great strength, and defended by a large number of machine-guns. A thick creeping barrage was fired by the Machine-Gun Battalion and the Divisional Artillery, augmented by four additional Brigades. The 15th Brigade were held up by three thick belts of wire, until a magnificent advance by the 37th Division and the effective work of two Tanks on their front enabled the line to get forward. The Bedfords were again checked near the final objective, when Lieut.-Col. Courtenay personally led up two Platoons at the critical moment, and captured the ridge. This gallant Officer, who had been so well known as a member of the Divisional Staff for over two years, was, unfortunately, killed. The 16th Warwicks advanced without a halt to the final objective, overcoming a formidable trench system on their way. Two Companies of the Norfolks were sent up to thicken the 15th Brigade front, and the captured ground was consolidated.

At the same time the East Surreys (Lieut.-Col. Minogue) gained their final objective, but on the extreme right the attack of the Gloucesters had been held up short of Irles. The strength of the position may be judged from the fact that at one point 23 machine-guns were captured on a front of 50 yards, each with a great heap of empty cartridge cases by its side. Strong patrols from the Gloucesters and the D.C.L.I. (Major Gent), who had been moved up from support, pushed forward into the village, but by 4 o'clock it had not been captured.

It was therefore decided to move up the 13th Brigade to complete the capture of Irles, and exploit the success of the morning's attack as far as Loupart Wood. During the day the Divisional Artillery had moved forward, and the 15th and 27th Brigades (the latter having only just returned to the Division after supporting the 63rd Division) were in position near Achiet-le-Petit.

Zero hour was fixed for 7.30 p.m. The order of battle from right to left was, West Kents (Lieut.-Col. Johnstone), 14th Warwicks (Lieut.-Col. Wilberforce), and 15th Warwicks (Lieut.-Col. Miller), with the K.O.S.B. (Major Dudgeon) in support. The attack was successful, though on the right the West Kents lost direction slightly, and only one Platoon entered Irles. However, at the same moment, Lieut.-Col. Colt of the Gloucesters organised an attack on the village on his own initiative. He formed up his men and led them through Irles and out at the other side, gaining the objective of his original attack. He was, unfortunately, seriously wounded, and his Adjutant was killed.

By midnight the situation was clear ; the line had been advanced to Loupart Wood (which had stared us in the face since the beginning), Irles was in our hands, and the West Kents had a defensive flank as a protection against Miraumont, which the Germans still held. At 4 a.m. on the 24th the N.Z. Division passed through the front, and continued the advance.

The first three days' fighting had been crowned with success, the captures of the Division being 2768 prisoners, 25 guns, over 350 machine-guns, 37 trench-mortars, a large number of anti-Tank and other rifles, two dumps of Engineer's material, a complete Quarter-master's Store, and much Signal and other equipment. Our own casualties were 70 Officers (including 4 Battalion and 3 Battery Commanders), and 1600 other ranks.

On the 25th the Division received orders to be ready to relieve the 37th Division and continue the advance. The 13th Brigade was concentrated West of Grevillers, whilst the Artillery, advancing in support of the 37th Division, was in action North of Biefvillers. There was much hostile shelling, especially on the roads and Artillery positions, and there were a good many casualties. Major Moreton, 119th Battery, and his Battery leader, and Major Anderson, commanding A/15 Battery, were killed.

The 37th Division had been fighting hard for the possession of Favreuil, and had finally established their line East of that place. Orders for relief came very late (12.40 a.m. on the 26th), and the darkness of the night added further to the difficulties. The units of the 111th Brigade (37th Division) had become very much mixed ; guides were not available, and the positions were difficult to ascertain. Undaunted by these difficulties, the K.O.S.B. passed through the front and formed up East of Favreuil, ready to co-operate

with the New Zealanders on the right in an attack at
6.30 a.m. This was successful, the K.O.S.B., supported
by a section of the Machine-Gun Battalion, gaining
their objective in spite of heavy fire from Beugnâtre.

A further attack against Beugnâtre—part of the
plan for the envelopment of Bapaume—in conjunction
with the N.Z. Division was arranged for later in the
day. The Artillery meantime moved up to positions
between Sapignies and Bapaume.

At 6 p.m. the K.O.S.B., commanded by Captain
Lake (Brigade Major, 13th Brigade), who had taken the
place of Major Dudgeon (wounded earlier in the day),
advanced against Beugnâtre under a creeping barrage.
Little resistance was met until the middle of the village
was reached, when enemy machine-guns became very
active ; but the troops pushed through the village, and
formed up on the crest beyond, being rewarded by
splendid targets of Germans, who were running away
in hundreds. Two Companies of the 14th Warwicks
were sent up to re-inforce the line, and by nightfall
the position was entirely satisfactory, touch being
maintained with the N.Z. Division on the right. An
attempted counter-attack about 11 p.m. was broken up
by Artillery fire.

For three days there was a pause. On the 29th
patrols were pushed through Bapaume by the New
Zealanders, and a combined attack along the whole of
the IV. Corps and part of the VI. Corps front was
ordered for the following day. Two objectives had been
allotted : first, the " Old Army Line," West of Beugny ;
and, second, the village of Beugny and the high ground
East of it. The advance to the second objective was
dependent on the success of the Divisions on either flank.

The attack was carried out by the 95th Brigade,

the D.C.L.I. on the right and the Devons on the left;
four Tanks advanced with the Infantry, who were
preceded by a creeping barrage.

The ground over which the advance was made was
overlooked from the enemy's position on both flanks
and from the East. On the right the D.C.L.I. encountered fire from Frémicourt, but eventually advanced to the high ground South of Beugny, where
they maintained their position with the help of the
East Surreys, and kept touch with the Division on the
right. On the left the Devons, in spite of the fact
that Vaulx-Vraucourt remained in the enemy's hands,
pushed forward to the high ground North-West of
Beugny, and sent patrols into the village. They were,
however, met with intense rifle and machine-gun
fire from both flanks, and had to retire to their first
objective, the " Old Army Line," which they consolidated.

The Hill 120 on the " Old Army Line," the most
important part of the first objective, had been secured,
but further advance was impossible, as the line held
formed a pronounced salient overlooked from both sides.

In the fight the 37th Battery (Major Evans) gave
very valuable assistance to the Devons, the Battalion
and Battery Commanders being side by side throughout. D/15 Battery (Captain Mayne) performed a
notable feat, galloping up through a heavy barrage in
full view of the enemy and coming into action not
700 yards from them.

On the night of 1st September the 15th Infantry
Brigade took over the front, preparatory to attacking
on the following morning, in order to assist the major
operation of breaking the Drocourt-Quéant line on the
First Army front to the North. When marching up, a

Company of the 16th Warwicks was caught by a German night-bomber, which dropped six bombs in quick succession, causing 80 casualties and practically wiping out the Company. Further, during the night, the Division on the right of the Corps advanced their zero hour eight minutes, with the result that a heavy counter-barrage was put down on the Divisional Front, causing a large number of casualties during the seven minutes prior to the attack.

At 5.15 a.m. the assault was launched. On the right the Norfolks gained their objectives, with few casualties, and captured about 250 prisoners. On the left the Cheshires got well into Beugny, where they were brought to a halt about the sunken road running North from the centre of the village. About noon the enemy counter-attacked on the right, but were repulsed.

Gallant efforts were made by the Artillery to deal with hostile machine-guns by running forward 18-prs. in close support of the Infantry. One gun of the 124th Brigade R.F.A. (37th Division), which was magnificently handled, was knocked out almost at once, every man of the detachment being killed or wounded. Another gun of the 52nd Battery (Major Fellowes) was run up to a position 1000 yards from the enemy soon after zero. Second-Lieut. Podmore, in charge of the gun, remained in action under heavy fire for three hours, firing over open sights on German machine-guns and re-inforcing troops.

It was decided that the attack should be continued the following day. Brig.-Gen. Oldman's plan was to advance up the spur from the South, with two Companies of the Bedfords, whilst two Companies of the 16th Warwicks converged from the North-West of the village. Beugny itself was to be subjected to an intense bombardment during the attack by three Brigades of Artillery.

The advance took place, and the complicated programme of Artillery fire was described by the Infantry as " magnificent " ; but most of the enemy had decamped during the night, and very little opposition was met with.

When it was found that the Germans had gone, the Bedfords and 16th Warwicks proceeded in pursuit, throwing out advance-guards, with the Norfolks and Cheshires in support at about 1000 yards' distance. The advance was carried out by " bounds," the 27th Brigade R.F.A., supporting with two Batteries, with two guns pushed well forward.

After advancing some 7 miles through Lebucquière and Vélu, the enemy were found on approximately the line Hermies-Havrincourt Wood, but orders were received from the IV. Corps that no further advance was to be made, and that the 37th Division would take over the positions gained.

During the night the relief was completed, and the Division, less the Artillery, who remained in to cover the 37th Division, were withdrawn to near Bihucourt and Favreuil.

The Division had been fighting almost continuously since 21st August, during which time it had advanced close on 14 miles. The casualties had been severe— 210 Officers and 4065 other ranks—but not out of proportion to the results gained. The losses in Officers had been unfortunately heavy, no less than 8 Commanding Officers having been killed or wounded.

Considering that the Division had been almost continuously in the line since April, and had therefore little opportunity for training, the handling of their men by subordinate Commanders and the initiative displayed by all ranks was remarkable. Again and again instances occurred of N.C.O.'s, and even Privates, taking charge of situations when the Officers had been killed, and carrying on successfully.

All this time the weather was intensely hot; the few wells in the tiny villages were either drunk dry or had been destroyed by the retreating Germans. Lieut.-Col. Homer and his Engineers had followed up closely in order to re-open up the water-supplies, or bore new wells, and, in addition, Tank Lorries had been used, so that at no time was there a real shortage, though the problem of watering horses was difficult. The Divisional Train, under Lieut.-Col. Wood, also gave great assistance by improvising water-carriers out of petrol-tins, and in converting G.S. wagons to water-tanks by the use of tarpaulins.

Two new methods of supply for Infantry ammunition and stores had been available, and proved most useful. First, three gun-carrying Tanks were attached to the Division, and used to carry forward stores, following on the heels of the attack. Secondly, arrangements had been made with the 59th Squadron, R.A.F., to drop boxes of ammunition by parachute; this was found most satisfactory, as the ammunition was supplied in nearly all cases within half an hour from the time of demand.

From the 4th to the 12th the Division remained resting, while the 37th Division continued the advance to beyond Havrincourt Wood. The 15th Brigade R.F.A. was withdrawn for a short rest from the 6th to 9th, but otherwise the Artillery remained in action under the command of the C.R.A., 37th Division.

During this period of rest the Division sustained a

heavy loss by the death of Brig.-Gen. L. O. W. Jones, who had commanded the 13th Brigade since the end of 1915, and to whom their success in so many operations had been in the main due. After gallantly leading his Brigade through so many dangerous battles, he succumbed to pneumonia, and was mourned by all ranks of the Division.

About this time the Americans opened their attack at St. Mihiel, and captured over 20,000 prisoners ; and the Allies in the Balkans were at last beginning to move. Austria, too, was flying peace kites, which met with a very curt answer.

On 13th September the 5th Division took over from the N.Z. Division with the 13th Brigade in front, the line running from the high ground East of Gouzeaucourt Wood to the South-West of Trescault Spur. The left flank afforded good observation, but on the right neither side could see the other.

Our rôle now was to advance the right of the line some 400 yards, and form a defensive flank for the larger operations by the Corps and Army to the right.

At 5.20 a.m. on the 18th, in pouring rain, the K.O.S.B. on a two-Company front attacked African Trench under a thick creeping barrage. They met with extremely heavy fire from machine-guns. The left Company obtained their objective—a sunken road— but only some of the right Company reached African Trench. Thus the position of the left Company was very exposed, and, although gallant efforts were made to extend the captured position, Lieut.-Col. Furber was finally forced to withdraw his Battalion back to their original line. But the attack to the South had been successful, and Gauche Wood, South-East of Gouzeaucourt Wood, was captured.

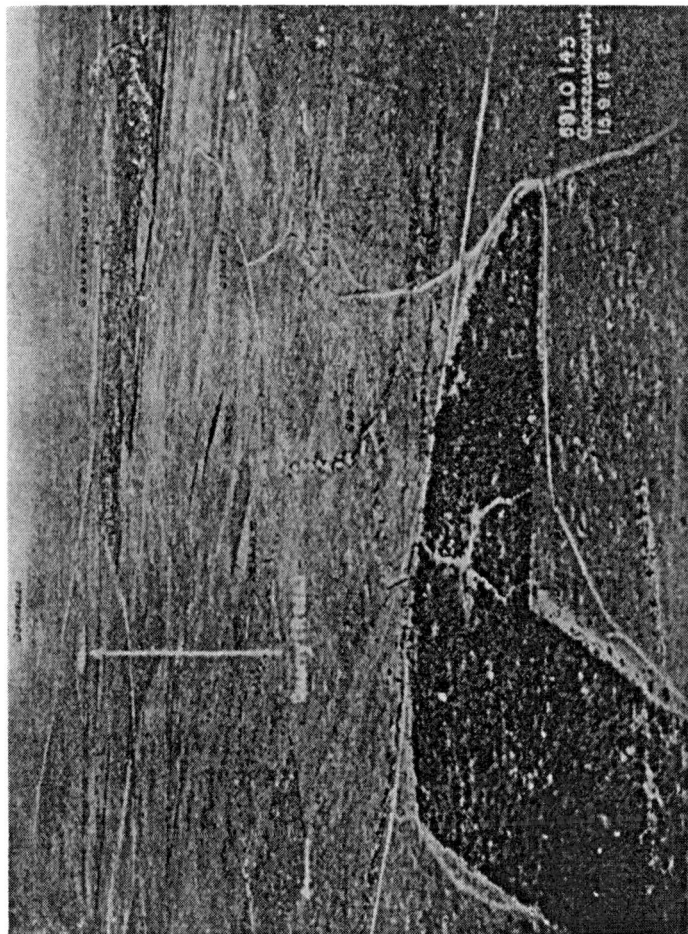

GOUZEAUCOURT.

[*To face p.* 240.

On the 27th the offensive was once again resumed, the Division forming the pivot for an attack by the Corps and Army on the left. The 13th Brigade, under Brig.-Gen. A. T. Beckwith, was in the right portion of the Divisional Front, and the 15th Brigade in the left. After the capture of the African Trench by the 13th Brigade the 15th Brigade were to advance and take the village of Beaucamp and Highland Ridge to the East of it. In the event of success, the 95th Brigade were to pass through and continue the advance to Welsh Ridge, North-East of Villers Plouich.

At 7.52 a.m. the 13th Brigade attacked with the West Kents on the right, 15th Warwicks in the centre, and 14th Warwicks on the left; the Bedfords on the right, and the Cheshires on the left, directed on Beaucamp, led the 15th Brigade. To support the attack, the Divisional Artillery was increased by the 3rd N.Z. F.A. Brigade and the 223rd Brigade R.F.A., and the medium trench-mortars of the 5th, 63rd, and N.Z. Divisions, under the command of Capt. Plummer, D.T.M.O., were also used, and fired some 4000 projectiles.

On the right the West Kents met with intense machine-gun fire from African Trench, and were only able to get forward a short distance. All the Company Officers had become casualties, but the Battalion Intelligence Officer, Lieut. Corke, took command of the line and succeeded in getting the position consolidated. The 15th Warwicks bombed their way into the enemy trenches, where Sergt. Jones distinguished himself in continuing the attack when all his party had become casualties and subsequently leading forward another party; and 2nd Lieut. Shaw and Sergt. Young, of the Machine-Gun Battalion, captured 30 of the enemy

16

unassisted. The 14th Warwicks started well, and, after some opposition, made good their objectives on the centre and left, connecting up with the 15th Warwicks. On the left the Bedfords and Cheshires were successful, but the 16th Warwicks, who were to pass through the former, could not do so owing to the enemy having penetrated between them and the 42nd Division. Captain Abbott's Company of the Machine-Gun Battalion did most valuable work, being specially commended by General Oldman.

General Ponsonby decided in the evening that the 95th Brigade should advance through the 15th Brigade early the next morning, whilst the latter would switch across and advance on the 13th Brigade front.

At 2.30 a.m. on the 28th the Devons and East Surreys went forward, the latter making good progress on the left and capturing their first objective; but the Devons could not advance far at first owing to the heavy fire from their right. During the initial stage of the attack the enemy concentrated his fire on the 13th Brigade front, but by 9.30 a.m. the resistance had weakened, and the West Kents moved forward into African Trench, followed shortly afterwards by the 15th and 14th Warwicks. The East Surreys, too, reached the Northern outskirts of Villers Plouich. African Trench was at last ours !

The 95th Brigade had now completed their first task, and the Divisional line ran from North-West of Villers Plouich to African Trench, North-West of Gouzeaucourt. This enabled the 15th Brigade to move forward from the 13th Brigade front, which they did with the Norfolks on the right and Cheshires on the left in advance-guard formation. Simultaneously with their advance the 95th Brigade resumed the offensive, and, by 8 p.m., the final objective had been captured and the line ran along the Gouzeaucourt-Villers Plouich railway on the 15th Brigade front and along the sunken road East of the railway on the 95th Brigade front.

During the battle the Artillery had moved forward by alternate Brigades, the 15th Brigade R.F.A. being in position West of Beaucamp, and the 27th and 223rd Brigades near Gouzeaucourt Wood.

In view of the weakening of the enemy resistance orders were issued by the Corps for the advance to be continued up to the line of the Canal de L'Escaut. Accordingly, the 95th Brigade were directed to continue the advance and the 15th Brigade to pass through them on the La Vacquerie-Gonnelieu road, and exploit. The D.C.L.I. and Gloucesters took over the front of the 95th Brigade, but it was found impossible to carry out a relief of the 15th Brigade front Battalions in time. The advance started at 8.30 a.m., and some 800 yards were gained, but further progress along the valley was impossible until La Vacquerie and Gonnelieu had been taken. Seeing that the advance was held up, the O.'sC. Bedfords and 16th Warwicks decided to push forward through the 95th Brigade, but very little improvement in the position resulted, though a few of the Bedfords and Warwicks managed to reach the La Vacquerie-Gonnelieu sunken road and captured about 130 prisoners, of whom 60 surrendered under a white flag. The advance of the Bedfords was largely owing to the skilful leadership of Capt. Wakefield, who, when the attack was held up, led a few men round the flank in the face of heavy machine-gun fire and captured 75 prisoners.

After dusk the D.C.L.I. were able to clear up a pocket of the enemy, who, although the New Zealanders had advanced to the Bonavis Ridge, 2000 yards East of the village, were still holding out in La Vacquerie. Over 200 prisoners and 50 machine-guns were captured in these operations, and orders were issued for the 15th Brigade to continue the attack on the following day. Gonnelieu on the South still remained in the enemy's hands, the attacks of the 21st Division against it having failed.

The 27th Brigade R.F.A. moved to positions close to the railway during the night, where, as they were only 1000 yards from the front line, any movement brought down a shower of bullets on them from Gonnelieu Ridge. The Cheshires and Norfolks now took over the front ready for the further advance.

The task before the 15th Brigade was the breaking through of the front and support trenches of the famous Hindenburg system, and the capture of the high ground overlooking the Canal. There was an immense amount of wire and many strongly-fortified trenches of the Hindenburg Line to be overcome. General Oldman decided to attack with the Cheshires, and that the Norfolks would pass through them. At 4 a.m. they started and were entirely successful ; 272 prisoners were taken, together with one field-gun and numerous machine-guns. The attack was only just in time to forestall a withdrawal of the enemy, and its success was in no small measure due to the excellence of the H.E. barrage, which gave the advancing troops a good guide to their objectives. About 7 a.m. patrols of the 16th Warwicks pushed into and captured Gonnelieu, thus enabling the troops of the 21st Division to come up into line on the right ; and in the evening the greater part of Banteux, in the valley, was cleared. The guns were all moved forward, 15th Brigade R.F.A. to near

La Vacquerie, and the 27th and 223rd Brigades to positions a mile North-East of Gouzeaucourt. During the night, the Division, less Artillery, was relieved by the 37th Division and moved back to rest, Divisional Head-Quarters remaining at Ytres, where it had been for the past few days.

This finished the second phase of the fighting. The enemy, though being steadily driven back, was by no means broken, and strenuous opposition had been met with throughout. The fighting had been over strange ground, and in many cases there had been no time to make reconnaissances, whilst the attacks themselves were made in darkness. The H.E. barrage was found most useful in such attacks, as it furnished a definite guide to the advance ; 18-pr. thermite shells, bursting in the air, were also tried in order to mark the flanks of the attack, but they were not reliable enough in their range to give much help. The later operations had all to be planned and carried out at short notice, and it reflects great credit on the Commanders and Staffs that on all occasions everything had been got ready by zero hour. The Artillery had a particularly hard and trying time, as the barrages, some of them very complicated, had to be worked out at night in a hurry in dark dug-outs ; but no mistakes were ever made.

The R.A.M.C. had worked throughout the operations in their usual gallant and efficient manner. While the 15th Field Ambulance was at Bus they suffered a most unfortunate loss, the C.O. (Lieut.-Col. Bradley) and the Second-in-Command (Major M'Cormack) being killed by a direct hit from a H.E. shell on the small shelter where they were sleeping.

During these months the deep throbbing hum of the

Gothas, bent upon their errand of destruction, was often heard, and their bombs caused much havoc in the Wagon and Transport lines. One night there was the delectable sight of one of them being brought down close to the Division Head-Quarters. It was caught in the beam of one of our searchlights and held there relentlessly, looking like a great white bird of ill-omen, when suddenly the rat-tat-tat of the machine-gun of one of our night scouts was heard. A tiny red spark appeared, which gradually spread till down came the raider in a sheet of flame. The German Officer escaped in a parachute and was taken prisoner, but six charred bodies of men were found in the wreckage.

While the Division was resting, the reduction from the twelve-Battalion establishment to nine Battalions, which had been avoided with so much success for many months, was finally peremptorily commanded. The 1/6th A. & S. Highlanders, who had worked so gallantly as Pioneers, returned to their old Division, the 51st, where they gained further honours in the subsequent fighting, being replaced as Pioneers by the 14th Warwicks. The 12th Gloucesters were disbanded, and their personnel was distributed among other units in the Division and other formations, whilst the 15th Warwicks were absorbed into the 16th Warwicks and posted to the 13th Brigade.

Although, with the exception of the Argylls, practically all the personnel of the disbanded units remained in the Division, it was a sad parting, and it is a lasting regret that they could not have kept their identity, and that the 5th Division could not have completed the remaining six weeks of the War with the twelve Battalions of which it had been so long composed.

During this and other short rests of the Division

the practice of " lorry-hopping " to Amiens was much in vogue. It was the only way one could get there, unless one was lucky enough to get a lift in a car or to borrow a motor-bike from the Signals. Amiens had been a little knocked about, both by bombs and shell-fire. Luckily the Cathedral had not suffered ; there was one small hole in the roof, caused probably by an anti-aircraft " dud," and some of the glass was broken, but the famous rose-windows were intact.

In other theatres of war events were moving rapidly. At the end of September General Allenby made a grand advance in Palestine, reaching Nazareth and capturing many thousands of Turks. On 30th September Bulgaria signed an unconditional surrender. On the Western Front the Americans and French were making large captures in the Argonne, and in the North the Second British Army and the Belgians were pushing forward. The end was fast approaching. .

On 8th October a " full-dress " attack (as the Corps Commander was wont to call it) by the Third and Fourth Armies took place. Cambrai fell, and on our Front the 37th and N.Z. Divisions advanced close to Le Cateau, over-running the villages of Ligny, Caudry, Béthencourt, Inchy, Viesly, and Briastre. All these villages were inhabited, and the problem was how our Artillery should deal with them and inflict the minimum amount of damage. The usual procedure was to shell the outskirts, where the Germans as a rule placed their machine-guns, and pass through the village with a light shrapnel barrage. The villagers were so over-joyed at their deliverance that they did not mind a few of their windows being broken, and, while the barrage passed over, took refuge in their cellars. At Caudry, a fair-sized town, where later the Division had their Head-Quarters, the inhabitants unfurled their Tricolors and sang the " Marseillaise " as our troops filed in. What joy it must have been to them after their four years of captivity !

In this advance the 5th Division guns covered the 37th Division, and moved, on the 7th, to positions North of Lateau Wood, and, on the 12th, to South-East of Viesly. While they were on the move the 15th Brigade R.F.A. (Lieut.-Col. Harvey) were called upon to fire an S.O.S. barrage, which they did with remarkable quickness, for which they were specially commended by the Army.

From the 1st to the 9th the Division was in Corps Reserve. On the 9th they moved to the Vauxelles-La Vacquerie area, and on the 10th to Haucourt and Esnes, with the 13th Brigade in Caudry. On the 12th they took over the line on the Selle River between Neuvilly and Briastre, with the 13th Brigade in front.

The 20th saw another " full-dress " attack, the objectives of the IV. Corps (5th and 42nd Divisions attacking) being the ridge South-West of the Solesmes-Ovillers road and thence North to the high ground East of Solesmes. The 13th Brigade, with the 16th Warwicks and K.O.S.B., who had been seven days in the line, were only to make good the road and railway East of the Selle River, and the 95th Brigade, with the East Surreys on the right and Devons on the left, were to pass through and capture the next two ridges. On our right was the 17th Division, and on the left the 42nd. The enemy position was very strong—a bare glacis-like slope with two rows of double-apron wire and a cow-fence—and not a vestige of cover for the attackers. The 527th Company R.E. built bridges over the Selle ; the trench-mortars did their best to

cut the wire; and the Artillery with four Brigades
and two Companies of the Machine-Gun Battalion
were ready to support the advance.

At 2 a.m., in thick mist and pouring rain, the
13th Brigade attacked, and, in spite of a good deal of
uncut wire, captured the enemy position after some
hand-to-hand fighting. The East Surreys and Devons
passed through, but, after taking the first ridge, could
not advance farther than the road just West of the
second ridge. The attack was resumed again at 4 p.m.
under cover of an excellent barrage of H.E. and smoke,
and the final ridge was gained, the enemy resistance
being completely crippled by the accuracy of the
machine-gun and Artillery fire. The following two
days were spent in consolidating; the D.C.L.I. took
over the front with three Companies, and the guns
moved across the Selle.

The next phase was to capture Beaurain and Petit-
Vendegies, and to advance to the high ground overlooking the Harpies River—part of a big attack by
the Third and Fourth Armies on the 23rd. This was
to be done by the 15th Brigade, with the Bedfords and
Cheshires and four Tanks, after which the 37th Division would pass through and exploit the success to
beyond Salesches. The enemy expected an attack,
and when the two Battalions were in their assembly
positions on the night of the 22nd they were caught
in a heavy barrage and suffered many casualties,
especially among the Cheshires; the D.C.L.I., too,
who were holding the original line, lost many men.

The battle was timed to start to the South of the
V. Corps at 1.30 a.m., on V. Corps front (on our right)
at 2 a.m., and on the IV. Corps front at 3.20 a.m.
The Bedfords and Cheshires, in spite of being somewhat

disorganised by the shelling, were ready at that hour, and jumped off behind the barrage. About the sunken roads and orchards round Beaurain they met with an obstinate resistance, the right of the Bedfords and the Cheshires being held up for some time at the Red House Estaminet. Lieut. Sanson, of the 120th Battery, handling his Section with great skill, shelled the place, and, on seeing the enemy retire, limbered up and occupied the house. By 8 a.m. Beaurain was ours, and the Norfolks, in support, were ordered up to mop up the village. By 9 a.m. the way was clear for the 37th Division to pass through.

In these two attacks (20th and 23rd October) the losses were 80 Officers and 1300 other ranks.

The Artillery, after moving forward to support the further advance of the 37th Division, were drawn out for three days' rest at Beaurain, where the 27th Brigade held a successful little race-meeting over jumps outside the village; some enemy aeroplanes, seeing a large concourse of men and horses, bombed the ground heavily in the night; but no one was there! No doubt the German communiqués chronicled a successful raid on a large concentration of troops.

On the 25th the 37th and N.Z. Divisions were close to Le Quesnoy; in three days the IV. Corps advance had been nearly 10 miles, and the Third and Fourth Armies had captured 8000 prisoners and 150 guns.

On 4th November the last great decisive battle of the War commenced, the First, Third, and Fourth British Armies and the First French Army taking part. As far as the Third Army was concerned the final objective allotted was the general line St. Rémy Chaussée—Pont-sur-Sambre—Bavai. The line from

the high ground between Landrecies and Locquignol—
East of Jolimetz—North-West of Gommegnies was
given as an intermediate objective. On the IV. Corps
front the 37th and N.Z. Divisions were to carry out
the initial attack and make good the intermediate
objective, after which the 5th and 42nd Divisions were
to exploit the success towards the River Sambre.
Prisoners brought stories of the masses of wire there
were in the Forêt de Mormal and the strong resistance
which would be put up there. The barrage was a
problem ; if the forest consisted of high trees shrapnel
would be of little use ; thermite was suggested, but
eventually it was settled to use 4·5 howitzers where
the forest was thick, and shrapnel where it was
open or scrub. As a matter of fact, half the forest
had been cut down, and the country was in many
places quite open, though in others there was dense
undergrowth.

On the night of the 3rd–4th the 15th and 95th
Brigades, who were to attack, moved to Neuville,
Salesches, and Beaurain ; Division Head-Quarters to
Neuville, in touch with the 37th Head-Quarters.

The morning of the 4th opened in glorious weather.
The 37th and N.Z. Divisions advanced and were
entirely successful ; by the evening the New Zealanders
had surrounded and captured Le Quesnoy, and the
37th Division had established a line on the Western
edge of the forest and sent patrols into it—how far
was not quite certain. However, the 5th Division was
ordered to relieve them in the morning wherever they
might be, and continue to press on. General Ponsonby
decided to advance on a two-Brigade front—on the
right, the 95th with the East Surreys right and the
Devons left, and on the left, the 15th Brigade with

the Bedfords in front and the other Battalions leap-frogging as they went on. The 15th Brigade R.F.A. and an extra Howitzer Battery, with two mobile 6-inch trench-mortars, accompanied the 95th Brigade, and the 27th Brigade R.F.A. (Lieut.-Col. White) with another Howitzer Battery and one mobile trench-mortar accompanied the 15th Brigade. Each Artillery Brigade sent forward one Battery, with two guns in close support of the Infantry.

The fine weather did not last; rain fell in torrents during the night, and the roads were in a shocking state. The Germans had blown mines at nearly every cross-roads or brook-crossing, and, until the craters had been bridged, the roads were almost impassable for wheeled traffic, and bad enough for the Infantry ; too much cannot be said for the way in which the R.E. and Pioneers accomplished their tasks both on this and the subsequent days.

In drenching rain the Battalions began their advance at 5.30 a.m. on the 5th. At first no enemy were met with, and they pushed on without any pause ; by 9.30 a.m. the D.C.L.I. and the East Surreys in the 95th Brigade and the Bedfords in the 15th Brigade gained their objective (La Grande Carrière—Foresters' House road). At the next objective (Embu Farm—La Por-querie—La Corne) opposition was encountered, and it was not until two mobile trench-mortars and a Section each of the 52nd and 121st Batteries had opened fire that the attack could be driven home. On information received from patrols of the 3rd Hussars that the New Zealanders on the left were well on, General Oldman decided to push the Cheshires forward and turn the enemy's flank ; by 4 p.m. the whole of the second objective was gained, and the first line was clear of the forest. By 8 p.m. the 15th Brigade were on the line of the Bachant-Pont-sur-Sambre-Bavai road, and patrols were sent down to the Sambre, where it was found that the Aymeries Bridge had been destroyed. Meanwhile the D.C.L.I., in spite of steady machine-gun and Artillery fire, had entered Pont-sur-Sambre with the help of two mobile trench-mortars, and at 6 a.m. on the 6th November the East Surreys moved forward in line with them.

Throughout the 6th the enemy maintained machine-gun and Artillery fire, and it was obvious that any bridging could only be done in the night. In the afternoon, however, Major Cloutman (Commanding 59th Company R.E.) visited the Quartes Bridge and found it intact. Seeing that the bridge had been prepared for demolition he rolled over the tow-path, swam the bullet-spattered river, and cut the leads, for which courageous act he received the V.C. A Platoon of the Cheshires and two trench-mortars were sent up at once, but they were too late to prevent the enemy repairing the leads, and the bridge went up, leaving intact the abutments, on which a bridge for heavy traffic was afterwards built. But meanwhile a pontoon-bridge, built by the 59th Company R.E., under cover of fire from the 27th Brigade R.F.A., was nearing completion, and the next morning (7th) the Cheshires and Norfolks crossed the river, and made good the railway East of the Bois Georges, with the left flank thrown back, as the 42nd Division were not yet up in line. On the right the V. Corps crossed at Berlaimont. By midday the 42nd occupied Hargnies and the road running South, but the enemy was still in the bend of the river by Boussières.

The 95th Brigade now crossed with the Devons,

who, passing through the Cheshires and Norfolks, captured the village of Fontaine, but failed in the attack on St. Rémi-mal-bati ; they gained touch, however, with the 21st Division of the V. Corps at Limont-Fontaine. A/15, D/15, and the 52nd Batteries of the 15th Brigade crossed the river, and came into action at Pantigny, the rest of the Divisional Artillery, with the 155th Brigade (Lieut.-Col. Congreve) attached, remaining in readiness West of the river.

On the 8th the advance was continued. The 95th Brigade, with the Devons, East Surreys, and D.C.L.I., preceded by a screen of the 3rd Hussars and Cyclists, moved forward ; the East Surreys passed through St. Rémi-mal-bati and took up a line on the high ground North-East of the village, and the D.C.L.I. reached a line just South of the Bois de Quesnoy ; these Battalions had comparatively heavy losses, the East Surreys losing about 50 men, and the Devons 90, including 9 Officers.

The 13th Brigade, who had been in reserve at La Porquerie, moved across the river in the course of the day in readiness to take up the pursuit. At 7 p.m. the K.O.S.B. on the right, and the West Kents on the left, each with a Section of " A " Company of the Machine-Gun Battalion, passed through the Devons. The night was pitch dark and it was raining hard, but by 1 a.m. on the 9th a connected line was formed, and by 5 a.m. the K.O.S.B. had a post on the Avesnes-Maubeuge road, and the West Kents a post about Le Paye. It was obvious now that the enemy was retiring helter-skelter, and orders were sent to keep pressing on, keeping in touch with units on either flank. In another hour the Brigade front had been advanced to the line Beaufort-Le Paye road, and was being pushed on in

MAJ.-GEN. J. PONSONBY, C.B., C.M.G., D.S.O.

[*To face p* 254

conjunction with the 52nd Infantry Brigade on the right and the 125th Infantry Brigade on the left. Brig.-Gen. Beckwith ordered two Troops of the 3rd Hussars and the IV. Corps Cyclists to push on in bounds and make good, first, the ridge West and North-West of Damousies; second, the railway line just West of the River Solre; and third, the high ground North and North-West of the Bois de Carnoy. Orders were now received for the Infantry to remain on the Avesnes-Maubeuge road and form a line of resistance, and for the Cyclists to hold the crossings of the Solre River, but before these orders reached the forward troops the K.O.S.B., with the 120th Battery in attendance, were already in Damousies, and the West Kents had crossed the Solre, where touch was gained with the enemy on the outskirts of Ferrière-la-Petite. A Section of the 119th Battery, under Lieut. Wintle, moved with the 3rd Hussars to Damousies and crossed the Solre stream by a bridge which they built with the assistance of the Cavalry and some villagers. The other Batteries of the 27th Brigade were in action about the Avesnes-Maubeuge road ; and Lieut.-Col. White, commanding the Brigade, had his Head-Quarters in the same village (Fontaine) in which he had begun the War in 1914.

The curtain was now beginning to fall on the last act of the World War Tragedy. On the 4th, Austria signed an Armistice ; on the 8th, we heard that a German General with a white flag was on his way to Compiègne, and on the 10th the news came that the Kaiser had abdicated and fled, that there was mutiny at Kiel, and revolutions in Berlin, Dresden, and other German towns.

On the evening of the 9th, orders came from the Army for the VI. Corps to continue the pursuit, and for the IV. Corps to hold the line of the Avesnes-Maubeuge road, which was done by the 42nd Division.

At 8 a.m. on the 11th, at Pont-sur-Sambre, the Division heard that the ARMISTICE had been signed, and that hostilities were to cease at 11 a.m. There was hardly any cheering ; indeed, the news was received with apathy and perhaps a tinge of disappointment that the pursuit of a routed and disorganised foe was not to be continued. When compared with the hysterical excitement and joy which characterised the receipt of the news at home, the callous manner with which it was greeted by those most closely concerned may appear strange. The lifting of the ever-present cloud of death, which had been before them for four and a half years, was not at first apparent to the muddy, rain-soaked, and exhausted troops, and, though the dramatic events of the past few days had prepared us for it, it took some time before its tremendous import could be fully realised. Our thoughts naturally turned to the immediate future. What would happen ? Should we be sent home ? Or to the Rhine ? Or where ? For the present, at any rate, the orders were for the Division to be cantoned round Le Quesnoy, and on this day and on the 12th the Division was withdrawn West of the Forest.

The difficulties encountered in the advance through the Forêt de Mormal can truly be described as stupendous. The rail-head of the Division was at Caudry, 20 miles back. Cunningly concealed mines with delay-action fuses were continually going up on the railways ; the bridges, culverts, and road-junctions were nearly all destroyed ; the rain was incessant ; and the labour of bringing up supplies and ammunition by horse-traffic was enormous. All Heavy Artillery had of necessity been left behind, and ammunition for the field-guns was brought up in relays by the extra Artillery Brigades who were echeloned in rear. The difficulties of command were much increased ; the less mobile Corps Head-Quarters were left miles behind, and communication, except by occasional dispatch-riders, was impossible. General Ponsonby and his Brigade Commanders, with only general instructions from the Higher Command, carried through the operations, and to them and their Staffs is much of the credit due. The services of the advanced Division Head-Quarters, in close touch with the troops, which had been maintained throughout these operations, were most valuable, and the energy with which Major Merchant and his Signal Company kept up communication calls for special commendation. The advance had been rapid, and the way in which all ranks conducted themselves, in this unaccustomed form of open warfare, reflects the greatest honour on their spirit and training.

Mention has been made at some point or other in this narrative of nearly all branches in the Division. One has been omitted. The record would not be complete without reference to the gallant and untiring work of the Chaplains. Regardless of their personal safety, they were always to be found in whatever part of the field they were required, while behind the line they were ever ready to help, not only in the spiritual welfare, but also in the comfort and entertainment, of the troops.

To sum up these final operations, the complimentary Order of the Third Army Commander (Sir Julian Byng) may be quoted :

17

To all Ranks of the Third Army.

" The operations of the last three months have forced the enemy to sue for an Armistice as a prelude to Peace. Your share in the consummation of this achievement is one that fills me with pride and admiration.

" Since 21st August you have won eighteen decisive battles, you have driven the enemy back over 60 miles of country, and you have captured 67,000 prisoners and 800 guns. That is your record, gained by your ceaseless enterprise, your indomitable energy, and your loyal support to your leaders. Eleven Divisions of the Third Army (Guards, 2nd, 3rd, and 62nd, 5th, 37th, 42nd, and New Zealand, 17th, 21st, and 38th) have been continuously in action since the beginning of the advance, and have borne the brunt of the operations.

" May your pride in your achievements be as great as mine is in the recollection of having commanded the Army in which you have served."

CONCLUSION

THE Division remained in the Le Quesnoy area till the middle of December. On 3rd December the King honoured them with a visit, and was shown the miniature Regimental Colour of the Cheshire Regiment. In 1914, during the Retreat, this flag was handed over to the Curé of a village, who had it walled up for safe custody, and now, four years later, the Regiment recovered their treasured relic of the War intact.

On 13th December the Division commenced a pleasant march to Belgium, and were cantoned in villages midway between Namur and Wavre. Mention must be made of a trooping of the Colours of the Bedfords and K.O.S.B., which took place in Namur on the 28th of January 1919, to celebrate the part these Battalions had taken in the relief of the town in 1695. The ceremony was performed in the main square, and caused much local interest.

In February demobilisation began ; by the beginning of April the Division had dwindled down to Cadre establishment, and by the 10th of May the last troops had left Charleroi and embarked for home at Antwerp. The 5th Division was no more ; the units composing it had been dispersed, some to the Army of Occupation, some to their Depôts at home to re-form, and others had been disbanded. In the Spring of 1919 it was re-born at the Curragh, its pre-war station, under the command of Major-General Sir H. S. Jeudwine, who will be remembered in connection with the magnificent stand of the 55th Division at Givenchy in April 1918. In their hands we may safely leave its glorious record, knowing that it will be maintained, and that its traditions will be worthily upheld.

The love of the grand old Division, the recollection of the many battles and the noble achievements of individuals, and lastly the memory of our fallen Comrades, to which this book is dedicated, will long be cherished in the hearts of those who have had the honour to serve in it.

APPENDICES

APPENDIX

ORDER OF BATTLE OF

1914.	1915.	1916.
13th Infantry Brigade.	13th Infantry Brigade.	13th Infantry Bde.
2/K.O.S.B.	2/K.O.S.B.	14th R. Warwick Rgt.
2/W. Riding Rgt. (Duke's).	2/W. Riding Rgt.(Duke's).	15th R. Warwick Rgt.
1/Royal West Kent.	1/Royal West Kent.	2/K.O.S.B.
2/Yorkshire L.I.	2/Yorkshire L.I.	1/Royal West Kent.
	9th London Rgt. (T.).	13th Bde. M.G. Co.
		13th Bde. T.M. Batt.
14th Infantry Brigade.	14th Infantry Brigade.	95th Infantry Bde.
2/Suffolk Rgt.	1/Devon Rgt.	1/Devon Rgt.
1/East Surrey Rgt.	1/East Surrey Rgt.	12/Gloucester Rgt.
1/D.C.L.I.	1/D.C.L.I.	1/East Surrey Rgt.
2/Manchester Rgt.	2/Manchester Rgt.	1/D.C.L.I.
1/Devon Rgt.	5/Cheshire Rgt. (T.).	95th Bde. M.G. Co.
	9/Royal Scots (T.).	95th Bde. T.M. Batt.
15th Infantry Brigade.	15th Infantry Brigade.	15th Infantry Bde.
1/Norfolk Rgt.	1/Norfolk Rgt.	16th R. Warwick Rgt.
1/Bedford Rgt.	1/Bedford Rgt.	1/Norfolk Rgt.
1/Cheshire Rgt.	1/Cheshire Rgt.	1/Bedford Rgt.
1/Dorset Rgt.	1/Dorset Rgt.	1/Cheshire Rgt.
	6th Cheshire Rgt. (T.).	15th Bde. M.G. Co.
	6th Liverpool Rgt. (T.).	15th Bde. T.M. Batt.
Divisional Troops.	Divisional Troops.	Divisional Troops.
1 Squadron 19th Hussars.	North Irish Horse.	
5th Cycle Co.		
Royal Artillery.	Royal Artillery.	Royal Artillery.
XV. Bde. (11, 52, 80 Batts.).	XV. Bde. (11, 52, 80 Batts.).	XV. Bde.(52, 80, "D" Batts.).
XXVII. Bde. (119, 120, 121 Batts.).	XXVII. Bde. (119, 120, 121 Batts.).	XXVII. Bde. (119,120, 121, 37 Batts.).

I.

THE 5TH DIVISION.

1917.	1918.	1919.
13th Infantry Brigade.	13th Infantry Brigade.	13th Infantry Bde.
14th Royal Warwick Rgt.	14th Royal Warwick Rgt.	16th R. Warwick Rgt
15th Royal Warwick Rgt.	15th Royal Warwick Rgt.	2/K.O.S.B.
2/K.O.S.B.	2/K.O.S.B.	1/Royal West Kent.
1/Royal West Kent.	1/Royal West Kent.	
13th Bde. M.G. Co.	13th Bde. T.M. Batt.	13th Bde. T.M. Batt.
13th Bde. T.M. Batt.		
95th Infantry Brigade.	95th Infantry Brigade.	95th Infantry Bde.
1/Devon Rgt.	1/Devon Rgt.	1/Devon Rgt.
12/Gloucester Rgt.	12/Gloucester Rgt.	1/East Surrey Rgt.
1/East Surrey Rgt.	1/East Surrey Rgt.	1/D.C.L.I.
1/D.C.L.I.	1/D.C.L.I.	
95th Brigade M.G. Co.	95th Bde. T.M. Batt.	95th Bde. T.M. Batt.
95th Brigade T.M. Batt.		
15th Infantry Brigade.	15th Infantry Brigade.	15th Infantry Bde.
16th Royal Warwick Rgt.	16th Royal Warwick Rgt.	1/Norfolk Rgt.
1/Norfolk Rgt.	1/Norfolk Rgt.	1/Bedford Rgt.
1/Bedford Rgt.	1/Bedford Rgt.	1/Cheshire Rgt.
1/Cheshire Rgt.	1/Cheshire Rgt.	
15th Bde. M.G. Co.	15th Bde. T.M. Batt.	15th Bde. T.M. Batt.
15th Bde. T.M. Batt.		
Divisional Troops.	Divisional Troops.	Divisional Troops.
Royal Artillery.	Royal Artillery.	Royal Artillery.
XV. Bde. (52, 80, "A," "D" Batts.).	XV. Bde. (52, 80, "A," "D" Batts.).	XV. Bde. (52, 80, "A," "D" Batts.).
XXVII. Bde. (119, 120, 121, 37 Batts.).	XXVII. Bde. (119, 120, 121, 37 Batts.).	XXVII. Bde. (119, 120, 121, 37 Batts.).

APPENDIX

ORDER OF BATTLE OF

1914.	1915.	1916.
Divisional Troops—*contd.* Royal Artillery—*contd.* XXVIII.Bde.(122,123,124 Batts.). VIII. Bde. (How.) (37, 61, 65 Batts.). 108th Heavy Battery. 5th Div. Amm. Col.	XXVIII. Bde. (122, 123, 124 Batts.). VIII. Bde. (How.) (37, 65 Batts.) 5th Div. Amm. Col.	XXVIII. Bde. ("A," 123, 124, 65 Batts.). 5th Div. Amm. Col.
Royal Engineers.	Royal Engineers.	Royal Engineers.
17th Field Co. . 59th Field Co.	17th Field Co. 59th Field Co. 1/2 Home Counties Field Co. (T.).	59th Field Co. 1/2 Home Counties Field Co. (T.). 1/2 Durham Field Co. (T.).
5th Div. Sig. Co.	5th Div. Sig. Co.	5th Div. Sig. Co.
5th Div. Train A.S.C.	5th Div. Train A.S.C.	5th Div. Train A S.C.
Medical Units.	Medical Units.	Medical Units.
13th, 14th, 15th Field Ambulance.	13th, 14th, 15th Field Ambulance. 5th Mob. Vet. Sec.	13th, 14th, 15th Field Ambulance. 5th Mob. Vet. Sec. 5th Sanitary Section.
	Pioneer Battalion. 5th Cheshire Rgt. (T.).	Pioneer Battalion. 1/6 A. & S. H.

I.—*continued.*

THE 5TH DIVISION—*continued.*

1917.	1918.	1919.
5th Div. Amm. Col.	5th Div. Amm. Col.	5th Div. Amm. Col.
"X," "Y," "Z" T.M. Batts. "V" H.T.M. Batt.	"X," "Y" T.M. Batts.	"X," "Y" T.M. Batts.
Royal Engineers.	Royal Engineers.	Royal Engineers.
59th Field Co. 491 (H.C.) Field Co. (T.). 527 (Durham) Field Co.(T.).	59th Field Co. 491 (H.C.) Field Co. (T.). 527(Durham)FieldCo.(T.).	59th Field Co. 491 (H.C.) Field Co. (T.). 527 (Durham) Field Co. (T.).
5th Div. Sig. Co.	5th Div. Sig. Co.	5th Div. Sig. Co.
5th Div. Train A.S.C.	5th Div. Train A.S.C.	5th Div. Train A.S.C.
Medical Units.	Medical Units.	Medical Units.
13th, 14th, 15th Field Ambulance.	13th, 14th, 15th Field Ambulance.	13th, 14th, 15th Field Ambulance.
5th Mob. Vet. Sec.	5th Mob. Vet. Sec.	5th Mob. Vet. Sec.
205 M.G. Co.	5th Batt. M.G. Corps.	5th Batt. M.G. Corps.
Pioneer Battalion.	Pioneer Battalion.	Pioneer Battalion.
1/6 A. & S. H.	1/6 A. & S. H.	14th R. Warwick Rgt.
208th Employment Co.	208th Employment Co.	208th Employment Co.

APPENDIX

COMPOSITION OF STAFF,

	1914.	1915.
G.O.C.	Maj.-Gen. Sir Charles Fergusson. Maj.-Gen. T. L. Morland.	Maj -Gen. T. L. Morland. „ C. T. Kavanagh.
G.S.O. 1.	Lt.-Col. C. S. Romer.	Lt.-Col. A. R. Cameron. „ R. A. Currie.
A.A. and Q.M.G.	Lt.-Col. A. W. Anderson.	Lt.-Col. A. W. Anderson. „ R. F. A. Hobbs.
B.G.C., 13th Infantry Brigade.	Brig.-Gen. G. J. Cuthbert. „ W. B. Hickie. „ R. Wanless O'Gowan.	Brig.-Gen. E. J. Cooper. „ C. C. M. Maynard. „ L. O. W. Jones.
B.G.C., 14th Infantry Brigade, exchanged in Jan. 1916 with 95th Infantry Brigade.	Brig.-Gen. S. P. Rolt. „ F. S. Maude.	Brig.-Gen. C. W. Compton.
B.G.C., 15th Infantry Brigade.	Brig.-Gen. Lord E. Gleichen.	Brig.-Gen. Lord E. Gleichen. „ E. J. Northey. „ M. N. Turner.
C.R.A.	Brig.-Gen. J. E. W. Headlam.	Brig.-Gen. J. E. W. Headlam. „ J. G. Geddes. „ A. H. Hussey.
C.R.E.	Lt.-Col. J. A. Tulloch.	Lt.-Col. J. A. Tulloch. „ C. E. G. Vesey.
A.D.M.S.	Col. R. H. Sawyer.	Col. W. T. Swan. „ A. J. Luther. „ F. W. Hardy.

II.

5TH DIVISION.

1916.	1917.	1918.	1919.
Maj.-Gen. C. T. Kavanagh. Maj.-Gen. R. B. Stephens.	Maj.-Gen. R. B. Stephens.	Maj.-Gen. R. B. Stephens. Maj.-Gen. J. Ponsonby.	Maj.-Gen. J. Ponsonby.
Lt.-Col. R. A. Currie. Lt.-Col. G. C. Gordon Hall.	Lt.-Col. G. C. Gordon Hall.	Lt.-Col. G. C. Gordon Hall.	Lt.-Col. G. C. Gordon Hall.
Lt.-Col. R. F. A. Hobbs.	Lt.-Col. R. F. A. Hobbs.	Lt.-Col. R. F. A. Hobbs. Lt.-Col. O. W. White.	Lt.-Col. O. W. White.
Brig.-Gen. L. O. W. Jones.	Brig.-Gen. L. O. W. Jones.	Brig.-Gen. L. O. W. Jones. Brig.-Gen. A. T. Beckwith.	Brig.-Gen. A. T. Beckwith.
Brig.-Gen. C. R. Ballard. Brig.-Gen. Lord E. Gordon-Lennox.	Brig.-Gen. Lord E. Gordon-Lennox.	Brig.-Gen. Lord E. Gordon-Lennox. Brig.-Gen. C. B. Norton.	Brig.-Gen. C. B. Norton.
Brig.-Gen. M. N. Turner.	Brig.-Gen. M. N. Turner. Brig.-Gen. R. D. F. Oldman.	Brig.-Gen. R. D. F. Oldman.	Brig.-Gen. R. D. F. Oldman.
Brig.-Gen. A. H. Hussey.	Brig.-Gen. A. H. Hussey.	Brig.-Gen. A. H. Hussey.	Brig.-Gen. A. H. Hussey.
Lt.-Col. C. E. G. Vesey. Lt.-Col. J. R. White.	Lt.-Col. J. R. White.	Lt.-Col. J. R. White. Lt.-Col. E. E. Homer.	Lt.-Col. E. E. Homer.
Col. F. W. Hardy. „ J. Thomson. „ H. Hewetson.	Col. H. Hewetson.	Col. H. Hewetson.	Col. H. Hewetson.

INDEX

18

PRINTED AND BOUND IN GREAT BRITAIN BY INTYPE LONDON LTD.

GENERAL MAP OF WESTERN FRONT.

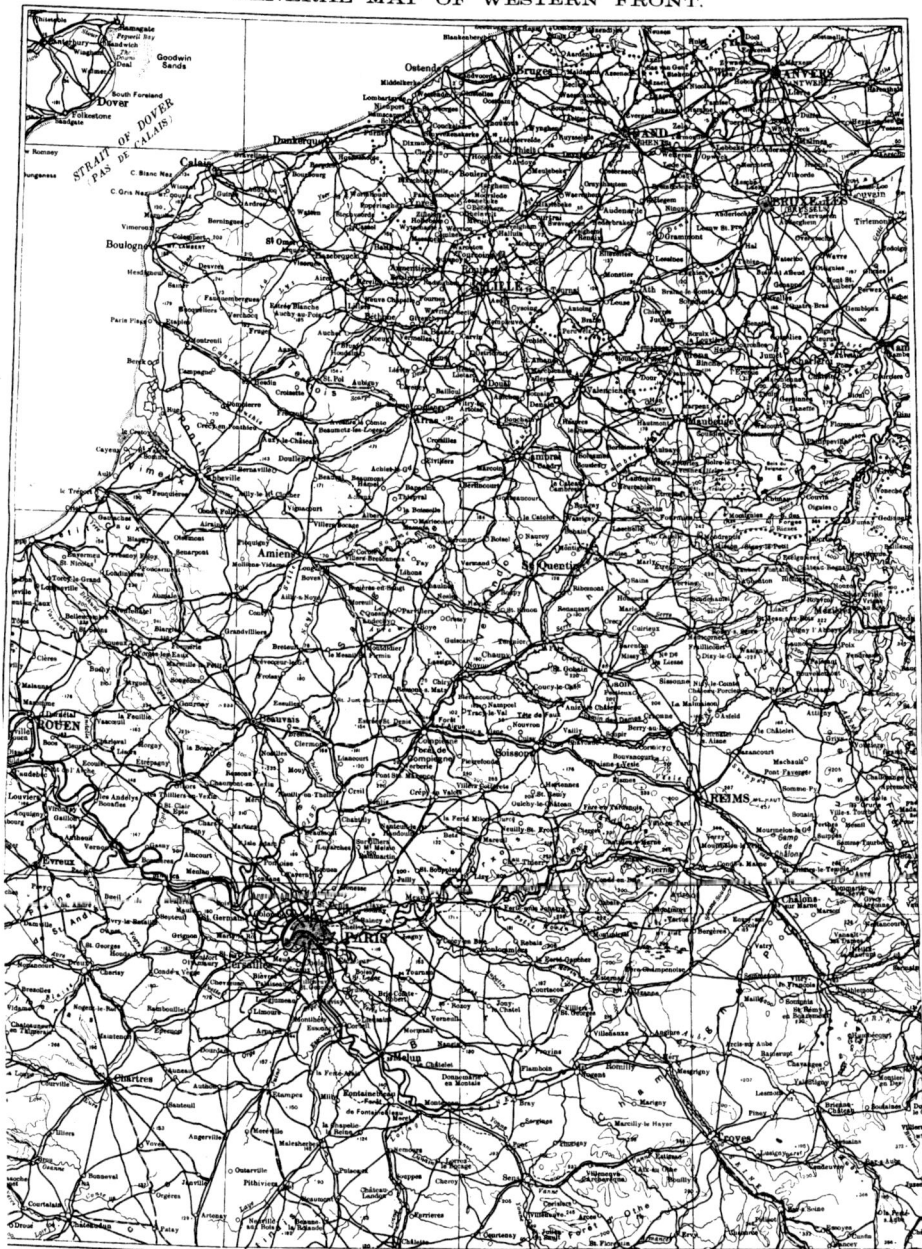

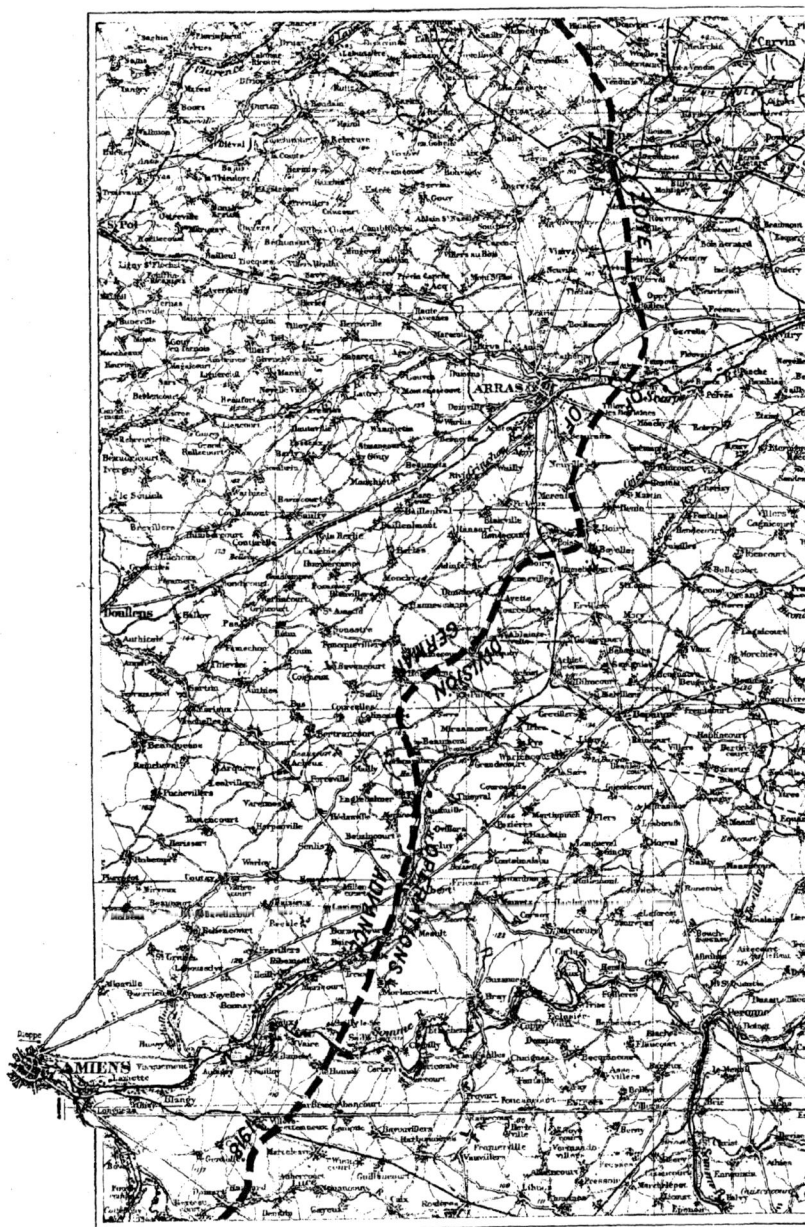

Miles 10 9 8 7 6 5 4 3 2 1 0   5

Scale 1 Inch to 3·95 Mile

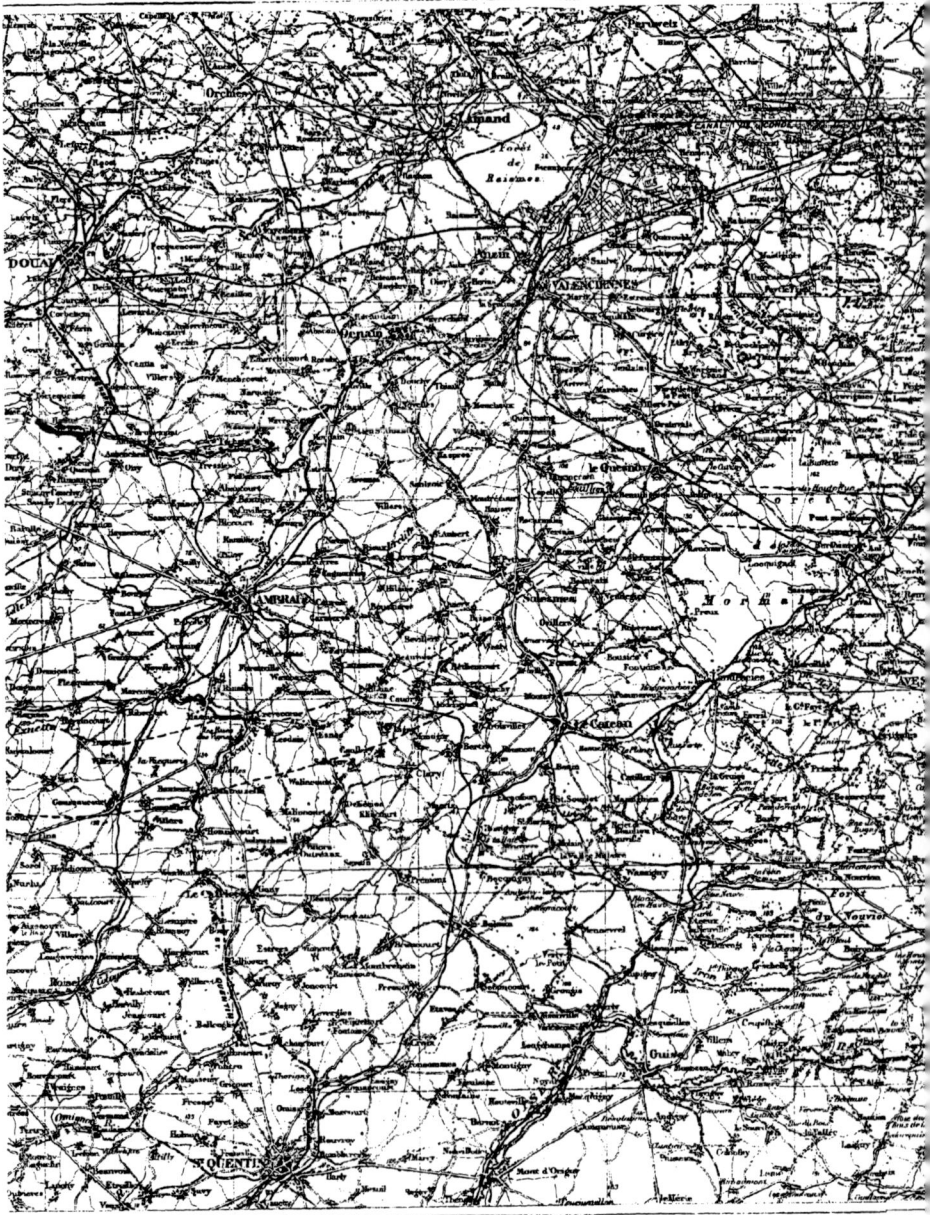

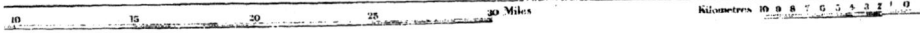

s . or 1·014 Inches to 4 Miles.

CHARLEROI

1 Centimetre to 2·5 Kilometres